MORAL PUZZLES

Moral Puzzles

Contractarian Fix

MALCOLM MURRAY

McGill-Queen's University Press
Montreal & Kingston

ISBN 978-0-2280-2907-6 (paper)
ISBN 978-0-2280-2974-8 (ePDF)
ISBN 978-0-2280-2975-5 (ePUB)

Legal deposit third quarter 2026
Bibliothèque et Archives nationales du Québec

Printed in Canada on acid-free paper that is 100% ancient-forest-free (100% post-consumer recycled), processed chlorine-free

This book has been published with the help of a grant from the Federation for the Humanities and Social Sciences, through the Scholarly Book Awards, using funds provided by the Social Sciences and Humanities Research Council of Canada.

Funded by the Government of Canada | Financé par le gouvernement du Canada | Canada

Canada Council for the Arts | Conseil des arts du Canada

We acknowledge the support of the Canada Council for the Arts.
Nous remercions le Conseil des arts du Canada de son soutien.

McGill-Queen's University Press in Montreal is on land which long served as a site of meeting and exchange amongst Indigenous Peoples, including the Haudenosaunee and Anishinabeg nations. In Kingston it is situated on the territory of the Haudenosaunee and Anishinaabek. We acknowledge and thank the diverse Indigenous Peoples whose footsteps have marked these territories on which peoples of the world now gather.

Library and Archives Canada Cataloguing in Publication

Title: Moral puzzles : contractarian fix / Malcolm Murray.
Names: Murray, R. Malcolm (Robert Malcolm), 1959– author
Description: Includes bibliographical references and index.
Identifiers: Canadiana (print) 20260150657 | Canadiana (ebook) 20260150703 | ISBN 9780228029076 (paper) | ISBN 9780228029748 (ePDF) | ISBN 9780228029755 (ePUB)
Subjects: LCSH: Contractarianism (Ethics) | LCSH: Ethical problems.
Classification: LCC BJ1500.C65 M86 2026 | DDC 171—dc23

This book was designed and typeset by Sayre Street Books in 10.5/13 Sabon.
Copyediting by James Leahy.

McGill-Queen's University Press
Suite 1720, 1010 Sherbrooke St West, Montreal, QC, H3A 2R7

Authorized safety representative in the EU: Mare Nostrum Group BV, Doelen 72, 4831 GR Breda, the Netherlands, gpsr@mare-nostrum.co.uk

Dedicated to David Gauthier, 1932–2023
Resurrector of contractarianism

Contents

Tables and Figures

TABLES

FIGURES

Gratitude

I am grateful to the colleagues I beleaguered as I worked on this book over the last nine years. At risk of missing some names, these include Paul Abela, Todd Calder, Don Desserud, Neb Kujundzic, Louis Groarke, Jason Holt, Mark Mercer, Duncan MacIntosh, Sohrab Saegh, and Scott Woodcock, as well as audience members of conferences spanning from Saint John's, Newfoundland, to Victoria, British Columbia. Very importantly, I owe much gratitude to the encouragement and challenges I received from anonymous reviewers. Thank you, too, to the great team at MQUP: Khadija Coxon, Filomena Falocco, Kathleen Fraser, James Leahy, and Joanne Pisano. As always, cheers to Jan Narveson who taught me how philosophy works. Lastly, to my grandchildren, Leon Layton and Iver Jack: I wish them well.

MORAL PUZZLES

Introduction

In this book, you will find nine moral puzzles, each with a review of previous attempts at solving them, followed by contractarian solutions.

1 WHAT ARE MORAL PUZZLES?

A philosophical puzzle provides us with at least two feasible, yet contradictory, answers. We want to say both answers are right, yet that cannot be. Whichever avenue we take, the other offers as much justification.[1] In terms of moral puzzles, we sensibly arrive at implausible moral stances.

Our task is to find the culprit that generates the antinomy and expunge it. Take, for example, Quine's solution to Russell's paradox. "We are asked to swallow a story about a village and a man in it who shaves all and only those men in the village who do not shave themselves. This is the source of our trouble; grant this and we end up saying, absurdly, that the barber shaves himself if and only if he does not. The proper conclusion to draw is just that there is no such barber" (Quine 1976, 2).

Contractarian analyses of moral puzzles are rarely found in the literature. This is not a minor omission, since, as I believe and attempt to show, most moral puzzles share the same problematic assumption that contractarianism eschews: namely the belief that morality is a metaphysical property. Admittedly, a few puzzles occur precisely by removing certain metaphysical assumptions. The ring of Gyges is a prime example. If contractarianism is a compromise between doing what you want and avoiding retaliation for doing so, then contractarianism cannot condemn someone's being immoral when repercussions to their actions are removed.

Contractarian answers to such puzzles tend to appeal to rationality (Gauthier 1990). I offer, instead, a more evolutionary account of contractarianism for my solutions.

2 THE PUZZLES

I have organized moral puzzles into two groups: common puzzles about which the literature has omitted contractarian solutions, and puzzles that beset contractarianism.

2.1 Omitted Contractarian Analyses

One never, or rarely, finds contractarian solutions to moral puzzles about supererogation, trolleys, cannibalism and incest, moral luck, moral dilemmas, and blackmail. These are the puzzles you will find in part I.

SUPEREROGATION

When thinking of moral injunctions, we can normally distinguish between actions that you must not do, actions you must do, actions you may do, and actions that would be nice to do. Those actions we must not do, like murder, we call negative obligatory actions. Those actions we must do, like paying our debts, we call positive obligatory actions. Those actions we may do, like playing the flute (assuming it is our flute and we are not playing it to irritate someone) we call prerogatory, or permissible. Those actions that would be nice to do, but not wrong to not do, like being excessively charitable, we call supererogatory. The puzzle concerns this last category: the supererogatory. Ought we aspire to do supererogatory acts? If so, is this *ought* a positive obligation? If yes, the supererogatory collapses into the obligatory and moral theory is faced with the ought-implies-can rule. If we cannot emulate saints, for example, can morality demand we emulate saints? If we ought not to aspire to do supererogatory acts, the supererogatory collapses into the merely permissible. We morally permit Mother Teresa to devote her life to help relieve suffering. Of course, we tend to praise her for that, whereas we do not tend to praise the doing of merely permissible actions. Can such a distinction be a reason to keep the supererogatory as a separate category, or is the praise we offer patronizing?

TROLLEY PROBLEMS

Is it moral to let one person die in order to save five? If so, is it equally moral to kill one person to save five? Is there – at least sometimes – a moral difference between killing and letting die? By examining runaway trolleys in various scenarios, we seek an explanation for believing a moral difference exists. A runaway trolley is heading toward five persons stuck on the track. If it reaches them, they will all be killed. You can pull a lever to switch the tracks so that the trolley avoids the five people. Unfortunately, one person is stuck on this side track. Under such a situation, is it morally permissible to pull the lever? If our only concern in determining good from bad, or right from wrong, is adding up happiness, subtracting pains, and not worrying about the individual distribution of pain and happiness, then would it be equally permissible to push someone onto the track to have their body (now corpse) stop the runaway trolley from killing the five? Saying, "Yes," to switching the track and, "No," to pushing a bystander requires fancy philosophical manoeuvring, manoeuvring that may ultimately fail. Saying, "Yes," to both is consistent, at least, whether advisable is another matter. Saying, "No," to both is a position hardly ever defended, but perhaps needs a fresh look.

CANNIBALISM AND INCEST

We tend to regard many things as simply wrong. To ask why they are wrong reveals an alien mindset. Any explanation for why it is wrong seems more inscrutable than that it is wrong. To persist with our question is to allow philosophy to "get in the way of good sense" (Gass 1957, 203). Another possibility, however, is that our good sense is sometimes foiled. Both cannibalism and incest have reasons against them related to health. In the case of cannibalism, at least among the Fore people in Papua New Guinea, individual practitioners are prone to Kuru, a degenerative disease transmitted through cannibalism and necrophagy (Lindenbaum 1979; Collinge et al. 2006). But many activities we deem morally permissible have associated health risks without our being so morally set against them. With incest, on the other hand, their offspring suffer the health risks. Incest, then, unlike cannibalism, has externalities. But what is wrong with homosexual incest, or recreational incest using contraception? Answers tend to devolve into the recognition that cannibalism and incest are just yucky. The puzzle now becomes whether morality is simply rooted in our ancestral sensibilities, or whether some reasoned explanation against cannibalism and incest (for example) can survive critique.

MORAL LUCK

We like to praise people for doing good acts and we like to blame people for doing bad acts. We make exceptions to this rule when we discover such acts were out of their control. When a woman suffers a stroke and consequently drives over a child, we do not call it a moral infraction. It is a tragedy. When a man saves a child from an oncoming bus only because he accidentally tripped the child, we do not morally commend his action. It was lucky. We like to imagine that moral praise and blame have no reliance on luck. When luck enters the picture, our moral assessment alters accordingly. At least so we suppose. Williams (1981a) and Nagel (1979) argue that luck plays a much larger role than we like to believe. This gives us a conflict between two seemingly correct propositions: "A person's moral standing ought not to be altered by luck" and "A person's moral standing is often, perhaps always, altered by luck." One of these propositions must go.

MORAL DILEMMAS

A moral dilemma occurs when someone has two conflicting duties that cannot both be satisfied. If I must do *A* and I must do *B* yet cannot do both, my doing *A* is a violation of my duty to do *B*, and vice versa. In serving one obligation, I fail my other. Perhaps my neighbour and I are having tea. Her husband arrives wielding a monkey wrench asking me where his wife is, promising to kill her once found. Two moral obligations seem to apply in my case: to not help a murderer, and to not lie. To tell the truth would seem to help the murderer, and we assume the best way to prevent the murder (at least presently) is to lie. Both obligations cannot be met. If obligations are arranged hierarchically – for example, preventing a murder always trumps telling the truth – then no *practical* dilemma exists. We still have a *philosophical* dilemma, however. Even if we come to believe that *A* is the preferred course of action, your doing *A* does not relieve you of your duty to have done *B*. How can any credible moral theory condemn us to being immoral?

BLACKMAIL

We know two wrong acts do not make a right act. The worry about blackmail, however, is the reverse. Can two right acts make a wrong act? If we think of blackmail as simply a seller offering information to a prospective buyer for money, and that buyer is free to accept or decline, as anyone confronted with an unbidden sales call should be, we should have difficulty saying that blackmail is immoral. If we think blackmail is immoral, then, we have to show that things are less simple than business proposals. The attempt to show the difference, however, is difficult.

2.2 *Puzzles Besetting Contractarianism*

Several moral puzzles are aimed at a group of reductionist moral theories of which contractarian is one. Other moral puzzles are aimed directly at contractarianism. The first group includes the is-ought problem and the problem with categoricity. The second group includes the ring of Gyges puzzle and the toxin puzzle.

THE IS-OUGHT PROBLEM

The is-ought problem (or fact-value problem) claims we cannot move from ises (descriptive statements, or facts) alone to oughts (normative statements, or values). If any is-ought move is a fallacy, then all moral reductions are fallacies. A moral reduction occurs when we try to explain morality in terms of non-moral utterances. To explain morality in terms of moral utterances would be a case of begging the question. If we start from a completely amoral initial position (an is), we will forever be unable to get to a morality (an ought) without committing the is-ought gaffe. Contractarianism is not alone in facing this worry, but it does face it. Critics proclaim that contractarians cannot get to a moral ought by their amoral derivations. They derive, at best, prudential advice, not moral mandates. Conversely, the concept of a prudence-irrelevant moral mandate is untenable.

CATEGORICITY

When speaking morally, we want to say, "Don't torture people," not, "Don't torture people if you don't want to be cruel." If for whatever reason one prefers the latter way of speaking, we would be obliged to add, "Then don't want to be cruel!" That is, it is hard to understand how morality can be anything but categorical. The categoricity of morality precludes morality's being conditional on anything. It is not a fully moral utterance to say, "If x obtains, don't be cruel." Morality wants to demand, "Don't be cruel whether x obtains or not." For if $\sim x$ obtains, what then? Who but terrorists want to say the prohibitions against cruelty may be waived if the right conditions obtain and then point out the existence of those conditions. To put it bluntly, those who maintain that morality is not properly speaking categorical are not merely misguided, but immoral. All fine sentiments, but for one problem: categoricity is an unsustainable concept.

THE RING OF GYGES

Contractarianism was the popular moral theory in Plato's day, according to Glaucon, a character in *The Republic*. Contractarianism was understood (still is, largely) as a rational compromise between what one hopes to get and what one can expect to get given social constraints. If we can remove those social constraints, we can remove the rationality of moral advice. The ring of Gyges is a magical ring that can make you invisible. Being invisible, we are to assume,[2] allows wearers of the ring the ability to bypass social constraints without repercussion. Can contractarians show that possessors of such a ring ought to remain moral? The question highlights two opposing views of morality. We may conceive of morality as having primarily intrinsic worth or as having primarily instrumental worth. If the value of morality is instrumental only, we are moral for some other gain, typically conceived of in terms of long-term net self-interest. By net interest, I mean the claim that morality is a prudential good. Just as prudence sometimes demands we relinquish the pursuit of one type of interest for the satisfaction of another type, proponents of instrumental morality see moral constraint on individual interests as sometimes a beneficial compromise to further other interests the agent endorses. This is the view of contractarianism. This is also the view that suffers from the ring of Gyges objection. On the other hand, the intrinsic view of morality, while avoiding ring of Gyges problems, cannot be maintained by any naturalistic ethic, one devoid of metaphysics.

THE TOXIN PUZZLE

Imagine a rich and inerrant mind reader who will insert one million dollars into your bank account at dawn tomorrow morning if, at midnight tonight, you commit to drink a cup of toxin at noon tomorrow. This multi-billionaire assures you that the toxin, while making you extremely sick, will not kill you or have any long-term adverse effects. Being inerrant, this mind reader can tell the difference between those people who really now commit to drink the toxin from those who are not earnest when they say they will drink the toxin. With this in mind, let us agree that, at midnight tonight, you earnestly commit yourself to drink the toxin at noon tomorrow. Given that commitment, the money is, at dawn tomorrow morning, in your bank. Come noon tomorrow, will you bother drinking the toxin? If not, was your original commitment sincere? Morality is a kind of toxin puzzle. With the toxin puzzle, we are to commit to drink the toxin even when, at the time of drinking, it seems no longer rational to do so. Likewise, we are to commit to being moral even when being immoral seems to be more rational. For example, you borrow money on Saturday with the promise to repay the money on Tuesday. On Saturday, you are committed to repay the money, otherwise you would not receive the loan. Come Tuesday, however, the commitment to repay the money seems against your interest. Your promise on Saturday was in order to get the money. On Tuesday, you already have the money, so giving it up seems irrational. If lenders knew that borrowers would be thinking about such things come due dates, they would not lend their money. They may give their money, but do not count on that. Thus, as with the toxin puzzle, your commitment at T_1 must extend to your being committed at T_3, despite the value of your commitment already being satisfied at T_2. Rationality seems to short-circuit our commitment to morality. If so, a morality based on rationality, as contractarians normally claim, cannot succeed.

3 CONTRACTARIANISM

What I hope to show is how contractarianism solves these puzzles. Before that demonstration, we should be clear on a few details about contractarianism.

3.1 The Basic Picture

Contractarianism is a moral theory arising from the ashes of metaphysics. There are no gods. There is no *summum bonum*, says Hobbes (1651, ch. 11). Morality is not independent of humans.

Does that mean morality is a myth? Nonsense. The myth part is the belief that morality is something to be discovered in the order of the cosmos and obeyed. The non-myth part is that morality is instrumentally beneficial to humans. Any intrinsic value to being moral (sanctity if moral, guilt if immoral) is secondary to the instrumental value morality provides. Once we know what we morally ought to do, we can internalize our moral disposition to enjoy doing good and dislike doing bad.

Contractarians argue that even amoral, self-interested, rational agents would accept constraints imposed on their social behaviour. Contractarians call those social constraints "morality." Without such constraints, we are vulnerable to the depredations of others, and with such constraints, we can all benefit from co-operation with others (Narveson 1988, 148). Otherwise, humans remain in a state where life is "solitary, poor, nasty, brutish, and short" (Hobbes 1651, ch. 13). So, humans agree to keep the peace, and to do that, they agree to a liberty rule, a rule to not interfere with others' pursuits, assuming others likewise agree. From this, humans get moral restrictions on their self-interested behaviour based on their own self-interested ends without appealing to any suspicious metaphysical notion of a human-independent moral reality.

Rejecting the *summum bonum* is not the central feature of contractarianism, but it is an often-forgotten piece, as we see when people object to contractarianism for failing to capture "true morality."

Contractarians conceive of morality as a necessary constraint on social life. They see moral rules as advice on how to live as best one can, conceived in terms of subjective self-interest, given the interests of others. Moral obligation is accepted only insofar as the benefit to the moral agent – the one asked to take on the duty – outweighs the cost of the duty itself. In this sense, contractarianism is a prudence-based moral theory. It explains why some kind of socially sanctioned moral conduct is worth the price to a wide range of individuals compared with no moral system at all. Since the comparison is to no morals, contractarians appeal to amoral motivations. Any moral claim entails a restriction on agents' freedoms. Since few like their freedoms restricted, we need to justify those restrictions. The only restrictions self-interested, amoral agents would be willing to endorse are those in which general adherence to such restrictions have net benefits to the adherents. By all adhering to the concept of reciprocal consent, no one will be forced to do with their bodies what they do not want. The cost to *A* is that *A* can no longer do to others without the consent of those others. *A* will deem the price worth paying if others reciprocate by not doing to *A* without *A*'s consent. Assuming general reciprocity, morality is worth *A*'s adherence when more harm can come to *A* from others doing ill to her than the benefits she may derive from doing ill to others. For example, you do better at whatever you want without someone stabbing you (Nozick 1974, 171). To get to such a state, you have to agree not to stab others. Such an agreement makes sense only so long as most of us reciprocate the rule against stabbing people; otherwise, stab away. To reciprocally agree to a rule not to stab is to agree to a system that would punish you if you do stab others. Once the enforcement system is in place, you have a prudential reason not to stab people, but you also have a prudential reason to agree to such an enforcement policy. For contractarians, reciprocal agreement based on self-interest is both the origin and stopping point of morality.

The moral restrictions against murder, assault, theft, rape, torture, and such things are all cases that pass a hypothetical test of being worthwhile for self-interested, amoral agents to reciprocally endorse. Should the reciprocal nature of such restrictions be missing, we change the moral descriptor of the act: it is not a boxing match, but assault; it is not the receipt of a gift, but theft; it is not sex, but rape. In all cases of uncontroversial moral wrongdoing, someone did something to someone else without the latter's consent.

3.2 *Central Features*

The following concepts will play a large role in my solutions to our moral puzzles.

EX ANTE

For contractarians, any moral rule as well as any condition to any moral rule must be justifiable at the *ex ante* position. An *ex ante* decision is what hypothetical agents would prudentially consent to in a premoral state. For Hobbes (1651, ch. 13), this is the State of Nature, a state that has less to do with a non-human world than with a human world in the absence of moral constraints. Gauthier (1986, 14–16, 131–4) refers to the *ex ante* position as the initial bargaining position. Rawls (1971, 17–22) calls his the original position. In contrast, an *ex post* agreement is made within the vagaries of human life. When deciding moral actions, contractarians do not look for consent among existing people immersed in conditions peculiar to them, the *ex post* conditions. Rather, they wonder to what rules reasonable agents suitably situated would consent (Gauthier 1986, 9–10). *Ex ante* agents are deemed to be rational, amoral, and self-interested not because contractarians have a dour view of human psychology, but because they wish to avoid begging the question when it comes to endorsing moral principles. The question is whether amoral people would agree to being bound by morality, not whether moral people would agree to be bound by morality. Following Hobbes, contractarians agree that rational, self-interested, amoral agents would, *ex ante,* derive conditional moral rules to help us live as well as possible given our social and environmental circumstances. Hobbes (1651, ch. 14) deems these edicts to be "Laws of Nature," each law being a "Precept, or generall Rule, found out by Reason." Modern moral contractarians content themselves with Hobbes's first three laws of nature: seek peace, lay down some of your freedoms, and stick to your agreements, all conditional upon others doing so as well.[3] The conditionality embedded at the root of morality is what distinguishes contractarianism from all other moral theories. Contractarianism conceives of morality as a reciprocal arrangement for the instrumental ends of peaceful cohabitation and enterprise. The reciprocity condition is ever-present. To say a moral rule binds you whether or not the other plays along is not something contractarians can stomach. "But shouldn't we be moral no matter what the other does?!" No. Such thinking comes from unsupportable myth.

Any duty to which general adherence would not serve the duty holder's long-term interests is not expected to be endorsed by amoral, self-interested, rational agents in an *ex ante* situation. Such conditionality cannot be in terms of *ex post* self-interest, admittedly, lest contractarianism collapse into ethical egoism. My not agreeing to pay my debts now does not invalidate my obligation to pay my debts given my earlier promise. I would not promise to do something unless I expect to benefit from doing that thing, all things considered, but once I promise, I am bound (all things equal). Similarly, *ex ante* agents in the state of nature would not promise to abide by rules governing their behaviour unless doing so stands to benefit them overall. If a proposed rule cannot be generally expected to benefit rule followers, then such a rule would not meet the conditions of being moral for contractarians. To say, "Ah, but morality needn't cater to self-interest!" is to presume a metaphysical origin of morality that contractarianism rejects.

To help ensure that people stick to their agreements (the compliance problem), these *ex ante* agents would also endorse a binding rule. Binding rules add external constraints to voluntary actions to lessen the chances of reneging. We do not want to fulfill our obligations *ex post* even when it is in our interest to agree to such obligations *ex ante*. But since rational, amoral, self-interested individuals would see the lure of breaking their promises (borrowing money without repayment, for example), and everyone knows that ahead of time, their *ex ante* agreements would include the installation of some binding rule. The cost of the binding rule (in implementation and being caught in its grip) is calculated when deciding the net benefit of any putative moral duty. Of course, the duty holder may at a different time be a duty recipient, and that is part of the calculation in long-term gain, but if one finds oneself facing the heavy cost of a duty without expecting to receive any offsetting benefit from others having a similar duty, the decision to be so bound was not well calculated. A right is granted only after *ex ante* agents would expect to benefit despite the overall cost of honouring their duty to uphold that right. Conceptually, duty comes before right. *Ex ante* agents do not look out at the world to see what rights exist and then conform their duties accordingly; they look out at the world and wonder what duties they are willing and can afford to take on, and thus they establish rights.

CONSENT

My notion of contractarianism assumes that *ex ante* agents suitably situated would agree to abide by an overriding principle that says not to do to others without their consent (Murray 2017). In my view, consent is of central importance at both the *ex ante* and *ex post* conditions. Consent means more than that agents agree. Their agreement must be voluntary, and by voluntary, their decisions must not be coerced, deceived, or manipulated. Such consent must be relatively steadfast throughout the process. Saying "Yes" in the kitchen does not preclude saying "No" in the bedroom. Apart from acting voluntarily, agents (or their proxies) must be competent and suitably informed. Another qualification is needed concerning *reasonably presumed consent* to accommodate those unable to provide consent (the very young or the incapacitated, for example) or for those situations where eliciting consent is not possible (throwing someone a surprise party or pushing someone out of the way of a falling piano).

The notion of a *concerned party* is needed to clarify whose consent counts and whose does not in any interaction. That two thieves have voluntarily agreed to rob me does not make their transaction moral; I am a concerned party: hence, my agreement is required. On the other hand, people who are morally opposed to homosexuality, call them homophobes, do not tend to agree to the sexual actions of homosexuals, yet their non-consent does not count. To ignore the homophobes' lack of consent to a rule permitting homosexuality, as contractarianism does, seems to conflict with their general principle that we cannot do things to others without their consent. But whom do *ex ante* agents mean by "others"? The answer must be only those who count as concerned parties. A concerned party to any agreement is one whose existence is required for the event to take place. Homophobes are not required for homosexuals to have sex, whereas the owner of money is required for a robber to steal it. The owner of the money need not be present, of course – in fact, the owner's absence can make it easier to steal the owner's money – but without the owner's existence, there is no owner's money to steal.

Accommodating all this, we get the following principle of consent: "Any act is morally permissible if and only if all concerned parties (or their proxies) are competent, suitably informed, and voluntarily, or would reasonably voluntarily, consent" (Murray 2017, 13).

Acts done to others without satisfying the above principle are generally immoral. When they are not immoral, special circumstances prevail. Killing another in self-defence, for example, is not done with the other's permission, but we deem it morally permissible (all things equal) because the other (the one threatening you, intentionally or not) is not honouring your consent. In such cases, your obligations toward them are dissolved.

STATUS QUO

So far, contractarianism gives us the following picture: *ex ante* agents would agree to moral rules that bind them assuming that being so bound makes their lives generally go better than not being so bound. Rather than list all the kinds of rules that may fit this requirement, they will agree to a general principle that says, "Don't do unto others without their consent." But what does it mean to do something to another? Typically, our concern is whether *A*'s action makes *B* worse off than *B* was before interacting with *A*. If so, we need to establish the position *B* was in before *A* interacted with *B*. Such a position is called *B*'s *status quo*. In an interaction between *A* and *B*, the status quo of *A* is *A*'s state of affairs just prior to the interaction with *B*.[4] When contractarians speak of the status quo, their focus is on time-sensitive individual states of affairs. They certainly do not mean to invoke the social-political status quo that sits atop legacies of historic injustice, as one might say. Identifying the status quo of any individual is aimed at not worsening their condition without their consent or presumed consent. If I pass a beggar without dropping money into his hat, this may not meet the beggar's consent. To say, therefore, I *must* put money in the beggar's hat, however, would not meet my consent. A moral theory based on consent *simpliciter* would be stuck. Allowing the status quo to be the default solves the problem. The status quo of the beggar is having his hat empty of my money. If I leave that a live option, which I do by passing by, I am not violating the contractarian principle of consent.

POSITIVE RIGHTS

If *A* has a positive right to *x*, *B*, either a specific individual or someone in general or society at large, has a positive duty to supply *A* with *x*. When people speak of welfare and food security, they speak of positive rights. If *A* has a *negative right* to *x*, no one can take or damage *x*. Rules against theft and vandalism are understood as preserving negative rights. The rule not to violate anyone's status quo well entrenches all our negative duties, those duties we have to refrain from worsening others' conditions. My not helping the beggar is not a violation of the beggar's status quo – he had an empty hat before my arrival and an empty hat after I passed – so is not a violation of the beggar's negative right. But ought we not help the beggar by raising the beggar's current status quo by a dollar or two? In other words, does the beggar have a positive right to my help? If so, my satisfying a negative duty (by not making the beggar worse off) may violate a positive duty I have to help others in need. If the example of a beggar does not do the trick, think of a drowning victim whom I can help, but decline to help. To say there is no negative-right violation in my declining to save the drowning victim is not to say I have a moral right to decline to save the drowning victim (all else equal). In fact, most people will think I have a moral obligation, a positive duty, to save the drowning victim, if I can. Contractarians can agree. Positive duties, suitably constrained, may be endorsed by *ex ante* agents.

Ex ante agents could accept positive obligations to help others (i) in need (ii) when doing so is not too onerous on the helper, (iii) the duty is evenly distributed across all agents, and (iv) everyone's taking on the duty benefits the duty holders overall more than their not taking on the duty. Ignore the vagueness in "need." For present purposes, we can agree that a drowning victim has a need, whereas the street beggar may not have a need. Also ignore the vagueness in "not too onerous." If the saviour's risk of drowning is high enough, the rescue attempt would be too onerous. In such a case, the positive duty is now void. Depositing a few coins into a beggar's hat is probably not too onerous, assuming you meet few beggars in your travels. It is one thing to give two dollars to a beggar, another to give two dollars each to eighty beggars in one afternoon. That may be too onerous. That the duty to save others is evenly distributed means only that *ex ante* agents wish to evenly distribute burdens. An amoral, self-interested, rational agent would not agree to a duty if they must abide by it more than others. A duty relegated to only a subset of the population is called slavery.[5] Concerning the third criterion, when you have an obligation to help another, your declining to help is a violation. Since declining to help is your status quo, the *ex ante* decision to endorse a helping rule (suitably demarcated) is a violation of the helper's status quo. *Ex ante* agents would agree to this, per hypothesis, only if living under such a rule would benefit the helpers, not merely the helped, more than not living under such a rule. The rationale so far is that when the cost of helping is guaranteed to be reasonably low, the benefit of being helped when in need reasonably high, the probability of needing help at some point in one's life sufficiently high, and the status quo violation of having to help relatively minor, one ought to help.

This is not a justification of contractarianism; it is an elucidation. Specifically, it is an elucidation of how a morality may come about in the absence of gods or the belief that morality is embedded in the fabric of the universe prior to and outlasting human existence. Even for those who have jettisoned belief in supernatural agency, the roots of such beliefs go deep. They permeate our conceptions of morality. By weeding them out, particularly those tendrils of moral objectivity, the moral puzzles discussed in part I dissolve. So I claim.

4 CONTRACTARIAN SOLUTIONS

Being faced with a moral puzzle is to recognize that we have an improper grasp on moral concepts. We know what sounds nice. What sounds nice and what we can support are not necessarily the same. Most of the fault, I believe, rests on old, often religious, lingering metaphysical assumptions that contractarianism explicitly rejects.

4.1 Contractarian Solutions to the Puzzles of Part One

SUPEREROGATION

The appeal to a supererogatory category comes from thinking morality is an objective thing-in-itself with an inherent value independent of any valuer. The ideal moral move is always just beyond human limits. To evict from our minds unsupported metaphysical claims is to remove the need to accommodate the supererogatory. *Ex ante* agents can agree to moral concepts that constrain individual behaviour only as long as such constraints provide an overall net benefit to the constrained moral agents themselves. Supererogatory acts benefit only the recipients, not the supererogatory agents. While we would like for you to be extra nice, we cannot mean that as a recommendation for you. Acts that do tend to benefit the agents themselves, little supererogatory acts we may call them, such as being kind and respectful, can be consumed under little moral recommendations. If so, not supererogatory.

TROLLEYS

A closer examination of contractarian ethics reveals, perhaps surprisingly, the claim that switching the path of a runaway trolley so that it kills one person rather than five is as egregious as pushing a bystander in the trolley's path to save five people farther down the track. Thomson (2008) also came to this conclusion, but for a different reason. I focus on the concept of the status quo and claim that any alteration to it cannot be done without the consent, or presumed consent, of any individual directly impacted. The person sitting on an unused spur is such a person, and would not, presumably, consent to being crushed by a trolley. That one ought to so consent cannot be supported by rational, amoral, self-interested agents in a pre-moral state. Besides, we could say the same to the bystander we push in front of the trolley. That she does not agree is irrelevant; she ought to agree to being sacrificed. Where is her community spirit? Your not pulling the lever, on the other hand, does not upset the status quo of the five in line with the trolley's trajectory. Tragedy yes, immoral no.

CANNIBALISM AND INCEST

That dumbfounding often occurs when we cannot express reasons for our moral beliefs is not sufficient to abandon moral cognitivism, at least when the alternative is to wean our moral repugnance toward fully consensual acts. We know to conceptually distinguish behaviours that disgust us personally from behaviours that we ought to morally condemn. Because I hate to eat mushrooms is not justification to prevent you from eating mushrooms. The same should apply to behaviours that disgust us collectively. As long as we do not have to partake, we should permit others to do so if they have proper consent among all concerned parties.

MORAL LUCK

If we believe that morality is a real, objective, human-independent fact of nature, we would be surprised and bothered to discover it ignores the role of luck that impacts our lives. On the other hand, the concern about moral luck dissolves once we stop believing that morality is an externally real objective thing that we must learn to recognize in the world and navigate our lives accordingly. We expect an ideal objective morality to be perfect. When moral luck enters our world, moral perfection is challenged. Those adopting an instrumental and conventional account of morality need not worry about perfection, and hence, one might think, can permit moral luck. That moral luck pollutes moral assessment need not bother anyone because morality is simply a human convention and, like any human convention, can only work with what it has available to it. This to-err-is-human stance is not the position I take. Rather, once we understand more clearly what an instrumental, conventional account of morality looks like, we see that no moral luck can occur at all. Moral luck occurs when luck impacts moral assessment, not outcomes. That is what I deny can occur, even when outcomes are morally assessed and those outcomes are largely due to luck. For comparison, it may be unlucky for me to have to compete against the best player in the first round of an elimination chess tournament, but it is not a matter of luck how success is determined during our match. In this case, I am eliminated early, whereas had I not met that best player until later in the series, my final position could be much higher. If there is money involved, such a difference in luck may have cost me considerably. Such is life, but life-luck does not impact chess assessment, and nor does it impact moral assessment.

MORAL DILEMMAS

The worry about moral dilemmas also rides on the belief that morality is a beautiful, ideal thing to which our humble conceptions of morality must aspire to match. For contractarians, having rejected the *summum bonum*, morality is simply a human tool to help regulate human behaviours to make social life as peaceful as possible. This tool, wielded in terms of adopted duties, is useful to the duty holder, assuming various circumstances apply. In cases of supposed moral dilemmas, one of these conditions no longer applies, and hence the merit of the tool can no longer be affirmed. If morality were real, the abandoned moral duty still lingers. If morality is a convention only, such a notion makes no sense. If construction forces us to drive on the left side rather than on the right side of the road, we may feel weird about not driving on the right, but few would feel guilty about it. Residual moral guilt for being unable to satisfy a duty that you would normally be able to satisfy would be as misplaced as an atheist still feeling the urge to pray.

BLACKMAIL

Most philosophers and legal scholars believe that blackmail is immoral. Assuming no independent moral violation is occurring as a component of the blackmailer's request (such as perjury, invasion of privacy, or threat of violence), and that blackmail cannot occur without some independent moral breach (per hypothesis), their reasons flounder. My approach is to argue for the imprudence of succumbing to blackmail. I offer a condemnation, not merely a moral condemnation. Only a paternalist ethic can morally condemn imprudence. Contractarianism is not a paternalist ethic. On the other hand, contractarian morality is a subset of prudence. All immoral actions are also imprudent actions, but not all imprudence is immoral. What makes an imprudent action also immoral concerns the status quo. As long as blackmailers permit balckmailees their status quo (which they do for our paradigmatic cases), there is no moral violation, despite the imprudence of succumbing to the blackmailer's offer.

4.2 *Contractarian Solutions to the Puzzles of Part Two*

While certain puzzles dissolve after expunging metaphysical assumptions lurking in our moral discourse, the puzzles discussed in part II loom – perhaps the very ones that originally invoked metaphysical appeal. This leads to a choice: accept unfounded metaphysics to explain our desired morality or accept that our desired morality fails to match the morality that can come from nature. Contractarians prefer the latter. While past contractarian defences of these puzzles have appealed to versions of rationality (Gauthier 1990), such thinking, I believe, gets mired. We can instead understand the mechanics of contractarian moral theory as a naturally evolved trait – that of reciprocal co-operation. As with all evolutionary traits, the benefits of a morality will be conditional upon the environment. Alter the conditions in which the moral trait benefits the moral trait holder, the merit of that moral trait dissolves. The puzzles that arise from jettisoning metaphysics (ring of Gyges, is-ought gaps, categoricity, and toxins), I argue, fail to properly understand this feature of naturalized ethics.

RING OF GYGES

Ring-of-Gyges cases suffer the absurdity of demanding that an evolutionarily successful trait (including the penchant to reciprocally co-operate) be successful *no matter* the circumstances. Alter the conditions in which an adaptative trait had success, we ought not to expect continued success. Thus ends the worry.

IS-OUGHT PROBLEMS

Morality is not a thing-in-itself. There is no *summum bonum*. Accepting an anti-metaphysical picture of morality permits a resolution to the is-ought puzzle by downplaying the magical feature of oughts. When contractarians claim an act is morally required, they mean adopting that action as a duty will, overall, for most people, under most circumstances, be in their long-term interests, given certain facts about human nature and resources and maybe a few other things. Thus, the moral ought is really a prudential ought – a subset of prudential oughts that concern strategic, interpersonal interactions. The "moral" part that is left out of such a reduction is precisely the metaphysical notion of morality that contractarians have expressly evicted.

TOXIN WORRIES

The toxin puzzle, as does the prisoner's dilemma, challenges rational models of morality. We may compare the toxin puzzle to the puzzle about loans. If we cannot rationally drink the toxin, we cannot rationally pay our debts. Since we are morally required to pay our debts, either morality is not rational, or some clever explaining is needed. One clever way of explaining the rationality of paying one's debts is not available in the toxin puzzle. It may sometimes be rational to *x* despite conditions in which *x*-ing made sense no longer apply, but only when some other condition is introduced that can rationally motivate the actor to *x*.[6] But when we alter the conditions such that there is no longer any reason to *x*, *x*-ing cannot be rational. The added condition in the case of debt paying (as with prisoner's dilemmas) concerns the prospect for future interactions. When I pay my debt, I keep a good credit score to help me get another loan. The reason I promised to pay back my loan is to get the loan; the reason I repay the loan is to better ensure prospects for future loans. The toxin puzzle, at least in its classic form, does not have this feature of repeatability. Admitting the irrationality of drinking the toxin, thereby, does not carry over to the irrationality of paying back one's debts.

Such is the summary of my arguments. Now for the details.

PART ONE

1

Supererogation and an Error Theory

A supererogatory act (i) goes beyond moral duty, (ii) is morally approved, and (iii) carries no moral condemnation for failure to comply. This demarcation raises the following puzzle: How can we morally praise an action that is not morally required? Conversely, we may wonder how acting outside the set of morality is still moral. Traditional moral theories (utilitarianism, virtue theory, and Kantianism) cannot well accommodate the supererogatory. Anything deemed to go beyond moral duty is either not morally recommended or is morally demanded. After all, how can we deem an extra-moral act to be morally better than what a complete moral theory already entails? Can contractarianism do better (assuming it is better for a moral theory to accommodate supererogation)? The answer, perhaps surprising given the dearth of positive obligations generated by as sparse a moral theory as contractarianism, is, "No." Not because supererogation will be consumed by obligation, but because anything beyond moral duty done for good reasons will be consumed by the category of the merely permissible. It is one thing to *permit* charity; another to *morally applaud* it. On the bright side, contractarianism has available to it, in a way other moral theories do not, error theories to explain our penchant to believe in supererogation.

1 SUPEREROGATION: A CLOSER LOOK

Moral theories tell us what to do and what not to do. We deem permissible anything outside those parameters. Moral theories may differ on how large or small that permissible space is, but they all carve out the positive obligatory, the negative obligatory, and the permissible (or prerogatory). A fourth category is possible. After all our moral acts are satisfied, we can perform extra morally, super

Table 1.1 | Moral categories

Type	*Action*	*Punishment (for failure)*	*Praise (for success)*	*Example*
Negative obligation	Must not do	Yes	No	Murder
Positive obligation	Must do	Yes	No	Debt paying
Prerogatory (permissible)	May do	No	No	Flute playing
Supererogatory (beyond duty)	Nice to do	No	Yes	Extreme charity

nice acts, not specifically required by our chosen moral theory, yet praiseworthy by moral standards. A soldier, for example, jumps upon a grenade to save foxhole mates (Urmson 1958, 202–3). This fourth category we call the supererogatory – morally praiseworthy acts that lie beyond moral obligation.

We morally condemn people for failing their moral obligations, but we do not (tend to) praise people for fulfilling their moral obligations. I did not kill anyone this week, yet nary a praise did I receive. We do not tend to praise people for paying their debts. The extent to which we praise obligatory acts may itself be supererogatory – a nicety of us, or we recognize in the debt payer a greater sacrifice than normal. We neither morally praise the commission of, nor morally condemn the omission of, permissible acts. With supererogatory acts, however, we praise the commission, but do not condemn the omission (see table 1.1).

As we mean it in moral theory,[1] the supererogatory is an action that goes beyond moral duty. That the supererogatory act goes beyond moral duty means it is not obligatory: hence we cannot critique the not going beyond moral duty (Zimmerman 1996, 234; Heyd 1982, 73). This may seem false. Someone who deliberately fails to hold a door open for another struggling with a baby carriage and groceries would be thought of as a "jerk," at least in Canada. Thinking of someone as a jerk is a kind of social condemnation, and the appellation, "jerk," seems to be a moral one. To be clear, we would not call someone a jerk for failing to make a large sacrifice for the benefit of a stranger. When we think of someone as a jerk for failing to do something, we expect people to do that thing (under normal conditions). But if we expect someone to do such a thing, the concept of its being beyond duty no longer seems to apply. If it were an action beyond morality, in the realm of the supererogatory, we would no longer expect a person to do it. If the extent of our moral condemnation of someone is to name them a jerk (and no longer interact with them, if possible) then the moral infraction is minimal. We think it wrong, but it is not worth our while to punish beyond social sanction. That there is no formal punishment for door-holding omissions, and similar weak moral rules, does not mean that door holding is not morally expected under suitable conditions: hence not supererogatory.

Contractarians can be more specific. If *A* fails to hold the door open for *B*, *B* might think of *A* as a jerk. But had *A* not been there at all, *B* would still have to contend with the door on *B*'s own. The status quo of *B*, then, is having no door held for *B*. *A* satisfies this: thus *A* cannot be morally condemned unless an argument can be made at the *ex ante* level, that rational, self-interested, amoral agents would agree to a door-holding rule. Such a rule would be constrained to cover the vagaries of physical distance (how far away is the person for whom you ought to hold a door open?), epistemic awareness (how aware are you of the need?), ability (how able one is to handle a door on one's own), numbers of people (for how many people will you have to hold the door in this instance?), and such. Assume such a rule. Then failure to satisfy the door-holding rule in the clear cases of the door-holding rule will deserve moral indignation, but not those who fail to hold the door in the less clear door-holding case. The first is not supererogatory, since it is covered by the *ex ante* agreement of hypothetical agents; the second is not supererogatory, because *ex ante* moral bargainers would not recommend it.

We also interpret "going beyond moral duty" as something that is still in the range of the morally good. Typically, when we define a set of something, say chairs, a thing beyond the boundary of that set is not a chair, but this is not so with the supererogatory. Or consider a marathon. Only when someone begins at the starting line and crosses the finish line are we able to say they completed the marathon. Imagine someone continues running after the finish line. We may say they are going beyond the boundaries of the race, but we would not think their current state of running is part of the race. Whatever they are doing is not part of the marathon game. We would not praise them for going the extra distance. But a supererogatory act, while not morally mandatory, is still, somehow, a moral act, hence morally praiseworthy (contra Archer 2015).

That the supererogatory is morally praiseworthy shows that the supererogatory is not merely a set of permissible actions. We do not morally praise someone for doing something that is morally permissible. My playing the tuba is a permissible act. We do not expect anyone to morally praise my playing the tuba. They may praise or blame my ability to play, mind you. But nor is the supererogatory a required act. We do not morally condemn someone for not going the extra moral mile; only for not going the moral mile.

Almost everyone agrees with defining the supererogatory as a non-obligatory act meriting moral praise without morally condemning omissions. Other demarcations of the supererogatory are sometimes offered. Perhaps only successful beyond-duty acts count as supererogatory. Poorly executed or poorly planned acts may not merit praise. Throwing yourself on a grenade when doing so saves no one and you had a chance of escaping harm, for example, may not be deemed a supererogatory act, especially so if we think supererogatory acts must benefit someone. Or in response to an evacuation due to fires, someone offers bibles instead of needed food, water, or blankets. Despite sloppy, ineffectual acts that merit no moral praise, some unsuccessful acts may still be deemed supererogatory. A person dying in a fire while attempting, yet failing, to save another may still merit a hero's praise. To withhold praise because she was not successful seems an insult.

Another limiting move is to suggest that the supererogatory requires the act to be "extremely valuable" in terms of benefit (Zimmerman 1996, 234). One dying instead of five dying, as in the foxhole case, would be extremely valuable. Offering a 20 per cent tip when a 15 per cent tip was the norm is not especially beneficial to the world. Reputedly, Saint Francis of Assisi preached the gospel to birds and largely for that reason was deemed a saint. I am not clear how valuable such an action is even if the birds understood Saint Francis, but it does seem like a case of the supererogatory.

Another suggestion is to limit the supererogatory to only those acts requiring great sacrifice (Feinberg 1961). Generosity, even someone's frequent generosity, may not count as a supererogatory act, whereas jumping on a grenade to save your foxhole mates is.

Jumping on a grenade may not be a great sacrifice if the alternative, doing nothing, is also death. But that one does so ahead of others is the great sacrifice. Conversely, we qualify supererogatory acts into three sorts: big (great sacrifice), medium (middling sacrifice), and little (small sacrifice) (Chisholm 1963; Richards 1971). To the extent we mildly condemn people who do not make even little self-sacrifices for the benefit of others, however, is the extent to which we think little supererogatory acts are not supererogatory. For example, if someone does not follow the norm of gratitude and civility, we think of that person as rude. Whereas failing the supererogatory is supposed to carry no condemnation at all.

One other distinction of note is whether the supererogatory concerns the act, the agent, or both. According to Heyd (1982), it is the intrinsic value of an agent going beyond duty that makes supererogation uniquely meritorious. As Kant (1797a, 6:397) thinks, "the worth of virtue itself, as its own end, far exceeds the worth of any usefulness and any empirical ends and advantages that virtue may still bring in its wake." This explains why we deem Saint Francis a saint, not because of his good works (if preaching to birds were his only accomplishment), but his being a really good, selfless person. It is true that we sometimes praise the action and sometimes the actor. A worry, however, is whether the intrinsic and extrinsic values have equal strength. Is a useless sacrifice better than a useful non-sacrifice? Case 1: *A* tries to rescue *B* from a fire, but both *A* and *B* die. Case 2: *A* accidently rescues *B* from a fire, I am not sure how, and both *A* and *B* survive. While the intrinsic value of *A*'s act outshines the intrinsic value of *B*'s act, you would think the extrinsic value to *B* in case 2 outweighs the intrinsic value we ascribed to *A* in case 1. Benefiting someone is generally good for the person benefited whatever the motivation behind the benefactor. One way to read Wolf (1982) is that the only value we should attach to supererogatory events is the good it does, not the goodness of the agent, since, as she thinks, the extra goodness of the supererogatory actor is not really of much value at all. We certainly would not encourage our loved ones to be supererogatory agents (at least in the big sense). And if not – although she does overstate her case – the intrinsic value in supererogation is suspect.

Besides, moral praise of a selfless action presumes the notion that self-interested actions are morally bad. From where does this idea originate? They certainly cannot be bad in themselves, lest sleeping and eating are sins. Sloth and gluttony are terms to describe excess, not self-interest. That we ought to sometimes put others ahead of ourselves does not entail that it is morally better to always do so, despite religious messaging to the contrary.

At any rate, not all helping acts are morally good. Should *B* lack, but desire, child pornography, for example, *A*'s self-sacrificially offering *B* child pornography is not likely to be what anybody would call a morally good act. To assign an intrinsic value to *A*'s selfless act – a value unconnected to any instrumental value *B* receives – seems to reveal the worthlessness of intrinsic moral value. Or even if we could identify a residue of moral niceness in *A*'s offer of child pornography, the residue could not override the badness of the act, in which case the intrinsic value of voluntarily giving to another what that other likes is not so strong a concept as we might think.

The value of the sacrifice and the value of the benefit are, for the most part, independent. The value to the one being saved from a fire, for example, should generally be independent of the degree of sacrifice to the saviour. Exceptions may occur. Jim buys Della a cashmere sweater, which Della loves, until she discovers that Jim sacrificed nothing to get it. Conversely, Jim buys Della a cashmere sweater, which Della loves, until she discovers that Jim sold one of his eyeballs to get her the sweater. The sweater's value may now pale in comparison. The problem of valuation is that there is nothing of value in itself; value is an ascription a beholder makes, and such ascription is influenced by social, economic, circumstantial, and environmental conditions, to name a few. Nevertheless, we can ascribe value to the things we need and want independently of the power to get it – a wouldn't-that-be-nice kind of value. But we cannot, as far as I can see, ascribe a value to a sacrifice independent of its result. Sacrifice by itself just seems to be a bad.

Perhaps the value of self-sacrifice is emphasized only when there is great benefit, or the intention of great benefit, to others. Then we can sensibly praise the actor and the act. The question remains: are we double-counting the moral value? If we praise the sacrifice of the agent as a separate category of praise more than the praise of the good done to the one who benefits, we have a theory of moral value unconnected to self-interest. Typically, we imagine duties of beneficence stopping short of self-sacrifice. Morality does not demand I save a drowning victim when my chances of drowning are large enough. I plunge into the water anyway and save the drowning person. Assume my success is largely due to luck. After all, if my saving the person was not due to luck, then my chance of drowning was not that large, and if I had no such large risk, I would have had an obligation to save the person (all else equal). But in my case, I had a large risk of drowning, and, by luck, saved the drowning victim without drowning myself. My rescue seems more reckless than praiseworthy. Thus, we have a standoff: if not reckless, obligatory; if reckless, not praiseworthy. Where is the space for finding the intrinsic value of self-sacrifice?

In what follows, I treat the supererogatory as a category of non-obligatory actions that are morally good and that, since they are morally good actions, we morally praise the doing without condemning the not doing. The puzzle: how can we morally praise an action that is not morally required? How can acting outside the set of morality still be moral?

Heyd (2024) claims that any moral theory unable to accommodate supererogation will be "distressingly impoverished,"[2] although his (1982, 166) defence of the supererogatory as a viable category seems based more on the *fact* of acts that we would call supererogatory. People do go out of their way for good causes, but this hardly shows that moral theory must accommodate it. All it shows is that people sometimes act for reasons they take to be good.

In the following section (2), I briefly explore how supererogation poses a problem for the standard moral theories. The section after that (3) will examine how contractarianism fares with supererogation.

2 UTILITARIANISM, KANTIANISM, AND VIRTUE THEORY

How can an act not required by morality be morally merited?

Utilitarianism tells us that the right or good action is that which maximizes social net utility. Whenever two or more actions are possible, you must always choose the one that increases overall net happiness. We might add, "… among all affected people," but if one is unaffected, one's utility remains zero, so the addition is idle. Between my giving nothing to charity and my giving one dollar to charity, we can suppose the latter action increases net social happiness more than the former. Yet my giving two dollars to charity may increase net social happiness even more than my giving one dollar. This derivation will keep going up to the point where my giving any more to charity will now yield less net social happiness overall than the previous point, when the cost to me outweighs the benefit to others. Imagine we have reached that point of maximal happiness. Morally, I can neither donate less nor more. To go beyond this perfect point cannot be moral; nor can it be morally praiseworthy. If we can reach this sort of tipping scale for every type of action, the category of the supererogatory is not possible for utilitarianism. Singer's (1972) argument for famine relief is a telling example. Because we feel morally obligated to save a child from drowning in shallow water, we ought to admit our moral obligation to save everyone from suffering everywhere up to the point where the constraint on our well-being is comparable to the suffering of those in need of our help. Our lives become dominated by moral obligation; there is no room for the supererogatory (McConnell 1980).

In a similar vein, one might complain that utilitarianism leaves no room for the permissible (Fritts and Miller 2023). If I have reached the point of maximal benefit to my charity, it would not be permissible, let alone praiseworthy, to donate more to charity, on the grounds that doing so would decrease net social utility. Nor can I offer less, since doing so would be suboptimal. We can make this calculation for every action. If our every action must increase net happiness, we cannot permit any action short or long of that. For example, I could not play my tuba unless my tuba playing increased net happiness compared with my not playing the tuba. Therefore, I morally must play my tuba.

Utilitarians may consider a weaker law: Whatever you do, do not decrease net happiness. This will not work. Utilitarianism is a person-indifferent model; every person has an equal value. While my utility is not weightier than yours, it is a value to be counted in the overall score. Assuming my wanting to play the tuba is to increase my happiness, I will not be able to morally not play the tuba, for that would be to decrease net happiness (since it decreases my happiness and we assume everyone else's happiness remains at their status quo). Being mandated to do that which one would do anyway does not make doing that thing morally permissible.

Whether successful or not, some utilitarians have resisted these sorts of arguments. Slote (1989, 3) and Dreier (2004, 142) appeal to satisficing instead of maximizing. Zimmerman (1996, 244–7) distinguishes between deontic rules and axiological ideals and thinks supererogation is possible under the latter. Benn (2018) appeals to how rule utilitarianism would recognize the general disutility of a demand for perfection.

Kantians have an even more difficult time with admitting the supererogatory.[3] Ought I to harm others? No. Ought I to help others? Yes. Is my contribution to world aid a case of helping others? Yes. At what point ought I to stop helping others? Here lies a mystery. On the one hand, the imperative to give aid is an imperfect duty, such that we would not prosecute non-aid. On the other hand, moral duties are determined by the categorical imperative and apply whether or not one's selfish interests come into play. A third hand, if we had such a thing, is to treat supererogation as an unattainable ideal that we must constantly approximate, nevertheless (Kant 1797a, 6:409). This would explain why we do not condemn someone for failing to go beyond duty, but it would not explain why we have no duty to try. Nor would it explain why we have no duty to perform any supererogatory action already achieved – jumping on grenades, turning the other cheek – since achievement proves attainability. Besides, since virtue is properly only one thing – to have the subjective disposition to fulfill one's duty (Kant 1797a, 6:410) – duties of virtue can (i) always be fulfilled such that coming short is a failure of moral obligation, and (ii) going beyond the disposition to do one's duty would be as impossible as making rounder a circle, or straighter a straight line (Kant 1797a, 6:433n). For Kantians, then, positive obligations consume the supererogatory. Never can we get to a point at which we could act beyond duty.

At least Kantianism permits the category of the permissible: all those acts the doing of which could be willed to be a universal law without contradiction, like tuba playing. Although if we imagine everyone always and at the same time playing the tuba, that would be a nightmare.

Neo-Kantians of a certain ilk like to put all the weight on Kant's principle of ends and ignore talk of a synthetic a priori moral law. As put, our moral task is to respect people as ends in themselves and never treat them as means to our ends only. The use of the word "only" permits us to use people for our ends, but to never do so without treating them as ends-in-themselves also.[4] Mutual using, thus, is fine. Little supererogatory gestures of gratitude and civility are both signs and symptoms of this required respect. Thus, little supererogatory acts, at least, are obligatory components of respect. But a social rule based on respect by itself is underdetermined. Can

I respect you yet not provide you with aid? Can I respect you and provide you with only minimal aid? Is it better for you that I provide you with maximal aid and not respect you than for me to respect you but offer no aid? This last question highlights, among other things, an ambiguity concerning the supererogatory. Even if we can go beyond duty in terms of providing amounts of aid to people, we cannot go beyond our duty in maintaining respect for people.[5] Respect seems to be an on-off kind of thing and our duty is to have it turned on all the time when interacting with people.

Whether successful or not, some Kantians defend supererogation's existence. For example, Hill (1971) proposes that Kant can permit supererogatory acts for wide imperfect duties, that is, duties of virtue (Kant 1797a, 6:410).[6] Heyd (1980) emphasizes that the Kantian respect of personal autonomy may sometimes trump objective judgments about the moral good: thus leaving room for the supererogatory.

Virtue theory is the clearest example of a perfectionist moral theory, and perfectionist moral theories seem impossible to allow room for supererogation (Benn 2014; Crisp 2013; Fritts and Miller 2023; Heyd 2015). Morality and well-being perfectly coincide in virtue theory. The value of being moral, behaving as the virtuous do, lies in psychological health. Vice tends to motivate immoral action. Greed, avarice, jealousy, hatred are the bedrock for immoral action and such traits cannot do the individuals who hold such traits any favours. It would be better for them if they, instead, learned to be patient, loving, kind, forgiving, generous. But there is no limit to kindness. You can always be kinder.

As Wolf (1982) says, striving for perfection is a kind of excess – a fanaticism. A virtue theorist may agree – to be excessive in anything, including saintliness, seems incongruous with the Golden Mean. Aristotle tells us that virtue lies in the middle, between excess and deficiency. If one is at the mean, then anything beyond that must be excessive. As it is excessive, however, it cannot be morally praiseworthy. If the Golden Mean is itself perfection, to go beyond that would be excessive. Since supererogatory acts go beyond moral demands, virtue theory cannot permit supererogation.

Whether successful or not, some virtue theorists defend virtue theory's allowance for the supererogatory. Swanton (2004, 177) takes a satisficing account, such that an act is right so long as it meets a general level of virtue. In a similar vein, Stangl (2016) recognizes that one may perform more than one virtuous act in a single gesture, and more than one way of hitting a virtuous target. This allows us to hit more or fewer targets in more or less skilled ways, opening a gap between satisfactory virtues and supererogatory virtues. Since virtue is relative to the situation (Aristotle 1941, 1106b), Hursthouse (2006, 111) suggests that one virtuous person's obligation may be another virtuous person's supererogation. Building on Hursthouse's account, Russell (2008), Kawall (2009), and van Zyl (2011) employ an ideal virtuous observer account to allow for supererogation in virtue theory.

3 CONTRACTARIANISM AND SUPEREROGATION

Neither virtue theory, Kantianism, nor utilitarianism can happily accept supererogation despite what appears to be the reality of supererogation. Can contractarians do better, assuming a moral theory that permits supererogation is better than one that does not?

As discussed in the introductory chapter, contractarians conceive of morality as a necessary constraint on social life. Moral rules advise us on how to live as best we can, conceived in terms of subjective self-interest, given the interests of others. Moral obligation is accepted only insofar as the benefit to the moral agent – the one asked to take on the duty – outweighs the cost of the duty itself. Negative rights are easily justified in this picture; positive rights with more difficulty. While many take the lack of positive obligations that contractarianism can generate as a reason to reject contractarianism, the dearth of positive duties is what allows room for the supererogatory, at least so it may appear. We can imagine contracting agents in suitable *ex ante* positions accepting an agreement to prevent nearby others from suffering when we can do so without too much cost to ourselves, but shy away from extending that help in any perfectionist quest. Of course, people are *permitted* to help others as much as they want, just as people are permitted to do whatever they want, assuming no infraction on others' like pursuits. The supererogatory is not supposed to be merely permissible, however.[7] We are supposed to praise people for going beyond duty without condemning others for not doing so. To call supererogatory actions morally praiseworthy and supererogatory people morally nice requires justification beyond pointing out that contractarianism permits space for people to do more than the morally required.

One reply is to count supererogatory actions as permissible, but nice to others. Many actions are permissible, buying myself a cup of coffee, for example, but buying myself a cup of coffee is not particularly nice to others. (It may be, if someone is selling cups of coffee for a charity.) When I buy you a coffee, on the other hand, a permissible action, not a morally mandatory action, it is also a case of doing something nice to others, you in this case. Thus, my buying you a coffee is a supererogatory act: morally nice but not morally required. This response will not do, however. The mistake occurs, I think, in conflating the niceness of receiving with the niceness of giving. *A* does something nice to *B* if the thing done to *B* is something *B* likes. But what makes it "nice" for *A* to do that which *B* appreciates? These two senses of "nice" are not the same; the first is amoral, the second moral, and the second is not obviously derived from the first. It is not just an objective fact that it is morally nice to do that which another finds nice. At any rate, contractarianism needs to explain the moral sense of doing something nice for another in terms that make it an overall prudential move of the first. There must be a reason that doing nice to others is worthwhile to the nice-doers, not merely the nice-receivers. If kind actions are due merely to the interests of the people who are kind, this deserves no more moral praise than someone doing something kind to themselves. A large gap exists between the amoral niceness of receiving and the moral niceness of giving. Recognizing this gap, I think, goes a long way to explaining why contractarians cannot place the supererogatory in the permissible-but-nice category, as might seem sensible.

Following Hobbes, the good is a purely subjective relative notion. "But Whatsoever is the object of any mans Appetite or Desire; that is it, which he for his part calleth *Good*" (Hobbes 1651, ch. 6). What an individual wants out of life is a good for them. Morality, for contractarians, comes into the picture merely as a prudential tool to guide each person through the travails of social life in order to secure, or at least not prevent, that individual's own notion of the good life. Morality is a restriction on an agent's behaviour aimed at maximizing that agent's own overarching interests given their social circumstance. The task is not to be moral for morality's sake, but to be moral for the individual agent's sake. For contrast, Dorsey (2012) solves the supererogatory problem by suggesting that while supererogation is morally obligatory, it is not rationally obligatory. From a contractarian perspective, this makes little sense. Contractarians conceive of morality as a subset of rationality, or prudence (Gauthier 1986, 4), and they conceive it this way because they regard morality as a tool to assist communal living as opposed to a fact of nature to which they must adhere. If the contractarian picture is correct, we would resist calling anything moral that would not be overall prudent. The upshot of this is that, for any action about which moral restrictions are lifted, no moral vocabulary may be used. To say, "Hey, that was nice of you," if "nice" is used morally, has no epistemic support.

Richards (1971, 196) demurs. Surely, we can imagine original contractors agreeing on an imperfect rule to benefit others when doing so costs the helper little and no one is plagued by the costs to agents of having the rule enforced.[8] The benefit to those being helped is obvious, and the benefit to the helper is twofold. Firstly, they, too, may find themselves in a spot of trouble and would appreciate living in a society where *ex ante* bargainers had committed themselves to a non-enforceable (but generally practised) helping policy. Secondly, in a society where civility (little supererogatory acts) is the norm, everyone avoids "various forms of arbitrary insult, crudity, annoyance, and the like, and [this] *generally facilitates the ease of social interaction*" (Richards 1971, 197). I emphasize the last phrase because, consistent with Hobbes, the point of morality is to help our society run smoothly: to seek peace so that each of us can pursue our own ends with as little molestation as possible. Since *ex ante* bargainers recognize the value of civility to each individual, they would adopt a policy of encouragement for those who practise civility. Thus, *ex post* agents will say to supererogatory agents, "Nice job! Keep it up!"

Extending such reasoning to big supererogatory acts is more difficult, since big supererogatory acts require great self-sacrifice. To explain why self-interested agents would voluntarily self-sacrifice for a greater good, Richards (1971, 206–7) posits that the sacrificing agent has an interest in sacrifice given excess Humean sympathy for others or for some adopted principle,[9] and that their sacrifice contributes to the benefit of others.

If someone wants to self-sacrifice and doing so does not harm anyone and furthermore helps someone, then of course, contractarians are not going to disapprove.[10] But that they will *approve* rests, according to Richards, on the fact that the approvers gain as well.

After all, the more we encourage people to be really nice – assuming they are so constituted to want to – the more we will benefit from their selflessness.

Lessons from game theory, however, disallow such parametric thinking. We know that in a prisoner's dilemma (PD), defection is the rational choice for each agent despite each agent's subjective desire to improve upon their status quo of mutual defection. They most prefer to defect while the other co-operates; but since the other also desires this, they remain in their suboptimal state of nature. If the only two strategies were to unconditionally co-operate (UC) and to unconditionally defect (UD), UDs win out. A third strategy is available, however: the disposition to reciprocally co-operate (RC) (Axelrod 1984; Trivers 1971; Gauthier 1986).[11] An RC will co-operate when the other co-operates, yet defect when the other defects. Players using the conditional strategy of RC benefit in terms of self-interest in ways that co-operators and defectors miss – through greater opportunities (both quantitative and qualitative) for mutual gain. This explains how self-interested, amoral agents in a pre-moral state could consent to be bound by rules (i.e., morality) governing their social interactions.

For demonstration, let us pit our three strategies against each other in a series of PDs. Assign 0 utiles to each player for mutual defection. Assign 1 utile to each player for mutual co-operation. Assign 2 utiles to any player unilaterally defecting. Subtract 1 utile to any player being unilaterally defected upon. The more utiles, the better for the agent adopting that strategy. Now imagine a world where the UD and RC strategies have two players each, while UC, being the underdog strategy, has only one player. The results (table 1.2) show how RC gains the advantage over the other strategies.

Since UDs benefit from UCs, the more UCs, the better UDs do, and the fewer UCs, the worse UDs do. This is an important detail, a detail that derails Richard's defence of the supererogatory. Since supererogatory agents sacrifice their own interests for others without demand for, or expectation of, reciprocity, a supererogatory agent must be a UC. While many people like to say such players display the *true* moral property, a kind of turn-the-other-cheek approach to life, this view is mistaken for contractarians. The only true moral agent is the one adopting the RC strategy, for it is only the RC strategy that offers a cure to the state of nature, a condition absent moral constraint. UCs persist by relying on the success of RCs. The presence of RCs diminishes the

Table 1.2 | Prisoner's dilemma results

	First player			
Second player	Unconditionally co-operates	Unconditionally defects	Reciprocally co-operates	Avg.
Unconditionally co-operates	1(1)	−1(2)	1(2)	0.2
Unconditionally defects	2(1)	0(2)	0(2)	0.4
Reciprocally co-operates	1(1)	0(2)	1(2)	0.6

success of UDs. The presence of UCs encourages the success of UDs. If we think a society with fewer UDs is preferable to a society with more UDs, we ought not to encourage UCs (Danielson 1992, 114–18).

An objection. If there were only RCs in a foxhole when a grenade gets tossed in, we would imagine a standoff: each waiting for the other to jump on the grenade, and all dying. To avoid such scenarios, it would seem prudent to encourage UCs. Yes, but such encouragement is duplicitous. It would be better for RCs if you were a UC; it is not better for you to be a UC. Contractarianism, meanwhile, is supposed to be founded on the expectation of mutual benefit, not one-sided benefit. So, if supererogatory acts are attractive to UCs only, and contractarians cannot sincerely encourage anyone to be a UC, then *ex ante* contractors cannot approve of a rule to morally praise supererogatory acts (on the grounds that we wish to curtail UDs).

4 ERROR THEORY

Where does this leave us concerning the contractarian view of the supererogatory? Since UC is a possible strategy, we could say that the category of the supererogatory is at least available, albeit not recommended. If we cannot morally recommend supererogation, however, the action can no longer count as supererogation, assuming supererogation is defined as morally praiseworthy. While we may not recommend becoming a UC to those we love, as Wolf (1982) notes, we really do praise supererogatory acts, often posthumously, as Urmson (1958) notes. If contractarianism is the best account of morality, our thoughts about supererogation must be in error. If any other moral theory is correct, supererogation will also be in error, but morally praising a morally obligatory act is a different kind of error than morally praising a morally permissible act. People do go out of their way for good causes. But this hardly shows that moral theory must accommodate it. All it shows is that people sometimes act for reasons they take to be good. Such a wide scale error must have a sensible explanation. I offer four: (i) short-sightedness, (ii) an overextended heuristic, (iii) non-moral praise, and (iv) definitional fiat. None are sufficient in themselves, but together present a formidable explanation.

(i) I live in an area populated by foxes. The suggestion given to us is not to feed the foxes since the food offered is not generally healthy for the foxes and also makes the foxes more demanding of people, leading to an increased risk of their attacking pets or children, forcing city officials to exterminate the very fox we were trying to help. But to feed foxes *seems* to be a moral thing to do. Similarly, it *seems* like the moral thing to do to encourage supererogatory acts, for people aim their supererogatory acts toward what we, prima facie, take to be a moral good: helping others. That it cannot be rationally recommended if the cost to the agent doing so is too great is not sufficient to discourage people who desire to do so – it is a permissible action, after all – but since such desires, the desires of a UC, widen the niche for UDs, nor can we encourage the desire itself. The UC strategy is based on insufficient vision. Just as we fox-feeders and fox-feeding-praisers see only the intrinsic value of helping, we miss the extrinsic harm our strategies produce.

In an important sense, the fox-feeding parallel fails to capture the UC worry. Fox-feeders may ultimately harm the fox they are trying to help; not so UCs. The harm UCs cause comes from opening niches for UDs, and they are the ones who harm the rest of us. A better parallel, then, may be our penchant to feed a wild species that, by its burgeoning population, invites other predators, say wolves, who feed on the burgeoning species but also our pets and children. At any rate, the idea here is to understand kindness in long-term and overall benefits, not short-term, short-sighted benefits, and we err by conflating a bit of kindness with the whole of kindness.[12]

(ii) An over-extended heuristic is a second possible explanation of the wide-scale error in our seeing UC's supererogatory behaviour as moral, if not ideally moral, as religious lore might have it.[13] Assume we have adopted the RC strategy: we co-operate with other co-operators yet defect against defectors. Reciprocity requires correct identification of the dispositions of other players. Mistakes can occur in two directions; we can mistake them and they can mistake us. Being correctly identified as an RC is more important to RCs than it is to UDs or UCs. UDs, in fact, would prefer being misidentified. RCs, therefore, will go out of their way to broadcast their RCness. This may create behaviours in them that would not be necessary absent the possibility of misidentification. For example, an RC need not co-operate with a UC, since a UC's co-operation is not contingent on the RC's co-operation.[14] But if another RC sees me defect against a UC, perhaps not knowing they were a UC, they may mistake me for being a UD, and thus remove their willingness to co-operate with me. If such a threat occurs often enough, it would be better for me to adopt a disposition to needlessly co-operate with UCs simply to prevent the *look* of my being a UD. As a result, my benefiting certain others needlessly will appear to be supererogatory.

Such a drive to preserve one's reputation as congenial to future co-operation will move a society of RCs to practise acts of charity and civility – little supererogatory behaviours. In fact, we expect social condemnation for failing to do so. Hence, little supererogatory acts would not count as supererogatory. On the other hand, an overextended heuristic cannot accommodate our praising big supererogation. My behaving as a moral saint is certainly not required to keep up appearances of my being an RC.

(iii) A third possible explanation of why we incorrectly believe in supererogation is that the praise we give for going beyond moral duty is not itself moral. We praise a fast runner for being best at running. Similarly, we may praise a supererogatory agent for being best (or among the best) at whatever it is they did. "You sure love helping people!" "You sure are one of the best at sticking to your ideals!" "You sure are good at putting others' interests ahead of your own!" Such praise need not have any moral content; we are simply praising best-in-class, someone's succeeding at goals they set for themselves, whether we think the goals themselves are worth anything.

Unlike most best-in-class praise, supererogatory acts tend toward providing goods for others. The act of running fast does not itself benefit others, typically. That supererogation benefits others seems to make supererogatory acts morally praiseworthy in a way that best-in-class praise does not. This leads us to a fourth possible error theory.

(iv) A fourth error theory appeals to the difference between definition and derivation. When we praise supererogatory acts, we may mean it is good that those sorts of actions have the goal of helping others when not morally required.[15] We can stipulate the meaning of a good act as those types of acts that help someone, or genuinely help someone, or possibly intend to help someone, without making it a moral requirement that we help anyone. Disconnecting the good of received help from the good of helping is easy. If a falling branch hits a person *A*, this is bad for *A*, but we do not call the branch bad, or the act of the branch falling bad. When a person, *B*, hits *A*, on the other hand, at least intentionally, the bad to *A* carries over to *B*. But the two senses of bad are not the same. The bad to *A* is amoral. The bad we attribute to *B* we designate as immoral. In saying this, we are not deriving the immoral bad from the amoral bad. Rather, we define the immoral bad as a case of someone's intentionally causing an amoral bad to another. Similarly, when *A* helps *B*, the good *B* receives is an amoral good, some bread, for example, but the good we attribute to *A* is a moral good, or so we like to designate it. The moral good is not a derivation from the amoral good received, but, again, borne by stipulation. Any act that provides a non-moral good to some other person (or animal) is defined as a moral good, in which case, supererogation would count as a moral good, recommended or not. A nominal category, of course, cannot account for any "true moral significance," as supererogatists (Raz 1988, 197, for example) desire. Expecting a nominal category to provide intrinsic goodness-in-itself is where people have gone astray: an expectation of a real morality, undoubtedly rooted in religion.

Combining the errors together, we get an understanding of supererogation as a non-moral praising of a best-in-class delivery of subjective goods to others. That people wish to call the delivery of non-moral goods a moral act stems from our liking to receive things or services that are subjective goods to us. Since we cannot derive a moral good from the delivery of a non-moral good, no moral obligation to do so can be found. While some of us might accept a lack of obligation to benefit another, especially at great expense to ourselves, most of us still sense a non-obligatory goodness in doing so. But this is based on an equivocation between our enjoying non-moral subjective goods to the ascription of moral good to others who provide that to us. As well, we often fail to see the long-term implications of our short-sighted actions, and we possess a useful, though often overextended, tendency to maintain a reputation of being someone with whom any co-operator can trust.

5 CONCLUSION

As with other moral theories, contractarianism cannot accommodate supererogation. Unlike other theories, however, it can offer error theories explaining why our penchant to morally praise supererogatory acts is a mistake.

2

Trolley Problems

The Trolley problem unearths a tension between competing moral principles, minimally that between helping and not harming, or between helping in one case but not in similar cases, or between whether numbers matter in ethical calculations. In section 2, I raise difficulties with the standard offered solutions. In section 3, I explain how contractarianism addresses the problem by relying on the concept of a status quo.

1 THE TROLLEY PROBLEM

In TROLLEY, a runaway trolley is heading toward five persons stuck on the track.[1] If it reaches them, they will all be killed. You, a bystander, can pull a lever to switch the tracks so that the trolley avoids the five people. Unfortunately, one person is stuck on this side track. Assume, as in all forthcoming variants, (i) the bystander has full information, (ii) the bystander is able to pull the lever (or perform whichever task trolley problem variant demands), and (iii) the people stuck on trolley tracks (or hospital gurneys) are equal in all relevant senses. Under such a situation, is it morally permissible to pull the lever? If all that matters in determining right from wrong is counting up happinesses and subtracting pains and not worrying about the individual distribution of utility, then why not, as in TRANSPLANT, pluck the organs of one healthy person for transplant into five unhealthy people?[2]

In SUMO,[3] a runaway trolley is heading toward five people stuck on the track. They will die if the trolley reaches them. On a bridge over the track, a sumo wrestler is leaning over the railing. With a slight nudge, you can push the sumo wrestler onto the track in front of the trolley. His bulk is great enough to be able to stop the trolley from reaching the five, but not so large as to protect the sumo wrestler from death. Should you push the sumo wrestler? If not, we see, again, that mere numbers are not the deciding moral factor. But what is the principle that distinguishes why it is permissible to pull the lever in Trolley, yet not operate in Transplant, nor push the wrestler in Sumo?

Even those who would not pull the lever in Trolley understand the lure of pulling the lever. The lure is that, all things equal, we should probably opt for the choice that involves less dying than more. To the extent that someone pulls the lever for that reason is the extent to which we might deem her action not morally blameworthy. In Sumo and Transplant, our intuitions shift. Most think such actions are morally atrocious. No difference exists in outcomes, of course.[4] If the only principle was "less death is better than more," we should find little difference between our moral judgments in the three cases. Most people do see a moral difference. The trolley problem forces us to come up with a reasonable and consistent principle to explain the difference that coheres with our other moral beliefs.[5] What is such a principle?

2 PROFFERED SOLUTIONS

2.1 *Letting Die vs Killing*

Letting someone die is different from causing that person's death. This conceptual distinction is also supposed to carry a moral distinction: letting die is morally better than killing (Foot 1967). In RESCUE I, an ambulance passes someone dying on the side of the road to attend to five people dying farther ahead. In RESCUE II, an ambulance has to run over a person in the middle of the road to attend to five dying farther ahead. That we think Rescue I is morally permissible while Rescue II is not, Foot (1967) explains, is because Rescue I is a case of letting die, whereas Rescue II is a case of killing. While killing is rarely okay, letting die is often okay. The distinction between positive and negative rights captures this. To fail a negative right is worse than to fail a positive right, especially if the reason to fail a positive right is the violation of a negative right, other things being equal.

This solution does not work well with Trolley, however. Killing the person on the spur track in Trolley would have to be deemed permissible because, apart from less death being preferable to more, *it is a mere case of letting die, not killing.* This seems implausible. My pulling the switch directly initiates an action that kills the person on the spur. How, then, is pulling the switch in Trolley a case of letting the person on the side track die as opposed to killing that person? Trolley is decidedly different than Rescue I. A REVERSED TROLLEY case could capture Rescue I. Imagine one person on the tracks in front of a runaway trolley. On a spur are five. To pull the lever to kill the five is not permissible. The moral decision is to do nothing and witness the death of the one.

Even if we imagine that pulling the lever in Trolley is a case of letting die, many counter cases exist against the belief that letting die is morally better than killing (Rachels 1975; Tooley 1980). Consider EMPTY TRACK. In Empty Track, a runaway trolley will stop on its own without hitting anyone unless someone pulls a switch to change the trolley's path onto a spur where one person is stuck. To switch the trolley from the empty track to the spur would seem wrong. Saying, "I didn't kill anyone, the Trolley did, I merely let the death occur," is hardly exonerating.

Another problem exists. A further distinction along with causing death and letting die may be made: what I shall call *witnessing death.*

When we *cause death*, the death would not have occurred without our actions. When the deaths we cause are unintentional, save for negligence, we do not tend to ascribe blame. Intentionally causing death will tend to be immoral, but not always. Other things being equal, it is moral to intentionally cause death to a villain to stop that villain from killing others, or when we stop an assailant from harming us. When we *witness a death*, as in vigils, a person is dying, there is nothing anyone can do about it, and we watch it happen with varying emotions. *Letting a person die* is an act that lies between witnessing a death and causing death. We let someone die when we can right now do something that would prevent that person's imminent death yet intentionally refrain from doing so. This distinguishes letting die from vigils. In vigils, there is nothing we are withholding.

Passive euthanasia is assumed to be a case of letting die, for had the medical team continued to provide life-sustaining treatment, the patient would not have died. Their withholding that treatment is partly why the patient dies. Most people deem passive euthanasia to be morally permissible when the medical team withholds treatment either because death is imminent despite further treatment, or the patient (or proxy) autonomously requests cessation of treatment. Absent those reasons, letting the person die may not be morally justifiable. If during an operation my heart stopped and all it would take is manual pumping to get it going again, a medical team that does nothing would seem negligent.

A problem exists, however. If the medical team is withholding treatment because treatment is deemed useless, then it is not correct to say the patient would not have died absent their withholding treatment.[6] If so, as seems obvious, then such cases of passive euthanasia are not cases of letting someone die. They would be cases of sitting vigil. A similar conclusion follows when the withholding of treatment in passive euthanasia is purely at the patient's request despite the fact that treatment would avoid imminent death. Assuming it is a wrong to violate a competent patient's consent concerning treatment to that patient's body, the medical team cannot morally proceed with treatment. Being bound in this way, it is misleading to say that the medical team could have provided treatment. They were forbidden. Hence, they could not. As a result, the medical team withheld nothing that they could have given to sustain life. The standard case of moral passive euthanasia, then, would not count as a case of letting die. This is an odd conclusion if the paradigmatic example of the morality of letting die is passive euthanasia.

Could letting die, as defined, ever be morally justified? Rescue I seems a plausible case. As Foot described it, however, the ambulance had already committed to rescuing five farther ahead. Other morally stronger obligations prevented the ambulance from stopping to help the person on the side of the road. As with passive euthanasia, then, it is not correct to describe Rescue I as a case where the ambulance *could have stopped.* Given their prior and morally stronger obligation, they were unable to stop. The moral obligation to save the five precedes the normal obligation of stopping to save the one; thus the moral obligation to save the five trumps the moral obligation to save the one. As put, the moral obligation to save the one is no longer on. If one has a moral obligation to do x, then one must not do that which will knowingly prevent x from happening. Passing the dying person on the side of the road, thereby, is more a case of witnessing a death (in passing), not letting a death occur.

Consider another rescue case, FIRE I. A fire traps two people (A and B) and you have time enough to save only one. In saving A, it appears that you let B die, since had you not saved A, you could have saved *B*. In electing to rescue *A* over *B*, you intentionally withheld doing a thing that would have saved *B*. Nevertheless, after your having saved *A*, no one would say of you that you let *B* burn to death. It would sound like an accusation, not a moral endorsement. That we would not say, "You let the person burn," fits with the distinction between vigils and letting people die. We let someone die only if we could have prevented the death. But in rescuing *A* in Fire I, we could not have prevented the death of *B*. Of course, we could have prevented the death of *B* by not saving *A*, but we could not have rescued *B* given that we rescued *A*. Consider FIRE II, a case where only one person is caught in a fire and you have the opportunity to save the person. Assuming no psychological, physical, or epistemological impediment, we would correctly say you let that person die in the fire if you could have saved that person but did not. We would also think it immoral of you to have wilfully failed to save a life when you easily could have done so, all else equal. Of course, we will find it difficult to know whether people wilfully opt out of saving a life when they knowingly could have saved that life without harm to themselves. An epistemological gap exists with letting die, but not with causing death. My point is not social-psychological; it is conceptual.

A complication: Consider RESCUE III (a reversal of Rescue I) in which an ambulance is on its way to save one and sees on the side of the road five dying, all of whom could be saved by the ambulance should it stop. Ought we to say that the prior obligation to the one trumps the requirement to stop and save the five? We know obligations may be overridden by other, more serious obligations. I ought to save a bystander in my path even if my doing so breaks my promise to meet you for tea.[7] Whether numbers ought to override one's prior positive obligation from an arising positive obligation is not, however, the problem Trolley poses: whether our positive obligations to help others (when the numbers are large enough) ought to override the negative rights of third parties.[8]

For another illustration, consider DRUNKARD. I am driving a car (with brakes and steering) and discover ahead of me in my lane a drunkard. Should I fail to brake or turn the wheel, the drunkard dies. Should I run over the drunkard, ought we to say I am the cause of the drunkard's death, or ought we to say I let the drunkard die? I am certain to be charged with causing the drunkard's death by running him over, but, really, the death would not have occurred had either the drunkard not been in the road, or I had done something – apply the brakes or turn the wheel. It is my refraining from doing either of those things that results in a corpse. So, I let the drunkard die. I am not saying letting the drunkard die in such a way is morally permissible. Compare a slightly different case, PEDESTRIAN. While I am driving along, I espy a pedestrian on the sidewalk and I turn the wheel so that the car runs over this pedestrian and the pedestrian dies. In Pedestrian, it is clear that I am the cause of the pedestrian's death. The death would not have occurred without my turning the wheel. Absent something I have done, driven onto the sidewalk, the pedestrian would have lived. I caused the death of the pedestrian on the sidewalk, but merely let the drunkard in the road die (despite our not being inclined to speak that way). Despite the let/cause difference, both acts are immoral. Compare PASSENGER. I am a passenger in a car, the driver of which collapses from a heart attack and runs over a drunkard in the road. Assuming I was unable to apply the brakes or turn the wheel, I, the passenger, neither caused the drunkard's death, nor let the drunkard die. I witnessed the drunkard die. My inaction is morally permissible. I focus only on ability to do something that would prevent death. Overlapping the distinction here is the assumed responsibility for avoiding harms that the driver, but not the passenger, assumes when getting behind the wheel. The driver neglects her duty, the passenger does not, since the passenger did not undertake that duty. Thomson removed this complication by switching the Trolley scenario from Driver to Bystander.

We can see this more readily in another version of Trolley I shall call EMPTY SPUR. Five people are on a track toward which a runaway trolley is heading. You are at a switch. To pull the switch, you divert the trolley onto another track. In this case, no one is on this other track. It is an empty spur. Imagine, however, you do not pull the lever. In such a case you have let the five people die, for you could have done something to prevent their death, but you did not do that thing. Absent physical, psychological, or epistemic constraints, we would think you are morally to blame. Had you suffered physical, psychological, or epistemic constraints that prevented you from pulling the lever, we would not (or should not) call it a case of a morally permissible letting die: your being unable to pull the lever would render your inaction no longer a case of letting someone die. It would be a case of witnessing death. Morally permissible. Whereas when you pull the lever in Trolley and the one person dies, we recognize that that one person would not have died had it not been for your action. This, then, counts as a case of causing death, not letting someone die. Whether it is morally permissible is another matter.

So far, then, letting die seems to be immoral. When it is not immoral, we refrain, or ought to refrain, from calling it a case of letting die. We ought to call it a case of vigilance. That said, people are dying all over the place. It may be true that we could be doing something to prevent death and, if so, our not doing that thing is a form of negligence. I could quit my job and go to a war-ravaged village to help dig wells so that someone may not die due to infected water. When I fail to quit my job for that good act, and someone dies from infected water in that village, I would be accused of letting that person die, an accusation of immoral negligence. Without offering here an argument against such an extension, I have deliberately curtailed it by adding *temporality* into the definition of letting die. I let someone die if I can *right now* do something that would prevent that person's *imminent* death, yet refrain from doing so. There is nothing I can do right now that guarantees the rescue of a person occupying space currently inaccessible to me. I did not let the person die; I stood vigil over it.

Given my analysis of letting die, pulling the lever in Trolley is not a case of letting someone die. Calling it a case of letting die in order to associate it with moral actions like passive euthanasia or Rescue I or Rescue III is misplaced for two reasons. (i) We are causing death when we divert the trolley in Trolley; we are not letting die. (ii) Actions that result in death that we deem moral, like passive euthanasia, ought not to be viewed as cases of letting someone die; they are more like vigils.

Whether pulling the lever in Trolley is a case of letting die or causing death, we may still ask whether it is morally acceptable under the circumstances. After all, we know it is sometimes morally permissible to cause death. For example, in self-defence, or, as I would argue, active euthanasia. Both are cases of causing death that, under suitable conditions, many count as morally permissible. The letting/causing (or active/passive) distinction has no role to play if we are to justify pulling the lever in Trolley without being committed to push the wrestler off the bridge in Sumo.

2.2 *Doctrine of Double Effect*

To say without contradiction Yes to switching the track in Trolley while saying No to the transplant in Transplant and No to pushing the wrestler in Sumo, some philosophers appeal to the doctrine of double effect.[9] The doctrine of double effect (DDE) claims that an action that causes harm as a side effect of promoting a greater good may be justifiable assuming the following four conditions.

1 The agent's ultimate goal and intention are good.
2 Although the agent may foresee a bad consequence in their pursuit of the good, they do not intend it, and they try to mitigate it where possible.
3 The bad consequence is neither pursued as an end in itself nor as a means to the agent's goal.
4 The good end the agent seeks outweighs the bad consequence.[10]

Trolley passes the doctrine of double effect, while Transplant and Sumo do not. Whether or not Transplant and Sumo meet criterion 4, they certainly fail criteria 2 and 3 of the DDE. The wrestler on the bridge in Sumo and the healthy individual in Transplant are both *means* to achieve the good goal of saving five others. Whereas our killing the lone person stuck on the spur in Trolley, even if foreseen, is neither a means to saving the five, nor intended. We would save the five by pulling the lever even if no one was on the spur, as in Empty Spur. We could not save the five without the wrestler in Sumo or the healthy patient in Transplant. DDE captures our saying Yes to Trolley and No to Sumo and Transplant. To this extent, the DDE sounds promising.

Thomson is dubious. Imagine LOOP, a variant of Trolley in which the spur loops back to the main track (Thomson 1985, 1402–3). On the main track are five people. On the looping spur sits the sumo wrestler. The runaway trolley is heading toward the five. You can pull the lever so that it turns onto the loop. In this case, Thomson tells us, the DDE is no longer satisfied, for without the sumo wrestler on the spur, pulling the lever would not save the five; the trolley will head through the loop and reconnect with the five on the main track. In Loop, the sumo wrestler's bulk is a *means* of saving the five. Since the wrestler's death is a means of saving the five, we also thereby intend the wrestler's death (or we intend to use the wrestler's body as a blockade) when we pull the lever. Loop fails criteria 2 and 3 of the DDE. But, says Thomson, if it is fine to pull the lever in Trolley, it is fine to pull the lever in Loop.[11] Since DDE does not allow Loop, DDE is flawed.[12]

One response is to say the reverse: since DDE tells us to pull the lever in Trolley but not to pull the lever in Loop, Loop and Trolley are morally different (Costa 1986). Thomson (1985, 102), however, wonders how an extra bit of track can make a moral difference.[13] Easy, I should think. Consider LONG TRACK. In Long Track, an extra bit of track lies between the runaway trolley and the five such that the Trolley's inertia will die out before it reaches the five. To pull the lever to crush a lone occupant on the spur would therefore seem impertinent. This shows that an extra bit of track can make a moral difference. It does not show that we should endorse the DDE, since we have other means than the DDE to explain why we ought not to pull the lever in Long Track.

My objection to the DDE concerns how costs to one person may be outweighed by a benefit to another, particularly. The standard objections to DDE, meanwhile, are our inability to clarify what counts as a means versus an end and what counts as intended versus merely foreseen.[14] For example, Davis (1984) argues that proponents of DDE equivocate between an *agent-interpretation* and an *event-interpretation* of means and intentions. An agent-interpretation pays attention to what the agent takes her intention to be. An event-interpretation takes a causal analysis of what events need to occur for the goal to be achieved. Accordingly, DDE proponents believe we are allowed to give a woman a hysterectomy that will kill her fetus if she is endangered by uterine cancer, but we are not allowed to crush a fetus's skull to ease its extraction so we can save a woman's life in labour (Quinn 1989). The idea is that we *mean* to crush the fetus's skull in CRANIOTOMY, so DDE prevents it, but we do not mean to kill the fetus in HYSTERECTOMY, so DDE permits it. According to Davis, such an interpretation is plausible only if we take an agent-interpretation in Hysterectomy and an events-interpretation in Craniotomy. An agent-interpretation would permit both hysterectomy and craniotomy, and an events-interpretation would permit neither. To think one is permissible and not the other is to equivocate.

In the case of Loop, an event-interpretation would point out that we causally require the death of the lone person on the spur. An agent-interpretation of Loop, however, would not run afoul of the DDE: we really do not intend the lone person's death in Loop any more than in Trolley. If the Trolley gods replaced the sumo wrestler with a sufficiently large sack of potatoes, we would still pull the lever.

One might suggest the DDE is saved if, following Davis's lead, we adopt an agent-interpretation of means. This is not Davis's intention. An agent-interpretation of Sumo passes the DDE test. Our intention is not the death of the sumo wrestler; we would instead push a sack of potatoes from the bridge if we could.

Can we do better by sticking with an event-interpretation? Again, this is not Davis's intention. An event-interpretation would not permit track switching in Trolley. If we intend to do *B* and the only way to do *B* is to do *A* first, a causal event of doing *B* is necessarily the doing of *A*. Doing *A*, then, is not merely foreseen, but required. As put, to save the five by shunting the trolley onto the spur and killing one, the killing of one is causally connected to saving the five. Even if we would use a sack of potatoes instead of a person to stop the trolley, killing the one is causally related to saving the five in Trolley. If we wish to say pulling the lever in Trolley is fine and pushing the wrestler in Sumo is not fine, an appeal to the DDE is not helpful.

2.3 Use

According to Kant (1785, Ak 429), we ought not to use anyone as a means only to our ends. Applying the Kantian model of not using anyone as a means can capture the intuition that we ought to pull the lever in Trolley and to refrain from pushing the wrestler in Sumo.[15] In Sumo, we need the participation of the wrestler to achieve our goal of saving the five, whereas in Trolley we do not need the participation of the lone person on the track. We can see this by imagining the sudden disappearance of the individuals we are about to kill. In Sumo, the sudden disappearance of the wrestler means the five will die. In Trolley, the sudden disappearance of the lone person on the spur would not make the five die. We *need* the sumo's death to save the five in a way that we do not need the death of the one person on the spur. We are *using* the sumo wrestler for our ends in a way that we are not using the person on the spur for our ends.

The dictum to never use anyone has the advantage of being simpler to interpret than the DDE. We need not enter the murky domain of intentions, nor get mired in comparing different kinds of benefits or harms. We simply ask whether the task could be accomplished without the sacrificed person. If Yes, then we have a case of not using anyone and we may morally proceed, other things being equal; if No, then we have a case of using someone and, for that reason, we may not do so.

One problem is that the nice demarcation above is not accurate. Kant admonishes us not to use people as means *only*. This means we *can* use people as long as we also treat them as ends in themselves, permitting respectful market transactions. This little detail creates a major problem for appealing to the use criterion in Trolley. Can I not push the sumo wrestler in front of the trolley with all due respect? If so (and I do not see why not), the use criterion is as open to interpretation as the DDE. We could amend Kant's principle to allow mutual use, however. Assuming one consents to being used if they stand to benefit in some other way, our amended use criterion would look something like the following: *Do not use anyone as a means to your ends unless they consent.* Presumably the mutuality condition is missing in Sumo.

Thomson uses Loop to reject the use principle as well as the DDE. Without the person on the spur, the trolley would circle back and kill the five, making it the case that we *use* the person on the spur to save the five. My worry with this objection is the same as earlier. That the use criterion is deemed idle follows only if we ignore the difference between Loop and Trolley, but to ignore the difference between Loop and Trolley is to presuppose that the use criterion is idle.

A bigger problem with the use criterion is seen in Foot's Rescue II. Running over the injured person on the road is not a matter of *using* that victim to save the five farther ahead. If the fallen victim were not there, the action would be the same, driving on. If Rescue II is wrong, it cannot be on the basis of the use criterion. Presumably we are looking for only one principle to explain all cases of permissible and impermissible sacrificing of others for a greater good.[16]

2.4 *Same Threat and Stringent Rights*

The negative right to life of someone, as we know, ought to prevent our redirecting a trolley to barrel down upon them, all things equal.

Sometimes things are not equal. Rights have exceptions. My right to use my body as I wish is constrained by your right not to have my body intentionally smash into yours without your consent. The negative right to life may be overridden in cases of self-defence, for example. Another occasion to acceptably override someone's negative right to life may be to intervene against a rights holder attacking a third party. The rights of self-defence and intervention are tempered by the rule to cause as minimal harm as possible to secure one's safety. Can we also waive the right to life (if suitably tempered) to minimize number of deaths, as in Trolley? In her second attempt at the Trolley problem, Thomson provided her composite formula to capture our intuitions about trolleys. "[T]there seem to me to be two crucial facts about what the bystander does if he proceeds in Bystander at the Switch. In the first place, he saves his five by making something that threatens them instead threaten the one. And second, he does not do that by means which themselves constitute infringements of any right of the one's" (Thomson 1985, 1407). The second "fact" is hardly plausible. In both Empty Track and Long Track, recall, a runaway trolley is barrelling down a track but will not hit anyone. If I knowingly shunt the trolley so that it switches tracks and kills someone, I would be, correctly, accused of violating a stringent right of the person killed. We cannot say initiating an act that kills someone is a rights violation in the one case but not the other. Shunting the trolley where it kills a person to save five may be the justification for violating the stringent negative right of someone, but we cannot say there was no stringent rights violation.

To capture my friendly amendment, I shall reframe Thomson's 1985 solution as follows:

> Apart from self-defence and intervention (each with their own restrictions), someone's stringent negative right to life may be overridden by us so long as we are (i) intending to cause fewer deaths than more, and (ii) merely redirecting an existing threat.

While both Trolley and Sumo violate stringent negative rights, such rights may be justifiably overridden in Trolley, but not Sumo. Pulling the lever in Trolley redirects an existing threat (runaway trolley), whereas pushing the wrestler off the bridge introduces a new threat (apart from being crushed by a trolley, also being pushed off a bridge, presumably). In Transplant, five would die by organ disease, and one by organ extraction, a different threat. In HOSPITAL, to save five patients dying from illnesses, pharmacologists manufacture a drug that leaks toxic gas into a sixth person's room and kills her. A different threat is created, and is therefore thought to be impermissible (Thomson 1985, 1407–8). In BICYCLE, we imagine a case where we can push a bystander's bicycle onto the path of the trolley to effectively stop the trolley from reaching the five trapped persons. Here is a case where we can say there is no stringent rights violation, at least in comparison to saving a life in the process.

While the distinction captures our intuitions so far (excepting Hospital, perhaps), how morally relevant is the appeal to a same threat? To counter Thomson's same threat principle, we need a case that is a rights violation with a different threat that we nevertheless think is fine, and we need a case that is a rights violation with the same threat that we think is not morally fine. I will start with the second. Consider a case I call GARBAGE. Your side neighbour tosses garbage onto your lawn. You erect a fan that sends that garbage into a back neighbour's yard. Would Thomson's same threat principle absolve you of wrongdoing? True, if *A*'s garbage suddenly lands on *B*, *B* may reflexively toss it elsewhere, alas on *C*. We would say *A* harmed *C*, not *B* harmed *C*.[17] But in GARBAGE, reflexive action is not in play. The action is deliberate. Since deliberation came into play, why not have the fan send the garbage back to its owner? Admittedly, littering may not be a stringent rights violation, but I take Thomson's point to apply to all same-level rights violations.

For the second counter, imagine a case I call NITROGLYCERINE. A runaway trolley carrying relatively well-packed nitroglycerine is going to run over five people. Running over the five people will not upset the trolley sufficiently to ignite the nitroglycerine, although all five will be crushed. We can shunt the trolley to a spur where one person is stuck. In shunting the trolley, however, the jolt will cause the nitroglycerine to explode. If we do nothing, five will be run over by a trolley, if we pull the lever, one will be blown up. To shunt the trolley, then, we introduce a new threat. To that extent, Thomson's position tells us not to shunt the trolley in Nitroglycerine. Perhaps that is correct (we are dealing with intuitions, after all), but given her penchant to deem Loop no different than Trolley, I suspect she would have difficulty accepting the conclusion in Nitroglycerine.

Given that the nitroglycerine *might* explode when hitting the five, Thomson could suggest it is really the same threat diverted. How about LIQUID CEMENT, then? In Liquid Cement, you have the option of dumping a sufficient amount of liquid cement onto the track to effectively stop the runaway trolley from hitting the five, but in doing so, you know that excess glue will slip down the spur suffocating a person stuck there. (Or, if you prefer, the liquid cement raises noxious fumes that you can predict will kill a bystander who does not have time to get out of the way). A new threat is introduced. Thomson would have to say one ought not to stop the trolley in Liquid Cement, but one ought to shunt the trolley in Trolley. Again, perhaps she would, but the differences in threat seem artificial.

Lastly, consider CLIFF. A runaway trolley heading to kill five can be diverted onto an empty spur by pulling a lever. Unfortunately, a bystander who has no intention of pulling the lever is blocking your way to the switch. You can either push the bystander off a cliff or onto the track in front of the trolley and then pull the lever. Not being a sumo wrestler, the bystander's falling onto the track will not stop the trolley's momentum. It will continue along the tracks to run over the five. Pushing the bystander in either direction is simply to get at the switch. Once the lever is pulled, however, the trolley shunts tracks and the five are saved. By pushing the bystander off the cliff, we have introduced a new threat (falling off a cliff as opposed to being run over by a trolley), so is impermissible by Thomson's reasoning. If we pushed the bystander under the trolley instead of over a cliff, however, the same threat is preserved, and Thomson would have to say, Go ahead.[18]

Such subtleties in facts affecting moral judgments seem unfounded to me. This is hardly an objection, admittedly, since the deciding factor is our varying intuition. For intuitions to be reliable avenues for moral appraisal, we would have to believe they derive from some inerrant, authoritative place. I do not pretend so.

Another consideration may help. Normally, when we morally appraise an action, we do not tend to consider whether threats are the same. That someone is murdered seems to be the relevant point; not that they were murdered by stabbing or choking or shooting. This shows that varying threats of death do not usually alter moral appraisal. That it should count in life-saving gestures seems a bit ad hoc.

Perhaps what Thomson's same-threat principle is capturing need not be taken literally. The idea, I take it, is that if one of two tragedies is unavoidable, everything else being equal, choose the lesser tragedy. Typically, such scenarios will involve same threats. In SANDBAGS, a flood redirected by sandbags saves a city by destroying a village. That it is the same threat seems less the point. In DAM OPENING, a fire might be doused to save a city by causing a flood that destroys a village. To say Sandbags is fine but Dam Opening is not, seems, again, disingenuous.

2.5 Non-Cognitivism

Another option to explain the apparent inconsistency in the Trolley problem is an appeal to non-cognitivism. Non-cognitivism is the meta-ethical notion that morality is no more than a subset of emotional displeasure (or pleasure). For example, we may find no good justification for forbidding homosexual incest, or incest without protection. The only thing consistent is our gut reaction about incest. Presumably we are moved by traits deeply rooted in our evolution that may not always cohere with our more recently developed cogitation. Neuroscience research may agree. Studies show that moral judgments are mediated by two classes of brain processes, one emotionally intuitive and the other a deliberative system. These two systems typically overlap in making moral judgments, but can oppose each other as in Trolley scenarios (Greene 2014; Greene, et al. 2004; Greene et al. 2001).

According to psychological research, people are more apt to pull the lever in Trolley when pressed for time or distracted by extraneous matter, but neither time pressure nor extraneous distraction affects their disinclination to push the wrestler off the bridge in Sumo (Cecchetto, Rumiati, and Parma 2017; Corey et al. 2017; Suter and Hertwig 2011). Similarly, inducing positive feelings in participants reduces the aversion against pulling the lever in Trolley experiments.[19] One explanation of this fits well with non-cognitivism. That people pull the lever under time pressure or distraction is consistent with their being moved by canalized non-cognitive reflexes. When given more time to think about it, they may change their behaviours. Whereas with Sumo, the sense of touch triggers an evolutionarily older part of the brain resulting in an emotional shutdown. Participants were more inclined to nudge the sumo wrestler off the bridge with a joystick in virtual reality than those claiming they would do so in real life (Francis et al. 2016). In TRAP DOOR, you stand by a control box operating a trap door in the bridge upon which the sumo wrestler happens to be standing. By a simple push of a button, the sumo wrestler drops onto the track in front of the runaway trolley and the five are saved. The wrestler dies, of course. Accordingly, respondents are twice as more likely to say they would push the button in Trap Door than they say they would push the wrestler in Sumo.[20] Such results need not propel us on a search to find some philosophically justifiable explanation between Sumo and Trap Door other than admitting that people's moral senses are not rationally motivated. Support for non-cognitivism.

Tracking how people behave in moral situations (or say they would behave)[21] is relevant to moral philosophy, I believe, but hardly sufficient. Even if most people say they would pull the lever in Trolley, that cannot qualify as proof that pulling the lever in Trolley is morally justified (Berker 2009; Kumar and Campbell 2012; Rini 2013). The interest we have in the puzzle is seeing if we can find a plausible principle to explain pulling the lever in Trolley and not pushing the wrestler in Sumo that is consistent with our other accepted moral conceptions. Non-cognitivism rejects the search for a consistent moral principle to explain it, preferring, instead, an explanation consisting in cognitive science and biology. I (with Thomson 2008) agree that there is no consistent and plausible moral principle to be found that could justify pulling the switch in Trolley and not pushing the wrestler in Sumo, but not because the search for a plausible and consistent moral principle is wrongheaded from the start. Compare the altered views on sexuality over the last half-century. Popular opinion was that only heterosexual relations were moral. Ought we to have left it at that? That people had strong negative gut reactions against homosexuality probably did influence the belief that homosexuality was immoral, but the lack of philosophical justification for deeming homosexuality immoral helped, I would say, to wean society of at least one rights violation. I would further propose that the recognition of homosexuality's moral permissibility is what helped wean society of its negative gut reaction towards homosexuality, not the other way around.

Other solutions have been offered for why diverting the trolley onto a person to save five persons farther down the track is morally permissible,[22] but I shall leave those aside. Before I explain why contractarianism would not permit pulling the lever in Trolley, I shall briefly examine Thomson's 2008 account that comes to the same conclusion via a different track.

2.6 *Thomson's Final Argument*

Thomson (2008) follows Foot (1967) in believing that one's negative right not to be killed trumps another's positive right to be saved. This means, pulling the lever in Trolley is inadmissible. To demonstrate the reasonableness of this conclusion, Thomson offers us an extra option to the one standing at the switch; we may call it MARTYRDOM TROLLEY. Option 1 is to do nothing with the result that five will die farther down the track. Option 2 is to turn the switch to the right with the result that one will die on the side spur to the right. Option 3 is to turn the switch to the left, resulting in one's own death – a case of martyrdom. Since we have a right to not martyr ourselves, we should also recognize a duty not to martyrize someone else (Thomson 2008, 364). If I have a right not to die to save the five, then anyone else has that right as well. I would violate that same right by turning the trolley onto anyone. Similarly, while it is fine I give my money to charity, it is not fine I give your money to charity (Thomson 2008, 365). The same thinking ought to apply under the original Trolley case. We ought not to have someone else pay the cost for our good deed (Thomson 2008, 365).

I agree, but the explanation Thomson gives is not quite correct. First, although we do not think we are bound to martyrize ourselves, we are morally permitted to martyrize ourselves. If I were not allowed to turn the trolley onto myself, then, feasibly, I am not allowed to turn the trolley onto another person. But since I am allowed to turn the trolley onto myself, the simple parallel ought to be that I may turn the trolley onto another. If I cannot turn the trolley onto another, we should seek the explanation elsewhere. Rather than the notion that I cannot do unto others what I cannot do unto myself, we need to recognize a limitation on what I can do unto others despite my being able to do unto myself.

Secondly, the reason we have a right not to let ourselves be killed is an appeal to self-defence. I am allowed to kill another if that is the only way to avoid my own death. Krusty the Clown has a right to kill Bart who has been hypnotized by Sideshow Bob to kill Krusty. And sometimes, we may be in a situation where *other-defence* is permissible: perhaps Sideshow Mel has an opportunity to kill hypnotized Bart before Bart kills Krusty. If we agree with self-defence and *other*-defence (suitably limited), it no longer follows that because I opt to avoid my death, I must avoid your death.[23]

On the other hand, we can get to Thomson's 2008 conclusion by contractarianism.

3 CONTRACTARIAN ANALYSIS

Contractarianism is often shunted to a sidetrack in moral philosophy, so the absence of a contractarian analysis of the trolley problem is not surprising.

As discussed in this book's Introduction, contractarianism is a metaphysic-free moral theory. There is no *Summum Bonum*, says Hobbes (1651, ch. 11). Morality's benefit is purely instrumental. Any intrinsic value to being moral is secondary to the instrumental value morality provides. Contractarians argue that even amoral, self-interested, rational agents would accept constraints imposed on their social behaviour. They call those social constraints "morality." Without such constraints, we are vulnerable to the depredations of others, and with such constraints, we can all benefit from co-operation with others. Otherwise, they remain in a state where life is "solitary, poor, nasty, brutish, and short" (Hobbes 1651, ch. 13). So, agents in the state of nature agree to keep the peace, and to do that, they agree to a liberty rule, a rule of not interfering with others' pursuits, assuming others likewise agree.

Two features are important for our discussion: status quo and *ex ante* decisions. An *ex ante* decision is what hypothetical agents would prudentially consent to in a pre-moral state.[24] The *status quo* is a feature of the *ex ante* agreement. My protecting your liberty means I cannot harm you without your consent (or presumed consent). We define harm as making you worse off than before my interaction with you.

3.1 Status Quo

The status quo for contractarians solely concerns the situation of individuals in relation to their interactions with other individuals. Contractarians do not mean to invoke or endorse "fat-cat" social-political conservatism. In an interaction between *A* and *B*, the status quo of *A* is *A*'s state of affairs just prior to the interaction with *B*. If I pass a beggar without dropping money into his hat, despite the beggar's druthers, I do not violate the beggar's status quo of having his hat empty of my money. If I leave that a live option, which I do by passing by, I am not violating the contractarian principle.

The status quo condition is in some sense the opposite of the use criterion. Distinguish for the moment between an *initiator of* and an *initiant to* an agreement. The initiator proposes a bargain and the initiant accepts or declines the proposal. In mutually initiated situations the distinction is idle, but in the interaction between the beggar and myself, the beggar was the initiator and I the initiant. In Trolley, the bystander at the switch is the initiator. "Hey, how about I cause a trolley to run you over?" The person stuck on the spur is the initiant. "No, thank you." The *use* criterion considers what happens if the *initiant* was not present. Would the bystander pull the switch? Yes. The *status quo* criterion asks what would happen if the *initiator* was not present. Would the person on the spur be spared from having a trolley run them over? Yes.

In Sumo, the wrestler's status quo is being on the bridge. If I push him off without his consent, I have violated the contractarian principle. Hence, I cannot morally do so. Since I am not allowed to push the sumo wrestler, my doing nothing is not a case of letting the five die. I merely witness their deaths. The death of the five people is a tragedy, not a moral infraction. When no one is on the side track (as in Empty Spur), you violate no one's status quo by switching the track and saving the five people on the main track. Your doing so, therefore, is morally permissible, if not morally mandatory.

Recall Long Track. A runaway trolley is heading down a track where it will eventually stop and not kill anyone. If you pull the lever, the trolley will switch tracks. Unfortunately, a person is stuck on this other track, and the trolley will kill that person. Knowing this, ought you to pull the lever? Presumably we should answer No. In Long Track, switching the trolley's path from killing no one to killing one person violates that one person's status quo, the state of not having a trolley about to hit that person. You intentionally do something that alters that person's current state of affairs, having no trolley barrelling upon them. If you were not present, the trolley would not have been shunted, no one would have died. But if Long Track shows the violation of someone's status quo absent consent, this must also be true in Trolley. In Trolley, the lone person's status quo is being stuck on a side track without (currently) a trolley coming. My pulling the lever (even if for a good motive) robs that person of their status quo, and to the extent that I anticipated it seems to make me morally culpable. If I were not present, the lone person on the side track would be fine. Being fine, though stuck, is that person's current status quo relative to my arrival on the scene.

The status quo of the five people is less rosy. If I were not present, the trolley would kill them. Their status quo is being about to die. My not switching the track is not a violation of their status quo. Presumably, they would consent to have me alter their status quo, as would the beggar. The status quo of the lone person on the other track, however, is being stuck on a track with no trolley threatening death. For me to save the five by switching the track would be a violation of this other person's status quo. Hence, for contractarians, at least prima facie, it is a morally wrong action. Whereas not doing anything and letting the five die is not a violation of the status quo of any of the five people stuck on the track: hence morally permissible – a vigil to a tragedy. Calling it morally permissible to do nothing to save *A* without violating *B*'s status quo (as in Trolley) does not imply it is morally permissible to do nothing to save someone without risk of violating anyone else's status quo (as in Empty Spur).

For contractarians, consent counts as an overriding factor against the rule of not worsening someone's status quo. In active euthanasia, for example, we alter the status quo of people – from being alive to being dead – but we do so with their consent. We do not suppose consent in any of the Trolley cases. Perhaps, however, moral people *would*, or possibly *should*, consent to being run over by a trolley if they knew the full story. Can contractarians claim that *ex ante* bargainers in the state of nature would consent to an "except-when" clause that may sometimes justify status quo violations in Trolley scenarios?

3.2 *Ex Ante Agreement*

Any status quo violation is prima facie wrong, not necessarily an all-things-considered wrong. Is it possible that *ex ante* agents in a state of nature would include the permissibility of pulling the lever in Trolley despite the status quo violation?

Except-when claims cannot be ad hoc. For contractarians, they must be justifiable at the *ex ante* position. When deciding moral actions, we do not look for consent among existing people immersed in conditions peculiar to them. Rather, we wonder to what rules reasonable agents suitably situated would consent (Gauthier

1986, 9–10). *Ex ante* agents are deemed to be rational, amoral, and self-interested to avoid begging the question when it comes to endorsing moral principles. Even these barely human agents have reason to endorse morality – and by doing so have reason to endorse being human. But they are not human yet. An *ex ante* agreement to pull the lever in Trolley cases needs to satisfy the long-term prudential interests of self-interested, amoral agents.

The thought that more deaths are worse than fewer deaths cannot be accepted for its moral value in the state of nature (moral value does not exist yet, per hypothesis), but it may seem that *ex ante* agents can reasonably expect to benefit from such a principle, since the odds of anyone dying are less in a world with a choose-fewer-deaths-than-more rule than a world without it, and we assume ex ante agents prefer not dying to dying.

If for some reason you cannot help but violate someone's status quo no matter what you do, an addendum rule claiming less status quo violations the better would come into play. Consider Y SPLIT.[25] In Y Split, a driver has an option of turning the trolley to the left or to the right. On the left track are stuck five people. On the right track is stuck one person. Since the driver can turn in either direction, each stuck person has 0.5 odds of being run over. But since there would be more status quo violations turning left than turning right, even *ex ante* agents can see the lure of turning to the right.

A complication. What if the driver opts to do nothing in Y Split? Two possibilities come into play. The first possibility I shall call Y SPLIT CLIFF, where, if the driver does nothing, the trolley goes straight off a cliff killing all aboard but avoiding all persons stuck on the track. Y Split Cliff has two versions. In Y SPLIT CLIFF 1, only the driver is on board; In Y SPLIT CLIFF 10, ten people are on board. The second possibility I will call Y SPLIT RANDOM. In Y Split Random, not turning in either direction when a Y track is present invokes a randomizing algorithm built into the trolley.[26] The smart trolley has a 50 per cent chance of turning to the left.

In both Y Split Random and Y Split Cliff 10, turning to the right will, or has a greater chance to, reduce the number of status quo violations than other available options. Contractarian analysis would permit it. Y Split Cliff 1 poses a worry, however. First off, suicide cannot count as a status quo violation. What you do to yourself counts as consent. We may rightfully interfere with a person's doing something to themselves only when we doubt their competency or their knowledge. Since suicide is not a status quo violation while the other options are, suicide would be the preferred option if our only *ex ante* rule is to avoid status quo violations. *Ex ante* agents would never recommend suicide over harming another, however. While we would say of such drivers that they are martyrs to drive the empty trolley off the cliff rather than run anyone over, our amoral, self-interested *ex ante* bargainers would call them suckers. In any event, the inevitability of a status quo violation is not occurring in Trolley as it is in Y Split. Letting the five die in Trolley is not a status quo violation. Hence violation of someone's status quo is not inevitable in Trolley. Hence the inevitability except-when clause cannot be invoked in Trolley as it may in Y Split.

An *ex ante* endorsement of helping prevent another's death at your own status quo violation (suitably demarcated) would cover the moral requirement of pulling the lever in Empty Spur, but not Trolley. Merely helping others at the helper's cost is not what the Trolley problem is about. In Trolley, another status quo violation takes place other than that imposed upon the helper: the one who gets killed. To justify pulling the lever in Trolley, *ex ante* agents would have to agree to permit a status quo violation not only of the helper, but also of a bystander (the one stuck on the spur). Would endorsing this rule be in the long-term self-interest of *ex ante* agents?

Ex ante bargainers might believe they would have a greater chance of being among the five stuck on the trolley track than being the one stuck on the trolley track alone. Think of a lottery where five citizens are chosen to be placed onto a trolley track on which a runaway trolley approaches and one citizen is chosen to be placed on the spur. To be among the five is to have five chances of being picked from the citizenry. To be the one on the spur has only one chance of being picked. Thus, the odds of being on a trolley track with four others are five times greater than the odds of being on a trolley track alone. Similarly, the odds of pulling the five of diamonds from a deck in five tries (5/52) are greater than the odds of pulling a five of diamonds from the deck in one try (1/52). If probability favours *ex ante* agents being among five on a trolley track compared to being only one person on a trolley track, endorsing a rule to divert runaway trolleys from killing five to killing one makes sense to rational, self-interested, amoral *ex ante* agents. Of course, having five times more luck being stuck on a trolley with others than by oneself is hardly a significant dent in probabilities. The difference between five chances out of seven billion (or whatever) from one chance out of seven billion is below normal people's range of calculation.

Even still, I think it the wrong way of looking at the odds. Compare tossing two coins simultaneously. The probability of both coins coming up heads are $0.5 \times 0.5 = 0.25$. If we toss the two coins sequentially, the odds of both coins being heads remains at 0.25. But what if, after tossing one coin that came up heads, we wonder what the odds are of both coins coming up heads. The answer is not 0.25, but 0.5, because the first coin being heads is already a given. All we are asking is what are the odds of the second coin by itself coming up heads. Similarly, so I suggest, calculating the odds of being among the five on the main line or the one on the spur, we are in a position of being stuck on a track. Our question is simply whether anyone else is with us. Given that we are already stuck, the odds of anyone else being stuck with us are the odds of our being stuck on a trolley track times two. Therefore, being stuck alone is far more probable than being stuck with others. (Compare the odds of your car having a flat tire at an intersection with the odds of four other cars each having a flat tire at the same intersection at the same time.) Thus rational, self-interested, amoral agents would not agree to a rule to divert runaway trolleys onto others.

Similarly, *ex ante* bargainers are unlikely to opt to live in a society that permits ambulances to run over people on their way to saving others, assuming that being a victim of an ambulance is more likely than needing an ambulance to save you. However many times we may need an ambulance, we have been passed by ambulances more often. However many times you may be run over by an undiverted trolley, the possibility of diverted trolleys running you over is greater.

Besides, an *ex ante* rule placing priority on *ex post* consent except when violation of that rule can produce fewer deaths than non-violation of that rule will permit lever pulling in Trolley, but also sumo wrestler pushing in Sumo and non-consensual organ harvesting in Transplant. An *ex ante* bargainer in the state of nature cannot complain about the immorality of non-consensual live organ harvesting, but they can recognize that they would likely do better in a world that does not allow such a thing, since the odds of your requiring a live organ are less than the odds of someone requiring a live organ.

SUMMARY
The status quo shows that it is as much of a rights violation to cause a lone person's death in Trolley as it is in Sumo. This is not to say that *ex ante* bargainers may never violate anyone's status quo. They may permit status quo violations only when

- i consent permits;
- ii in self-defence;
- iii to intervene in other status quo violations (without undue harms to self);
- iv status quo violations are inevitable.

Beyond that, nothing. Trolley is a case beyond that. It would be as immoral to pull the lever in Trolley as it is to push the sumo wrestler in Sumo.[27]

3.3 A Problem or Two

In Foot (1967)'s introduction of the Trolley problem, DRIVER, a driver of a suddenly brakeless trolley is heading toward five people, but the driver can turn the trolley to the right and run over one person. We are inclined to think the driver should turn the trolley to the right. Everything else equal, no overriding moral principle can hope to suggest going straight. But the *ex ante* solution says Go straight! The current state of affairs is the trolley heading toward five. The status quo of the five, then, is the state of being about to be hit by a trolley. The status quo of the person on the spur to the right is not having a runaway trolley about to hit him. If the driver were not present, the trolley would go straight and kill the five. To turn the trolley to the right, therefore, is a violation of the one person's status quo, but doing nothing and thereby running over the five is not a violation of anyone's status quo. While some may see the appeal of not pulling the lever in Trolley, few believe we ought not to turn the wheel in Driver.

Driver (and some would include Trolley) reveal an interpretation problem with the status quo. Perhaps we should say that being stuck on the track is not properly one's status quo. Perhaps we should interpret a person's status quo not with one's current, particular situation, but with one's *normal* state, or possibly one's *optimal* state, or possibly one's *subsistence* state. If the status quo of the five is not being stuck on the track and not having a trolley about to run over them, an interacting agent has the obligation to *return* them to their normal status quo, if possible, or their optimal status quo or at least their subsistence status quo, or return as many people as possible to whichever state one picks.

While reinterpreting the status quo matches our intuitions in the cases of Driver and Trolley, it would overflood us with obligations. A cut finger is not one's normal status quo. Nor is a cold. It is unlikely that any rational, amoral, self-interested agent in a state of nature would agree to be bound to fix everyone's problems. Even if "normal" included cut fingers and colds but not being stuck on train tracks, it would not include being seriously ill, injured, or dying. That we may like to help such people is one thing, that amoral, self-interested *ex ante* agents would agree to be bound to do so another. Given the population size and state of wellness in the world, the task is too great, too constant, too liberty-interfering for amoral, self-interested *ex ante* agents deciding upon moral constraints. To say, "But that's not moral!" is to miss the point. Morality, for contractarians, is not part of the fabric of the world that we must recognize and obey. Morality is simply a tool to enable social agents to cohabit as peacefully and productively as possible. Anything beyond that is an appeal to some kind of moral myth.

Too drastic a reinterpretation of the status quo is imprudent. Perhaps, however, we could alter the concept of *a given interaction*. In Trolley and Driver, for example, I claimed that the status quo of the lone person on the side spur is not having a trolley barrelling upon them. Perhaps this claim is false. Given what is happening on the other track, they certainly are in danger of having a trolley run them over. If so, making it such that a trolley does run them over would not count as a violation of their status quo.

Such an interpretation cannot hold, however. Consider MUGGER. A mugger does not offer the status quo as a live option when she demands your money or your life. Having both your life and your money is your status quo. The whole point of mugging is to make it so that your status quo is no longer an option. But if we think of the mugging victim's situation to include being presently confronted by a mugger, or even being in a district where mugging is possible, the mugging would no longer be a violation of the status quo – it is the status quo! If mugging does not violate anyone's status quo, mugging is morally fine. Since mugging is not morally fine, in fact one of the ills our *ex ante* agents were trying to protect themselves against, such an interpretation of an *ex ante* situation is hardly plausible.

I would rather claim that Driver is like Y Split – they are cases of inevitable status quo violations, thus permitting the except-when clause. I say this because the driver of the trolley in Driver, in lieu of being a licensed driver for the Trolley Company, has voluntarily assumed an added duty not to run over anyone, or at least to minimize the number of people to run over. The driver's obligation is *in personam*. It applies only to the driver who voluntarily undertakes the role of being the trolley driver. Under the crisis situation in Driver, the choice is between running over five or one. The bystander at the switch in Trolley has no such *in personam* obligation.

4 CONCLUSION: A SIMPLIFICATION

The many trolley variants in the literature (and this chapter) may overcomplicate matters. Let me simplify. Concerning Bystander cases (as opposed to Driver cases), we have only three variations to consider: (i) Self-defence, (ii) Sumo, (iii) Standard.

(i) Self-defence. A runaway trolley will kill you unless you pull a switch diverting the trolley onto five. Contractarian recommendation: Pull the switch. Rule: Self-Defence trumps.

(ii) Sumo. A sumo wrestler has enough girth to stop a runaway trolley from killing five. You do not. Should you push the sumo in front of the trolley to save the five? Contractarian recommendation: Do not push the sumo. Rule: Do not violate anyone's status quo without their consent. The status quo of the wrestler is not being shoved in front of a trolley. The status quo of the five is having a trolley about to run them over.

(iii) Standard. A runaway trolley is about to kill five people. You, a bystander, can pull a switch to divert the trolley onto a spur where the trolley would kill one. Contractarian recommendation: Do not pull the switch. Rule: Prevent fewer deaths assuming you do not violate anyone's status quo without their consent in the process. The status quo of the one on the spur is not being in threat of a runaway trolley. The status quo of the five is having a trolley about to run them over. The fewer-deaths rule is trumped by the status quo rule. The bystander stands vigil to the tragedy; she neither caused nor let the tragedy happen.

3

Cannibalism, Incest, and Dumbfounding

Studies in moral emotions describe three things: (i) our abject disgust toward incest and cannibalism, (ii) the failure of the standard arguments for the immorality of cannibalism and incest, and (iii) our trenchant resistance, or "dumbfounding" (Haidt 2001), against changing our minds, as if our disgust speaks for itself. Emotionists take our moral disgust toward incest and cannibalism as supporting the view that morality is *merely* an emotional response rooted deep in our evolutionary past. Emotionism, by the way, is Prinz's (2007) term for expressivism (with a few twists that need not detain us), a type of non-cognitivism that has roots in sentimentalism, sensibility theories, and emotivism. As a moral irrealist theory, emotionism is not claiming (unlike Kass 1997) that disgust justifies our moral beliefs. Rather, morality is nothing else but our evolutionary-rooted emotions and sentiments.

Contractarians can agree with emotionists that we have no rational reason to forbid incest and cannibalism. Contractarians can also agree that any complaint against cannibalism and incest is purely emotional. This would not show that moral judgments are purely emotional, however, since (i) the alternative that incest and cannibalism are morally fine has not been ruled out, and (ii) studies show only the effects of emotional dumbfounding on "crimes of nature" (specifically cannibalism and incest), as opposed to "autonomy" violations, crimes of interference. Since most moral theories (save divine command theories and virtue theories) eschew so-called "nature crimes" from moral restrictions, dumbfounding studies do little to undermine our confidence in cognitive ethics.

In the following sections, I: 1. distinguish types of cannibalism and incest, 2. offer a contractarian defence of consensual cannibalism and incest, 3. briefly explain how other theories can condemn neither incest nor cannibalism, 4. describe some of the psychological studies on moral disgust that emotionism uses to its advantage, and 5. show how those psychological studies on moral emotions fail to support emotionism, or, for that matter, any moral theory – mainly because their results apply only to violations of "nature," as they put it; not violations of "autonomy" as they put it – the focus of most moral theories. Lastly, 6. I distinguish two ways of looking at the evolution of morality, one involving moral content and one involving moral structure. Those focusing on moral content, such as what we see in the psychological studies on moral emotions, are misguided. Evolutionary game theory supports only an architectural structure of moral dealing. Those who reciprocally co-operate tend to do better in social situations than those who do not. The benefit of adhering to the structure of reciprocal co-operation supports contractarian moral theory without pretending that humans have evolved to deem any particular content, such as incest or cannibalism, to be immoral.

1 TYPES

1.1 Cannibalism

Cannibalism is a case of eating a member of one's own species. The term, anthrophagy, eating human flesh, is sometimes used, but would not differentiate a cannibal from a lion. For that matter, fish who eat their own young are cannibalistic but not anthrophagic. The name, cannibal, is a misnomer given to us by Columbus. He was told that the Caniba tribe in the West Indies ate people and were not to be messed with (Burley 2017, 488–9).

A variety of cannibalistic practices have been recorded. Wisniewski (2014) distinguishes three types: ritualistic, survival, and fetish. The first includes religious sacrifice, funereal rites, and prisoner-of-war handling. The second occurs when, for example, your plane crashes in the Andes or you are shipwrecked at sea and the only food available is your mates. The third category includes those who just like the taste or the concept of eating other people. Burhenn (2004) (adopted by Burley, 2016) offers a two-set categorization: that between exocannibalism and endocannibalism. The first is eating people from other groups, typically as the means of handling captives in war. The second is when members of a group eat other members of their own group, typically in sacrifice to the gods or in funerary practices.[1] The term "transumption" has been used to describe the eating of dead kinfolk as a means to help free the spirit of the dead (Alpers 2007, 14). Endocannibalism tends to be a sign of respect to the one eaten, a counter case to Kass's (1994) claim that eating humans is always disrespectful to the eaten. Even endocannibalism was sometimes performed with respect to the bravery of the enemy warrior (Harris 1977, 232–3).[2] Irvine (1989) (followed by Lu 2013) adopts an active-passive distinction. Active cannibalism is a case of killing a person to eat them. Passive cannibalism is a case of eating someone already dead. Nussbaum (2004, 80) conceives all cannibalism to be active.

Other forms of cannibalism seem to defy categorization. Medicinal cannibalism, common in China up to the nineteenth century and Europe during the sixteenth to eighteenth centuries, was the practice of eating parts of humans for supposed medicinal benefits (Schutt 2017). The practice of eating afterbirth placenta may be a type of medicinal cannibalism, although Milburn (2016, 260) calls it a type of "waste cannibalism." Autocannibalism is a case of eating parts of one's self (Dole 1962). Symbolic cannibalism is the symbolic ritual of eating human flesh, as in the Catholic practice of parishioners eating the body of Christ and drinking his blood (Wisniewski 2014). Milburn (2016) recommends producing in vitro human meat as a kind of "victimless cannibalism."[3] Some people – whether literally or metaphorically – suggest organ transplants and blood transfusions are cases of cannibalism (contra Zwart 2014). For Kant (1797a, 6:359), carnal sex, as opposed to marital sex, counts as cannibalistic.

Cannibalism is not just for humans. Fish and plankton eat their own eggs and larvae. As hatchlings, snowy owls, egrets, and vultures will eat their own siblings if not enough food gets to their nest. Sand tiger sharks eat their own siblings in utero. Toad larvae eat their own brood mates. Polar bears consume other polar bears. Male lions eat the cubs of rivals. Pigs and chickens are cannibals when quarters are cramped. Female praying mantises eat the head of their spouse as protein for her offspring. A black lace-weaver spider mom gives her own body as food for her young (Birkhead, Lee, and Young 1988; Elger and Nash 1988; Gallucci and Ólafasson 2007; Schutt 2017). That cannibalism is relatively common in nature does not count toward our calling it moral. It does count against our calling it "unnatural" or "against nature" (contra Kass, 1997).

Despite the variety of cannibalisms, the principal distinction I will use (apart from the active-passive one) is whether cannibalism occurs with consent or without.

1.2 *Incest*

Incest is less diverse. Other than varying the relations, incest is sex among close blood kin. Sex with one's biological parents, uncles, aunts, grandparents, siblings, half-siblings, nephews, nieces, and cousins counts as incest. Some of these relations are non-consensual, in which case we are dealing with rape. For consent, we require agents to be competent and informed and voluntarily consent. Coerced sexual relations violate that condition, as do sexual relations between adults and children below the age of competency. Determining an age and level of competency is problematic,[4] but suffices for present purposes.

As with cannibalism, my concern in this chapter is with whether incest is consensual or not, that is, incest among competent, informed, and voluntarily consenting agents. From here on, when I say "cannibalism" or "incest" I mean "consensual cannibalism" and "consensual incest," unless otherwise stated.

For the following discussion, I have two cases in mind, one fictitious, but probable, the other factual, but improbable. The fictitious case is about incest and was given for commentary in a psychological study discussed by Haidt (2001). It involves Julie and Mark, two adult siblings who happily and without ramification engage in protected sex once and only once. The factual case is about cannibalism in December 2002, Germany. Armin Meiwes advertised for "a young, well-built man who wants to be eaten." Several candidates opted out once discovering that Meiwes was not speaking metaphorically. Bernd Brandes, however, happily consented to let Meiwes kill and eat him, which Meiwes did.[5]

2 CONTRACTARIANISM

As discussed in my introductory chapter, contractarianism is a liberal theory that lets people do what they want to do except when using other people without their consent. "Consent" means more than that agents agree. Their agreement must be voluntary, and by voluntary, their decisions – throughout the entire event – must not be coerced, deceived, or manipulated. Apart from acting voluntarily, agents (or their proxies) must be competent and suitably informed. Another qualification is needed concerning *reasonably presumed consent* to accommodate those unable to provide consent (the very young or the incapacitated, for example) or for those situations where eliciting consent is not possible (throwing someone a surprise party, or pushing someone out of the way of a falling piano). Another criterion is needed to clarify whose consent counts and whose does not in any interaction. That two thieves have voluntarily agreed to rob me does not make their transaction moral; my agreement is required. On the other hand, homophobes do not tend to agree to the sexual actions of homosexuals, but their non-consent does not count. A concerned party to any agreement is one whose existence is required for the event to take place. Thus, "[a]ny act is morally permissible if and only if all concerned parties (or their proxies) are competent, suitably informed, and voluntarily, or would reasonably voluntarily, consent" (Murray 2017, 5). Acts done to others without satisfaction of the above principle are generally immoral. When they are not immoral, special circumstances prevail. Killing another in self-defence, for example, is not done with the other's permission, but we deem it morally permissible (all things equal) because the other (the one threatening you, intentionally or not) is not honouring your consent. In such cases, your obligations toward them are dissolved.

Contractarians will morally permit consensual incest, as in the Julie and Mark case. To the extent that the offspring of incestuous couples are adversely affected parties who did not consent, we can limit our focus to consensual incest for those without intending to have offspring. This will not exclude accidental offspring issuing from incestuous couples, but, presumably, nor ought we to ban couples with genetic markers for disease to have sex in case of accidental offspring (Tralau 2013, 98–9; Singer 2016, 136). Whether contractarians should deem immoral incestuous couples who *intend* to have children requires further discussion. As Parfit (1986, 361) notes, it seems better for the children to be born malformed than not to be born at all. My claim, however, is only that the grand taboo against incest is unsupported, not that no incest is immoral.

Contractarians will also morally permit consensual cannibalism, as in the Armin and Bernd case, assuming Bernd was competent. I admit difficulty in accepting Bernd's competence, but we have to be careful not to assume competency merely on the basis of what we would choose. Non-consensual incest and non-consensual active cannibalism are wrong even for contractarians. Non-consensual passive survival cannibalism may be deemed morally fine. Eating someone without their consent may be morally justifiable assuming the other has already died and other food sources needed for one's own survival are unavailable. This can be deemed as morally permissible as killing another in self-defence. I would not go so far as to claim that non-consensual active survival cannibalism is morally fine, however, but my reasoning for that takes me further afield than is necessary for my basic claim. Mortuary or funerary cannibalism is morally fine under the assumption that the practice is implicitly accepted. Canadians, for example, accept being dumped in a hole post-death, but few actually gave consent to it: it is simply implied. Assuming contractarians do not understand war as a reversion to the state of nature (contra Viminitz 2005), where nothing can be immoral, contractarians can argue that *ex ante* bargainers would settle on rules of war, including the prohibition of cannibalizing (or torturing) prisoners. Ritualistic cannibalism to appease gods without the consent of the sacrificed is immoral on contractarian grounds. Consensual sacrificial cannibalism is fine assuming the sacrificed did not suffer non-autonomous indoctrination. As with competency, however, we have to be careful not to assume autonomy merely on the basis of what we would choose. Catholic families, for instance, indoctrinate their children, yet we let their children consent to Catholic rituals just the same.

A practical difficulty exists with consensual cannibalism. How can we tell whether consent occurred? We cannot ask them when they are dead. For that reason, Baggini (2017) deems it wise to prohibit cannibalism even while admitting that consensual cannibalism would be moral. I do not have a nice answer to this worry, other than that my concern here is theoretical. The same worry plagues active euthanasia cases, and so, perhaps, can be addressed in a similar fashion, i.e., by credibly documenting pre-consent. Meiwes did attempt this with Brandes, to not much success.

A theoretical challenge to contractarianism's excessive permissibility may be framed as so: cannibalism and incest are so wrong that even properly consensual cannibalism and properly consensual incest are wrong (Gass 1957; Kass 1997). In fact, one might say, any theory that claims cannibalism and incest are morally fine counts as a *reductio ad absurdum* against that theory (Gass 1957).[6] As put, the reason (reasonable) people *would not* agree to be eaten or engage in incest is *because* those practices are wrong. If so, consent cannot be the reason for morality, but the reverse. The objections would resonate more if at least some credible moral theory can show cannibalism and incest are wrong without appealing merely to our gut.

3 OTHER THEORIES

Assuming no health harm, act utilitarianism is likely to support passive cannibalism. Eating the dead provides a new food source and limits the space required for cemeteries.[7] Under certain conditions, cannibalism in non-human species helps stabilize an ecosystem (Rault, Benoît, and Gouzé, 2013). Rule utilitarians might object if enough people are made sufficiently unhappy to live in a world where cannibalism was a thing. Ditto with incest. According to psychological studies, however, people do tend to mind, and the disgust may be unexcisable since it is buried deep in our ancestral heritage. Thus, rule utilitarians can condemn incest and cannibalism on the grounds of making us all worse off. The circularity of such reasoning is apparent. Why would people be unhappy (per hypothesis) to live in a world where people are made happier (per hypothesis)? The same argument can be applied to homosexuality. Homophobes, those against homosexuality, minded. Once the norm caught on, however, homophobic reactions waned. Between two options, one where homosexuals are extremely unhappy being forbidden from having loving relations and homophobes being a little happier for quashing others' joy, and the other where homophobes are a little bit bothered by what their neighbours are doing for a relatively short period of time until they get used to the idea and homosexuals being much happier, a rule utilitarian can opt for the second. Over time, greater happiness is accommodated by permitting homosexuality. A similar line can be used for incest and cannibalism. The anguish of unconcerned parties will wane over time; the overall net happiness is increased by permitting consensual relations, including incest and cannibalism.

Kantians cannot plausibly condemn either consensual cannibalism or consensual incest. Applying the supreme categorical imperative, we will find it is logically possible to consume others with consent in a world where people are universally permitted to consume others with consent. One might suggest that if everyone ate everyone, no one would be left. This is a consequentialist worry, however, so is not permitted for Kantians. Besides, it is implausible. That is like saying in a world where everyone dies (our world), no one would be left to die (not our world, yet). We need not assume everyone dies *at the same time*. Nor need we imagine a world where everyone consumes everyone, let alone simultaneously. The argument is to permit cannibalism under certain conditions, not demand it. The other Kantian approach concerns treating people as means rather than ends. Kass (1997), for example, complains that cannibalism is a case of lacking due respect for the one being eaten. Cannibals *use* the other as fodder, after all. But a lack of respect is not evident in funereal cannibalism, nor need it be evident in consensual active cannibalism. Meiwes respected those who opted out as well as the one who opted in.

The normal arguments against incest are off limits for Kantians. Arguments about birth defects and about bad things that will happen to those engaging in incestuous relations (given the intolerance of society, mainly, as opposed to anything particular about incestuous relations) are appeals to hypothetical consequences and interests of agents. Meanwhile, the a priori manoeuvre of the supreme categorical imperative cannot work for condemning incest. In a world where incest was universally permitted, it would not be logically impossible to engage in incest. And assuming incest is consensual, no obvious violation of the principle to treat people with respect occurs.

Other than a divine command theory, virtue theory is the best candidate for claiming incest and cannibalism are wrong, assuming we can show that these are activities in which virtuous people would not engage. Many theories of well-being concern themselves with healthy and moderate diets. A desire for human meat would not be on the virtuous person's menu, presumably, but nor would a desire for a hotdog or an extra serving of cake. This points to one worry about virtue theory: advice about how to live well need not conform to moral advice. In any event, funerary cannibalism may well be practised by the virtuous person. It would be unvirtuous, in fact, to refuse to eat a bit of the deceased; an act of utter disrespect. And since, per hypothesis, Meiwes cautiously verified Brandes's consent, we can say Meiwes respected Brandes as an ends-in-himself, a kind of action we expect from a virtuous person.

While agreeing with Wisniewski (2004; 2007) and Shand (2010) that neither deontological nor teleological theories can succeed, Lu (2013) attempts a virtue theory condemnation of cannibalism.[8] For Lu, "Human corpses are vulnerable in virtue of some sort of residual humanity" (2013, 458), and that residual humanity is in lieu of its once housing a soul (453). Though the corpse no longer has a soul, the corpse (before putrefaction) offers a reflection of the person who was (454). Ignoring talk of souls, the idea, I take it, is that violating the corpse is like violating a photo of a deceased person. The wrongness need not be in terms of the harm to the deceased, but the kind of vice displayed by the person to do such a thing. It does not follow, however, that one cannot permit one's corpse to be consumed any more than one may permit one's organs to be harvested, or, for that matter, put in one's will to have all one's photos shredded.[9]

Virtue theory does better condemning incest than cannibalism. Incest, especially incest without procreation, is putting sexual appetite ahead of philosophical contemplation and virtue (disregarding that we have not yet established that recreational sex is not a virtue, or, for that matter, that philosophical reflection is). But incest would be banned by virtue theory along with all recreational sex. It is not incest, per se, that is the problem: recreational sex is. That no virtuous person would engage in recreational sex is a non-falsifiable claim.

While no well-standing moral theory can show incest or cannibalism to be wrong, only contractarianism can unequivocally say such activities are morally fine. Does this show a problem with moral theory (or contractarianism in particular), or is thinking something must be wrong with moral theory for permitting cannibalism and incest itself a case of dumbfounding?

4 DUMBFOUNDING

Dumbfounding is Haidt's (2001) term for a person being unable to explain why something is wrong while adamantly maintaining its wrongness. Dumbfounding consistently occurs in people confronted with tales of consensual cannibalism and consensual incest. Haidt offered the tale of the happy, harmless recreational sex among consenting adult siblings, Julie and Mark. Each used contraception, enjoyed the experience, never had sex with one another again, and lived happily ever after. When presented with the scenario most people thought what Julie and Mark did was immoral. When asked to explain why they thought so, study participants spoke of genetic mutations, or deleterious effects on the relationship between Julie and Mark, or their future intimate relations with others. After being told that such concerns were not relevant in the Julie and Mark vignette, few changed their minds about the wrongness. They simply gave up trying to justify why they thought it wrong, other than offering dumbfounding expressions like, "It's just wrong!"

Such vehement assurance was commonly deemed an adequate guide to morality by moral philosophers of the not-too-distant past. Butler (1726) thought our moral insight came intuitively from God. Why something was wrong was less relevant than that it was wrong. Moore (1903) thought our dumbfounding is because morality is a simple, unanalyzable, non-natrual property. To ask why something is moral is to demand a non-moral explanation; as sensible as asking what colour a lemon is without using the term yellow. Gass (1957, 654) argued that any explanation for why cannibalism, for example, is wrong is always more inscrutable than that it is wrong. More recently, Kass (1997) argued that disgust is a perfectly adequate moral guide. We need no more defend our disgust or the connection between our disgust and our moral judgment than simply knowing the universal truism that we ought never to transgress what is "unspeakably profound" (20). These are not justifications for our moral judgments, of course; they are justifications for our being correctly dumbfounded by someone asking us *why* incest or cannibalism is wrong. We are dumbfounded at the incredulity of thinking anyone needs an explanation. We wonder if they even speak our language.

Intuitionism claims to justify moral actions by an internal radar that bypasses rational explanation. When intuitions clash with reasoning, however, it does not necessarily follow that we ought to keep our intuitions, especially when intuitions are based merely on the traditions in which we have been raised. Sometimes we ought to abandon the folklore. To rely merely on one's intuition is demonstrably problematic in epistemology. Why ought intuition to have more clout in morality than epistemology? Since moral obligations cost the obliged, at least in terms of restricted behaviour, we should expect justification beyond, "It seems that way to me." But recent psychological studies of the dumbfounding effect are not pointing toward a kind of higher-order intuitionism that humans possess by the grace of some divine presence or cultural inculcation. Rather, they see morality as being rooted in deep, primitive, naturally selected emotions – disgust and anger (Rozin et al. 1999; Prinz 2009; Schnall et al. 2008; Seidel and Prinz 2013; Russell and Giner-Sorolla 2013).

Anger is invoked when making judgments about "autonomy" violations, that is, crimes against persons, such as murder, assault, and theft. I put autonomy in quotes, since it seems either biased toward Kantianism, or completely misguided if by autonomy they mean the ability to choose one's desires. "Liberty" is probably the more apt term. Disgust is the emotion aroused when making judgments about "crimes against nature," as the literature puts it,[10] such as incest, cannibalism, bestiality, and necrophilia. Accordingly, neuroimaging makes vivid the different areas of the brain activated between moral disgust and moral anger (Borg, Lieberman, and Kiehl 2008; Greene et al. 2004; Greene et al. 2001; Haidt 2001; Vytal and Hamann 2010). Anger triggered by autonomy violations tends to be accompanied by ready external justifications consistent with one or another moral theory. Belief of an autonomy violation can be easily withdrawn with new evidence. Not so nature violations. Moral disgust is the more primitive reaction: quick to arise and slow to depart. Once disgust is invoked, the moral condemnation rendered stubbornly remains despite evidence to the contrary. The inflexibility of our disgust is itself deemed sufficient reason to morally condemn the disgust-invoking action (Russell and Giner-Sorolla 2013, 344). Conclusion: we draw on different emotions when arriving at moral judgments and thus we need to give up looking for a common essence to morality the way moral theory (including contractarianism) does (Seidel and Prinz 2013, 5). Hume and the emotivists seem vindicated.

That we deem incest and cannibalism to be both immoral and disgusting does not mean cannibalism and incest are immoral, let alone immoral *because* they are disgusting, although such an inference is made by Kass (1997). That we are disgusted by these kinds of things has empirical support. Such empiricism does not translate into believing that disgust is a *correct* reaction. Something else is required; presumably that the action toward which we show disgust *is* immoral ... unless disgust and anger (and their opposites) turn out to be the only things that – in fact – establish our moral views. This latter possibility – that our moral views are no more than emotional reactions embedded in ancestral evolution – is the theory of emotionism (Prinz 2007).[11] After all, what else could explain our confidence that incest among fully consenting adults is wrong? Yes, birth defects are associated with sibling incest, but what is wrong with incestuous relations with prophylactics? What is wrong with homosexual incestuous relations? The primitive part of our brain answers: "It's so disgusting we want everyone to deem it disgusting, too!"

For emotionists, it is not that incest is really wrong because we are disgusted by it. Rather, since we designate negative moral language to things that disgust us, and incest disgusts us, incest is deemed immoral. Unlike with Kass, Gass, Moore, and Butler, Prinz (2007) makes no claim that morality is a real thing out there in the world. Prinz is not saying that incest is *really* immoral: only that our account of morality stems from emotion. In fact, there is no such thing as morality outside of human emotion. Emotionism is an irrealist theory.

The nice thing about emotionism is it explains both our view that incest and cannibalism are wrong and our being dumbfounded about how to explain why we think it wrong. Not all of the psychological research appears to understand the moral irrealism of the argument, since many studies critique the notion that disgust is neither evidence nor justification of moral wrongdoing (Cofnas 2020, 47; Kelly 2011, 148; May 2014, 129). Others take great efforts to connect disgust with morality at some deep, evolutionary level (Borg, Lieberman, and Kiehl 2008; Plakias 2018, 5468), but the connection presumes what emotionism denies: that there is any real morality out there to begin with.

Two worries are left unexplained with emotionism, however. Firstly, the argument in favour of emotionism relies heavily on our deeming incest and cannibalism to be immoral. The evidence for that is that people tend to deem these things to be immoral. We also deemed homosexuality to be immoral (and disgusting, at least for heterosexuals), but that was not (in the end) the deciding factor. Secondly, the emotionist solution to the puzzle about cannibalism and incest seems to be at the expense of morality. This is not a fault if a justifiable morality is a fiction, but one may wonder whether a less drastic solution may be found instead, for example, contractarianism. The task ahead of us is to decide whether the evidence supports emotionism? My answer is no.

5 EVIDENCE

The standard approach to psychological studies of morality is to induce various emotions in subjects and get them to react to moral situations. Disgust may be invoked by vomiting sounds (Siedel and

Prinz 2013) or fart spray (Schnall, Haidt, Clore, and Jordan, 2008), for example, and then subjects so inflicted rate the morality of various scenarios. While disgust significantly raised the severity level of moral judgments compared to control groups, it never made subjects deem morally innocuous situations to be immoral (May 2014; Royzman, Kim, and Leeman 2015; Cofnas 2020). This indicates that actions are judged to be moral or immoral by issues *other* than emotional triggers of disgust or anger. At best, psychological studies show that emotions co-occur with moral judgments, but that is hardly surprising.

Royzman, Kim, and Leeman (2015) critiqued the moral dumbfounding literature. Replicating Haidt's (2001) study with "credulity checks," they found that most subjects failed to be convinced that no harm was to come to Julie and Mark, despite being repeatedly told by the experimenters that they were not harmed. People assumed that Julie and Mark's relation with each other – as well as their future intimate relations with others – would be damaged. Subjects simply did not believe that Julie and Mark lived, or could live, happily ever after. They continued to believe that the real peril of harm with incest is the irreparable relationship damage (Jacobson 2013, 301). Dumbfounding was not because subjects had no reason for believing incest was wrong; rather their reason for thinking it wrong (harm to the incestuous couple) was not permitted as an answer. Of course we would be dumbfounded to be told to come up with a reason for our moral judgment *without appealing* to the reason why we take the specific action to be wrong. It is like telling a child to come up with a reason to have a cookie without appealing to the fact that the child wants one. But that *is* the reason, we want to say. Royzman, Kim, and Leeman (2015) claim that subjects' dumbfoundedness led Haidt and company to erroneously assume that only pure emotion guides our moral responses.

Royzman, Kim, and Leeman (2015, 302) compare incest dumbfounding with drunk driving dumbfounding. If you were asked why drunk driving was bad, presumably you would mention something about the likelihood of harm to others. Being told that no harm was done in a particular case of drunk driving would not prevent you from still basing your reason of the wrongness of that particular episode of drunk driving on the likelihood of harm. To be prevented from using that argument would surely be met with dumbfounding. Similarly, dumbfounding in the moral psychology studies seems more directed at the questioner; it was not due to a lack of having a reason to say why incest is wrong.

Apart from offering teleological reasons (the potential harm) as legitimate grounds for condemning incest, Royzman, Kim, and Leeman (2015) found that their subjects offered deontological reasons, that is "foundational reasons" (311), against incest that did not rely on harms. Examples were given such as incest is "inherently wrong" (299, 305, 308), "inherently immoral" (303), "fundamentally wrong" (308), and not in "compliance with natural law" (310). Haidt treated such appeals as unsupported declarations (i.e., dumbfounding), instead of recognizing the long-standing deontological tradition (Royzman, Kim, and Leeman, 2015).

Royzman, Kim and Leeman's critique flounders. Deontological theories are not well expressed as a vague appeal to intrinsic wrongness, and to the extent that they are, is to commit dumbfounding. "Wrong in principle" is just another dumbfounding term; not an alternative moral explanation. And deeming incest to be wrong because of potential harm to the practitioners is different than deeming drunk driving to be wrong on the basis of harm to others. The first is a paternalistic justification, the second a liberal justification.

This is not to say that the dumbfounding literature supports emotionism. Brain scans and psychological studies claim to show different "moral" emotional channels, one for autonomy violations and one for nature violations. Ignoring the use of "nature" here, such evidence does not show two types of moral judgments without presuming that "nature violations," like cannibalism and incest, count as moral violations. An equally apt conclusion: disgust cannot be a basis for moral judgments because it occurs at a different level of the brain than moral reactions (those aimed at "autonomy" violations).

SUMMARY

The only persistent evidence of dumbfounding occurs with "nature" violations. This alone cannot support emotionism as a general theory; it can do so only in terms of our reactions to "nature" violations. If we think that "nature" violations are not even within the rubric of morality (as is the case with contractarians), such psychological studies have nothing to say about moral assessment at all.

But does an appeal to the evolution of morality not commit us to something akin to emotionism? I am afraid not.

6 EVOLUTION AND MORALITY

An evolutionary story of disgust is that it arises as a social alert for norm violations (Kekes 1992, Kahan 1999, Fischer 2016). Disgust initiates the flight response; anger initiates the fight response (Seidel and Prinz 2013). Since we want to imitate "good" norms and shun "bad" norms, disgust acts as a countermeasure to imitation, and in that sense, disgust can be viewed as an appropriate response to preserve the norm (Plakias 2018). As social creatures, we like to mimic things (Boyd and Richerson 2002). A danger is mimicking the wrong thing. Disgust helps us avoid mimicking wrong behaviours. Disgust's role is to communicate our rejection of norm-violating behaviours (Plakias 2018, 5471).

Nothing in the above is problematic unless we take our disgust reaction to nature norm violations as *evidence* of the norm violation being immoral, as Kekes (1992), Kass (1997), and Kahan (1999) do. Plakias (2018), at least, offers a response model of moral disgust. Disgust is viewed as an appropriate response to norm violations – a kind of norm-guardian, perhaps akin to danger calls in birds. Disgust is a response to, not evidence of, certain norm violations. The idea is that moral disgust evolved from contagion disgust: how we used to communicate to others not to consume or touch something contagious (Chapman and Anderson 2013; Kelly 2011; Plakias 2018; Rozin, Haidt, and McCauley 2008; Tybur et al. 2013).

A common example is given to highlight contagion disgust. Normally it is a good thing not to drink some juice with a cockroach in it, due to possible contagion. Upon being told that the cockroach has been sterilized before it was dropped in your glass ought to remove your reluctance to drink the juice. For most of us, such assurance is hardly satisfying (Rozin, Millman, and Nemeroff, 1986). Our disgust still prevails and we have no reason to offer why we are not drinking the roach-dipped juice other than our currently misguided disgust. That contagion disgust may be given an evolutionary backing need not be doubted; that moral disgust is co-opted from contagion disgust is not evident, however. My disgust to drink roach-dipped juice counts as my *reason* for not imbibing. It is incorrect to say I have no reason to drink it. For that matter, declining consent never needs a reason. When others persist that you offer a reason for declining their offer, they get the onus of consent backwards – a worry raised in date rape literature. "I don't want to" is as much of a reason as we need. On the other hand, refusing to let others do an activity when I am not a concerned party (or demanding others do an activity) requires a justifiable reason other than my disgust at their so doing (or not so doing).

Despite Plakias's critique of the evidentiary model in support of the response model, the response model requires the evidentiary model as a foundation for the claim that disgust is an apt response to a norm violation. Warning others not to imitate norm violators requires some justification that the norm is inviolable. Her idea seems to be that a norm is inviolable should it in fact be contagions (Plakias 2018, 5468). Littering and queue cutting, for example, are contagious to the extent that if we see enough people littering and queue-cutting, we tend to follow suit (Plakias 2018, 5469). If we wish to preserve the merit of cleanliness and queuing, we ought to react negatively against litterers and queue cutters. A difficulty with the evidential model is that disgust is also associated with racism and homophobia (Kelly 2011, 148). We are past the point of calling racism and homophobia morally apt reactions. In response, Plakias claims that homosexuality is not contagious (5466). Thus the disgust response to homosexuality is not apt. Disgust to only those norm-violations that are contagious is apt.

At least two issues leap forward. First, that *x* is socially contagious does not necessarily show that *x* is immoral. Some things are contagious because they are fun: the hula-hoop, for example. Playing with the hula-hoop is neither immoral, nor disgusting. Second, and leaving aside whether homosexuality is or is not socially contagious, racism is contagious while cannibalism and incest are not.[12] Since our rabid disgust is aimed more at cannibalism and incest than littering and line cutting, the worry about homosexuality and racism also plagues Plakias's response model.[13]

The standard claim is that evolution's weaning of incest is due to lowered genetic fitness (Ruse and Wilson 1986, 184). That the taboo extends to childhood co-residents is known as the Westermarck effect (Westermarck 1891). The suspicion is that childhood co-residence serves as a kinship cue, a cue that would have indicated genetic relatedness in ancestral environments (Wolf 2004). For example, studies with peer groups on kibbutzim found non-sibling children growing up together tended not to form sexual relations (Lieberman and Lobel 2012). Meanwhile, we have accounts of happy sexual relations between unknowing siblings whose experience of repulsion occurred only after they discovered their kinship.[14]

While Cofnas (2020) critiques the evidence for the Westermarck effect, a greater worry about tying evolution to morality is what he calls the moralization problem (47) – or what Mackie (1977, 23–4) might call the motivation problem. We can accept that evolution instills in us a personal aversion to incest, but how does that extend to a social taboo against incest? Personal disgust may lead to a personal prohibition but cannot automatically convert to a social prohibition. My disgust of mushrooms, for example, leads me not to eat mushrooms, but it does not lead me to forbid you from eating mushrooms.

The emotional reactions accompanying a cultural norm violation are part of what it means to endorse the norm, and to prevent it from being eroded, but none of this explains *morality*. If people do react negatively to you for being a norm violator, this gives you, prima facie, a prudential reason not to violate that norm, but such a reason cannot plausibly be a *moral* reason, since nothing prevents us from wondering whether the norm itself is moral. Suffragists violated the norm of keeping women from voting or owning property and were, as a result, kicked, spat at, and ridiculed in public (if not beaten in private). While entrenching norms have good aspects that can be given an evolutionary backing, it certainly does not follow that the best understanding of morality is to simply follow the operating norm.

We can agree that an evolutionary story explains our disgust towards incest and cannibalism. Does this mean incest is immoral for those who believe morality comes from evolution? The answer is no. The evolution of morality occurs at a deeper level: the trait of reciprocal co-operation, not the trait of punishing norm violators. When norms themselves fail to mesh with reciprocal co-operation is when those norms are due to crumble. An evolved morality is a strategy, not a content. We can give an evolutionary story to our penchant for dessert without thinking it is morally mandatory to eat sugar. We can give an evolutionary story about our fear of snakes without making any moral recommendations about snakes. Morality, to be sure, is a subset of our evolutionary lineage, but something else is going on to make a particular trait *moral* than that we can track an ancestral lineage. What is at root is the propensity to reciprocally co-operate, and having that trait helps us in our social dealing compared to non-reciprocally co-operative traits (Alexander 2001; Axelrod 1984; Binmore 1998; Danielson 1992; Gauthier 1986; Murray 2007; Skyrms 1996; Trivers 1971). A tendency to reciprocally co-operate with others curtails certain activities: those in which we do to others without their consent. It is this formal structure that presents the boundary of right and wrong. Right if you meet with reciprocal co-operation among all concerned parties who are competent and informed; wrong otherwise. But the content of such agreements is left untouched. All that matters is the structure: informed, competent, voluntary consent among all concerned parties (Murray 2017).

7 SUMMARY

Studies in moral emotions describe two things: (i) the unreasonableness of the standard arguments against incest and cannibalism, and (ii) our trenchant resistance to think cannibalism and incest are thereby morally fine. Such unreasonable reluctance is taken to support the view that morality is *merely* an emotional response rooted deep in our evolutionary past. Contractarians can agree with emotionists that we have no rational reason to forbid incest or cannibalism. Contractarians can also agree that any complaint against cannibalism and incest is purely emotional. This would not show that moral judgments are purely emotional, however, since (i) the alternative that incest and cannibalism are morally fine has not been ruled out, and (ii) studies show only the effects of emotional dumbfounding on "crimes of nature" (specifically cannibalism and incest) as opposed to autonomy violations. Since most moral theories (save divine command theories and virtue theories) cull so-called "nature crimes" from moral restrictions, dumbfounding studies do little to undermine our confidence in cognitive ethics.

Many of our moral shifts over time have been accompanied by emotional intransigence despite reasoned arguments. Our reluctance to think homosexuality could be morally permissible, for example, has been accompanied by extreme emotional resistance. That we expect emotional attachment to claims we deem moral does not show that claims we deem moral are what we ought to call moral. I am disgusted by mushrooms. My disgust governs my dietary choice; my disgust cannot justify the moral outrage I direct at people who eat mushrooms. To the extent we can alter our emotional reactions to x over time suggests that our emotional responses come after our moral conceptions, not before or coincident with them, and certainly not grounding them. That an evolutionary story can be given to explain our disgust toward incest and cannibalism, for example, does not show an evolutionary story for morality. This does not mean we do not have an evolutionary story of morality. We do, but it can only be in terms of structure, not content. Those who behave as reciprocal co-operators do better in terms of passing on their traits than those with other social dispositions. Such a structure cannot support a moral prohibition against properly consensual acts, including incest and cannibalism. Unlike emotionism, however, contractarianism does not come with a tidy error theory to explain dumbfounding other than that our society is still being influenced by obsolete religious doctrine.

4

Moral Luck and Williams Shifts

The problem of moral luck occurs when moral blame is affected by factors outside the control of those being blamed. So either our concept of moral responsibility does not hinge on what is in an agent's control (and we somehow deal with the unravelling threads of morality that precipitate), or we find a way to explain how the paradigmatic examples of moral luck are flawed. I opt for the latter. While others do as well, I suggest that their reasoning fails to account for a deeper rift lying between moral luck proponents and moral luck skeptics. I call that rift the Williams factor: when morality is seen as no longer supreme.

In section 1, I paraphrase the standard examples of moral luck. In section 2, I highlight why previous attempts at rejecting moral luck fail to be entirely convincing. In section 3, I offer math luck as an undermining parallel to moral luck. In section 4, I distinguish three ways in which morality may no longer matter and how that impinges on moral luck. In section 5, I explain why contractarianism views moral luck as myth.

1 MORAL LUCK ILLUSTRATIONS

We like to praise people for doing good acts and we like to blame people for doing bad acts. We make exceptions to this rule when we discover such acts were out of their control, that is to say, a matter of luck.[1] A man driving over a child because he suffered a stroke deserves no blame (all else equal). It is not a moral infraction; it is a tragedy. A woman driving over a pedestrian due to spite deserves blame. It is a moral infraction. In this sense, we like to imagine that moral assessment is never a matter of luck. When luck enters the picture, moral judgment alters accordingly. At least so we suppose.

Moral luck advocates, however, suggest that luck plays a much larger role than we like to believe – not merely in that certain things happen to us out of our control, but that the things that happen to us out of our control rightly affect our moral worth.

It is easy to admit how luck occurs regularly if not constantly in life, but whether we may infer *moral* luck from *life* luck needs to be illustrated. Attempts at such inferences concern three areas: (i) results, (ii) circumstances, and (iii) constitution (Williams 1981a; Nagel 1979). A fourth area, the general worry about free will, I ignore.

(i) Resultant luck concerns the luck involved in how things turn out despite intentions. Compare three drivers, Abigail, Bertha, and Clarissa. Abigail is sober. Bertha and Clarissa are equally intoxicated and ought not to be driving. In the cases of Abigail and Bertha, a child lurches from behind a bush in front of their cars and is struck dead. Neither had any chance to prevent the death. While being drunk slows reflexes, police investigation reveals that Bertha could do as little as Abigail in the situation. Although Bertha was drunk and Abigail not, the child's appearance was so sudden and unforeseen that neither could do anything to stop the tragedy. No child lurches out in front of Clarissa, although she is later stopped at a road check and charged for drunk driving. We expect to blame Bertha more harshly than Clarissa, but we do not expect to blame Abigail at all.[2] Is this ordering of blame unfair? Certainly it violates our notion that we withhold blame to the extent that the action is not the culprit's fault.

The three drivers illustration reveals different moral appraisal between Abigail and Bertha despite their outcomes being identical.[3] That we do not blame Abigail is because we deem her not culpable. Although Bertha (like Abigail) could not help but run over the child, she was drunk and so deserves more blame than Abigail. But since Bertha and Clarissa were equally intoxicated while driving, should not the blame we accord Bertha be equal to the blame we accord Clarissa? To think the child's death is relevant in our blaming Bertha more than Clarissa is to forget that the child's death is not relevant in the case of our not blaming Abigail.

So is blaming Bertha more than Clarissa and Abigail fair? Bertha is being punished for more than being drunk while driving. She is also punished for being culpable in the death of the child to a degree that was not her fault, either in terms of external result (compared to Abigail) or in terms of internal will (compared to Clarissa).

(ii) Circumstantial luck is the luck involved in placing you in a situation where you may respond immorally. Imagine two inner-city youths, Delilah and Edwina, who have identical dispositions. Delilah joins a gang and becomes a murderer. Just before she is about to join a gang, Edwina is pulled out of the inner city and grows up in a gangless community somewhere in Canada with her aunt. She does not become a murderer. We blame Delilah, but not Edwina, even though had the circumstances been reversed, Edwina would have been the murderer, and not Delilah.[4]

(iii) Constitutive luck is the luck involved in forming your character, specifically your moral character. Imagine two cases where a Jewish family asks a German citizen to hide them from the Nazis. Each German citizen, Ferdinand and Karl, wish no ill will on the Jewish family and are against the Nazi policy. Unfortunately for one family, Ferdinand is a coward, and declines. Karl, who is more courageous than Ferdinand, accepts. We would morally blame Ferdinand and praise Karl, even though the differences lie in dispositional traits they are unable to control.

My focus will be on resultant luck. Neither the constitutive nor circumstantial luck cases seem problematic. In the constitutive luck case, we would praise Karl for sheltering would-be victims at risk to Karl's life, but we would not blame Ferdinand for failing to shelter anyone at risk to Ferdinand's life. Whatever failing being a coward is, it is not a moral failing. Cowardice may prevent one from doing the moral thing, as in Ferdinand's case, in which case it can lead to moral failing, but cowardice itself is not a moral failing, contra virtue theory. Likewise, courage may well be a virtue, and courage is often needed to perform moral tasks, as in Karl's case, but that does not make it a *moral* virtue. Assassins, bank robbers, and terrorists require courage as much as saints. Therefore, the extent to which we morally blame Ferdinand is the extent to which we blame wrongly. We have no moral obligation to preserve the lives of others at our own expense.

In the circumstantial luck case, we avoid condemning people for what we think they statistically would have done had they been in different circumstances. Unless we have clear proof of immoral plotting, we follow the rule not to punish people for crimes not committed. That they were lucky not to have committed the crime is not to say we judge their moral worth on the basis of luck. Abused children tend to grow up to be abusers. We do not morally blame the abused for being abused, however (Card 1996, 41). There is no puzzle in our not blaming people who commit no crime even when they might have done so in other circumstances. If any puzzle exists, it concerns the fickleness of personal identity. We are largely who we are on the basis of circumstances beyond our control. It is true of all of us that we might have done a bad act had the circumstances been different. But we need not confuse the presence of circumstantial life luck with moral luck.[5]

2 PREVIOUS SCEPTIC ATTEMPTS

Moral luck proponents share the intuition that we morally blame Bertha (the drunk driver who killed the child) differently than Clarissa (the drunk driver who killed no one). I have never felt that particular intuition.[6] To blame others for actions you realize you may have done is hypocritical (Fritz and Miller 2018). To blame others for actions you are too insensitive to realize you may have done is self-righteous (Watson 2004, 254). When luck is involved, how could blame be other than hypocritical or self-righteous? One could blame oneself for actions one would excuse in others. We would tell Abigail, the non-drunk accidental killer of the child, not to blame herself, while knowing we would blame ourselves, as she does. Self-blame need not be moral blame, however, and, at any rate, cannot justify blaming others when we know it is not their fault.[7]

Four common responses to the puzzle about moral luck share my doubt. (i) Blame is being confused with blameworthiness and/or severity of punishment. (ii) Blame is due to epistemic gaps in the blamers. (iii) "Blame" is too vague a concept to be used without equivocating. (iv) Blame is appropriate for "optional" luck, but not "brute" luck. None of these attempts at discrediting the existence of resultant moral luck succeed, however. Something else is required.

2.1 *Blame, Blameworthiness, and Punishment*

Distinguishing blame from justifiable blame seems simple enough. That people morally blame someone does not mean moral theory approves of such blame. We condemn vigilantism, for example, where citizens assume the roles of both blamers and punishers. To say the issue of moral luck arises only because of mistaken blame (Enoch and Marmor 2007, 433), however, is too facile. That we differently blame our three drivers is not obviously a fault of the blamers (Sand and Klenk 2021). This is not to say people never get moral matters wrong. Our prisons reveal endemic racism. That we punish blacks who harm or are alleged to have harmed whites more harshly than whites who have harmed whites, hardly shows we are justified in doing so. Rather, it shows that people can let extraneous influences, like racism, affect their moral assessment. While we could concoct scenarios where racism, sexism, or ageism could influence blame, we cannot point to any non-moral extraneous matter affecting our judgments about our three drivers, save our emotional displeasure at someone's being killed. A dead child in the drunk-driving case seems more morally relevant than the difference of skin colour in a murder victim.

We may *punish* these characters differently,[8] and to the extent that we do may still seem (at least mildly) puzzling (Smilansky 2007, 33–41). One likes to imagine that equal punishment is owed to equal blame, but that we do not always follow this rule seems easily justified. We can be pluralists when it comes to the purpose of punishment. Punishment may be useful as retribution, deterrence, protection of other members of society, victim compensation, rehabilitation, and/or maybe even some sort of expressivist outburst. While people may get moral appraisal wrong, for there is little check on what people happen to think or say, to get formal punishment wrong (as in the racist charge) is a serious problem needing an immediate fix. The worry about moral luck is not resolved, however, by pointing out the truism that the aims of punishment are plural.[9] We can easily say that punishment is deserved only when culpability is present (retribution), but degree of punishment varies according to degree or extent of harm. Abigail is not culpable for the accident; so deserves no punishment at all. Clarissa is culpable of drunk driving, but not of killing anyone, unlike Bertha who is both culpable for drunk driving and for killing someone. Fair enough, a moral luck proponent may say, but this does not rule out the role of luck. Clarissa was luckier than Bertha and but for that luck they would have been treated the same. Thus we punish on the basis of luck. While Nagel may have obscured the distinction between blame and punishment (Sand and Klenk 2021, n. 10), most moral luck proponents clearly emphasize that they are primarily concerned with blame, not punishment (Hartman 2016). That is, ignoring punishment, we still blame Bertha more than

Clarissa. While I cannot fathom their intuition, as I have said, it is disingenuous to insist that moral luck proponents are confusing punishment for blame.

2.2 *Epistemic Gaps*

Another approach to refute moral luck is to accuse moral assessors of missing some key fact (Latus 2000; Enoch and Marmor 2007, 416; Wolf 2001, 7). Luck is involved merely in our coming to learn about the players' moral characters, not in our moral assessment of those characters (Rescher 1993, 154; Richards 1993). The problem, then, is not rooted in moral blame, but in our understanding all the relevant variables that a proper blamer ought to consider. To better eliminate epistemic gaps is why we prefer a formal judging process over vigilantism. My three-drivers illustration, however, is devised to avoid the worry about epistemic lack. Detectives confirm, we imagine, identical facts about speed and application of brakes between Abigail and Bertha. Moreover, we know that Clarissa drove drunk with the same degree of intoxication (as stipulated): she was charged. While epistemic gaps exist in circumstantial and constitutive luck cases,[10] they are not always present in resultant luck cases (Schinkle 2009.)

2.3 *Types of Blame*

Blame is not a uniform concept. Apart from demarcating moral from amoral blame, four distinctions in moral blame can be made: (i) between the scope and degree of blame; (ii) between blaming the character and condemning the act; (iii) blaming as retribution and blaming as a corrective; (iv) deontic blaming and supererogatory blaming.

(i) Distinguishing scope from degree of blame is another way to explain away moral luck (Zimmerman 2002, 560–1). Degree refers to the measure of internal culpability for acting. Someone may be fully or partially responsible for an act. Scope refers to the range of bad acts for which the person is being blamed. In the drunk drivers case, Bertha and Clarissa have equal extent of blame for driving drunk and risking harm to pedestrians, but only Bertha's blame extends in scope to include actual harm. Everyone agrees that *both* degree and scope matter in moral appraisal, however, and that we think so seems hardly a mistake (Cyr 2021, 10). A brutal killing is worse than a simple killing (degree), and a mass murder is worse than a single murder (scope). It would be surprising to discover we are wrong about that, or that moral luck proponents have been conflating the two.

(ii) When blaming, we may be focusing on the act or the person. Sometimes we want to call the person bad; other times we want to call what the person did bad without necessarily imputing that the person doing the bad act is bad.[11] Zimmerman (2002) refers to this distinction as hypological and deontic. Hypological blame focuses on agents' internal motivations – they acted with bad will. Deontic blame points out violations of obligatory acts. We may sometimes blame someone hypologically *because* of the egregiousness of the act. What Hitler did was so evil we infer *he* was evil. We may also blame someone hypologically without blaming them deontically. A selfish politician giving to charity may be too blatant and self-serving, for example. One may satisfy one's deontic duty without receiving hypological praise. My not murdering anyone today does not deserve applause. When the focus is on character, we think in terms of what they have a propensity to do. As put, the focus of character blame is often counterfactual. That Pinocchio has lied deserves deontic blame, but when we call Pinocchio a liar, we hypologically impute in Pinocchio a propensity to lie in the future. Deontic blame, or the blame concerning acts, must always be actual. Zimmerman's idea is that proponents of moral luck conflate the two. To say Bertha (the killer drunk driver) deserves *more* blame than Clarissa (the non-killer drunk driver) is to switch from hypological to deontic blame. Driving drunk opens the door for counterfactual manslaughter. Whether one actually commits manslaughter or not is irrelevant to hypological blame. But deontic blame focuses on actual wrongdoing, not counterfactual wrongdoing. To speak correctly, we ought to say that while both Bertha and Clarissa deserve equal hypological blame (their characters are equally blameworthy), Bertha may also be blamed deontically (vis-à-vis manslaughter), but not Clarissa.

I have no qualms about the hypological/deontic (or character/act) distinction in blame, but to say that moral luck proponents equivocate between the two is not supported.[12] Moral luck proponents claim that we hypologically blame the killer drunk driver worse than the non-killer drunk driver, despite equal counterfactual wrongdoing. Williams's talk about agent-regret, for example, is to highlight hypological blame independently of deontic blame (Williams 1981a, 28). I do not share such an intuition, as I have said, but I think it unfair to accuse moral luck advocates of equivocating between hypological and deontic blame. Besides, we do not deontically blame Abigail, although we deontically blame Bertha. Bertha's blame gets double-counted even under Zimmerman's distinction. Moreover, Zimmerman's introducing counterfactual considerations for hypological blame leads to peculiarities. Imagine three snipers. Sniper 1 shoots and kills her target. Sniper 2 sneezes and fails to fire the rifle at the opportune moment: the target lives. Sniper 3 has a bout of conscience just before he fires, so withholds fire: the target lives. Even admitting that hypological blame should be equal between Sniper 1 and Sniper 2, few would believe that Sniper 3 deserves equal hypological blame. Nevertheless, Zimmerman's counterfactual concept of hypological blame makes Sniper 3 as hypologically blameworthy as Sniper 1 (Zimmerman 2002, n. 43). The rest of us would think the pang of conscience Sniper 3 enjoys lessens his hypological blame. Similarly, Zimmerman's solution would have us blame Edwina (who left the gang without killing anyone) equally with Delilah (who remained in a gang and killed) (Hartman 2019b, 230). The hypological–deontic distinction does not eliminate the worry about moral luck, or at least resultant moral luck.

(iii) We may condemn an act, but blame a person. The purpose of such blame has some overlap with the purpose of punishment. When we blame someone, we may do so retributively (a kind of punishment), or correctively, to help teach them a lesson.[13] Corrective blame, or perhaps communicative blame (Enoch and Marmor 2007, 428; Hartman 2019b, 230; McKenna 2012), focuses on altering character traits, as is typical in parenting. As such, corrective blame assumes character traits can be intentionally altered and this clashes with constitutive luck. As far as circumstantial luck goes, to correctively blame Edwina, the would-be gang member, as much as Delilah, the actual gang member, would make no sense. There is nothing we need correct (vis-à-vis gang member activity) in Edwina. She is no longer part of a gang. The difference in blame, then, is not affected by luck; rather, the conditions governing the function of blame differ. Similarly in resultant luck cases, difference in blame may be less to do with luck than difference in types of blaming we accord the lucky and the unlucky agents.

When we keep constant the type of blame we are delivering, the worry about moral luck does not obviously dissolve, however.

In the three drivers' case, Clarissa, the lucky drunk driver, is still caught by police and suffers some sort of formal punishment, considerably less than the unlucky driver who killed a child. Had Clarissa not been caught, and we found out about Clarissa's action, our blame of her would include, presumably, a corrective component. Don't do that again! But since she was caught and given some formal punishment, the need for our blame to be corrective has dissolved. The state is handling that. The same goes for Bertha. Our need to offer Bertha corrective blame dissolves because she is being formally punished to an extent greater than that which Clarissa received. At any rate, the corrective for both is the same: Don't drive drunk. So the corrective component of the blame is the same. The retributive component of blame, however, can be aimed at both Bertha and Clarissa (and not Abigail), and moral-luck components claim the degree of blame is worse for Bertha than for Clarissa. One might even say it is this difference in retributive blame that justifies difference in punishment.[14]

(iv) We can blame someone for failing an obligation (deontic blame) and we can also blame someone for their failing to satisfy a supererogatory virtue. The focus here is on the *virtue* of taking responsibility at times when it is not deontically required (Wolf 2001, 17; Card 1996, 41). To apologize for snoring, for example, would be a case of taking responsibility even though one is not, in an agency sense, responsible for snoring. Wolf speaks of a vase falling off a table and breaking in the presence of a guest. The guest did not knock the vase over. Perhaps a loose floorboard is the real culprit. Nevertheless, one can offer a causal hypothesis that the vase would not have fallen at that time without the guest's presence. Despite not being morally responsible, a virtuous guest would take responsibility and offer to compensate the host for the loss of her vase (Wolf 2001, 13). To apply this to our resultant luck case, we can admit that Bertha and Clarissa are equally blameworthy for *being* responsible for their drunk driving, yet still blame Bertha more than Clarissa because of a supererogatory virtue to *take* responsibility for the death of the child. Similarly, we expect Bertha to take responsibility for the accident in a way we do not expect Clarissa to take responsibility. Thus, we may hold both Bertha and Clarissa equally responsible for driving drunk, yet our greater moral condemnation of Bertha is due to this added supererogatory virtue to take responsibility for compensating the victim (or the victim's family).

While we may agree that taking responsibility in this way is a virtue, we do not, in fact, blame the guest in the house for breaking the lamp. We praise her for taking responsibility for it. The vase case highlights how it may be nice to take responsibility despite being blameless. That is not what is going on in moral luck scenarios, however. Besides, we do not *stop* blaming the drunken killer of the child if she makes the grand gesture of paying for damages to the child's mother. Nor would moral luck proponents praise her for taking responsibility because they have already condemned her for *being* responsible. And for contractarians, at least, what virtues we ought to adopt to live well is a different discussion than what actions you ought to do or refrain from doing to satisfy moral demands.

2.4 *Optional and Brute Luck*

According to Otsuka (2009), brute luck is what happens to people without any record of their being responsible. Optional luck is when an agent opted to do something that led to a bad (or good) result. Being struck by lightning is an example of brute luck. Losing your bet on the horses is an example of optional luck. Since you opted to bet with the understanding of risk, we hold you responsible for the ensuing risk. The drunk-driving cases are cases of optional luck, not brute luck. The drunken driver opted to drive drunk and thus we can hold her responsible for outcomes that resulted from her choice. That we can hold someone responsible for an outcome that was a matter of luck is no longer seen as a mystery as long as we can recognize the luck was optional, not brute. Enoch and Marmor's talk of *ex ante* decisions is similar to Otsuka's optional luck (Enoch and Marmor 2007, 411). While the drunk drivers varied in luck *ex post*, they each had sufficient control *ex ante*, when they decided to drive drunk (or decided not to prevent themselves from the temptation to drive drunk). Thereby, we can rightly blame Bertha more than Abigail (who also accidently ran over the child, but did so soberly) *because* of Bertha's *ex ante* decision to drive drunk. To drive drunk is to knowingly assume a greater risk of running over a child than when driving sober.

Two problems prevent the optional/brute distinction counting as dissolving moral luck. The first is that we would have to rule out constitutive luck to convince moral-luck proponents that optional luck is really an option at all. To avoid contamination from constitutional luck, Otsuka claims that as long as a person *could have done otherwise* (for example, not drink and drive), then we are not unfair to blame that person (Otsuka 2009, 380). Even ignoring the charge that being able to do otherwise is both question begging and non-falsifiable, we do not retract our blame for murderers who proclaim, "But I couldn't do otherwise: I hated him so damn much!" (cf. Dennett 1984). The second problem is that the three-drivers case is set up to prevent Otsuka's appeal. Bertha (the killer) and Clarissa (the non-killer) had equal optional luck, yet we still blame Bertha more than Clarissa. More to the story than the distinction between optional and brute luck is needed.

The solution to the moral-luck problem is to be found at a deeper level, the level of meta-ethics, the level where we wonder what morality is supposed to be doing for us.

3 MATH LUCK

A preliminary argument against moral luck is to compare moral luck with math luck. The extent in which luck permeates our lives does not impinge on math luck. The comparison to make is that the luck that permeates our lives also does not impinge on moral assessment. Of course, math and morality are not the same. Whether that counts as an objection, however, requires (i) a clarification of the difference between math and morals, and (ii) a clarification of how that difference shows moral luck to be different than math luck. Satisfying (i) is simple; satisfying (ii) is not.

Constitutive Luck

If Jones is so constituted that he is poor at math, we do not let him get a passing grade even though the fault is not his. We feel no need to reassess education on this basis. Imagine if both Smith and Jones are good at math, but Jones has test anxiety that prevents him from performing. After the test, Smith passes but Jones fails, as one could predict. Perhaps different testing methods could be found for Jones, but if the counterproductive anxiety remains, the fairness of math assessment is not impinged. If Jones has math anxiety, and not mere test anxiety, such that Jones can never perform math problems successfully, we would have to say Jones is not good at math, even if the fault for that lies deeper than Jones's math ability.

Circumstantial Luck

Imagine if both Smith and Jones are poor at math. Smith is given the test and so her poor math skills are revealed. Jones is not given the test and so Jones's poor math skills are not revealed. Since only one is blamed in the form of a bad mark despite both being equally blameworthy, we would not think luck affected our math assessment. We would think luck affected who gets assessed. Assessment luck does not imply math luck.

Resultant Luck

Imagine in a test both Jones and Smith make a mistake in calculation, but while Jones gets the incorrect answer, Smith luckily gets the correct answer. If the teacher has only the final answer to correct, Jones fails and Smith passes. If the teacher has also the calculations to observe, the teacher will see that Smith got the correct answer by fluke, and thus the teacher will punish Smith despite her good result. This shows that the luck involved between Smith and Jones affects their being assessed, not the assessment itself. Conversely, the mistake Smith gets is due to a momentary glitch in Smith's vision, such that she read a "3" as a "5." Her answer would have been correct had the "3" been a "5" but otherwise incorrect. The glitch is unlucky. If she explains to the teacher about the glitch, the teacher is prone to reply, "Too bad, Smith. I can only assess results." Luck affected Smith's math assessment, but it is not a matter of math luck.

If Smith complains about unfairness, it is an appeal to a value external to math assessment itself. Can the same be said for morality? Are there extra-moral values that may trump morality, and if so, is this the domain wherein we find moral luck? In the following section, I explore and dismiss the thought.

4 ENDO-MORAL, EXO-MORAL, AND WILLIAMS SHIFTS

Perhaps Smith does not care about a poor math grade. Life is one thing, math assessment another. Similarly, we might complain about the unfairness of being morally blamed. Complaining about the unfairness of being morally blamed, however, can be understood in three ways: an endo-moral shift, an exo-moral shift, and what I shall call a Williams shift. *Endo-moral circumstantial shifts* affect the value of moral assessment of the same action, *x*, where *x* is deemed morally fine in one circumstance and not morally fine in another. For example, in C1, a white-skinned teacher gives extra time to a white-skinned student to complete an assignment, but not to a black-skinned student, despite everything else being equal between the two students. We would think this is unfair. We would accuse the teacher of racism. In C2, a black-skinned teacher gives extra time to a black-skinned student to complete an assignment, but not to a white-skinned student, but, unlike C1, differing circumstances between the two students reveals a moral justification for the different treatment – prior approval, documented illness, or past behaviour, for example. With endo-moral shifts, differing circumstances can change the moral assessment of similar outcomes. An endo-moral complaint about the unfairness of morality, then, is not a complaint about morality as a whole, only the failure of the current *moral accusation* to take into account relevant factors.

Exo-moral shifts are cases where morality itself no longer applies. Hume, for example, offered five exo-moral shifts where conditions favouring the usefulness of morality is absent (Hume 1751, sect iii, pt i). The value of charity, for example, applies only in a world of limited resources held unequally. In a world of pure abundance, the value of charity would be nil. And dystopia fiction may display conditions so harsh that the basic ingredient for moral behaviour is absent. The shift in moral assessment is not from good to bad or the reverse, as in endo-moral shifts, but from our thinking morality has a value (whether negative or positive) to our thinking it has no value.

A *Williams shift* views morality as merely one of competing values. When morality demands of you to sacrifice some other important value you endorse, abiding by morality no longer takes precedence. As Williams says, "[W]hile we are sometimes guided by the notion that it would be the best of worlds in which morality were universally respected and all men were of a disposition to affirm it, we have in fact deep and persistent reasons to be grateful that that is not the world we have."[15]

An exo-moral shift is not the same as a Williams shift. With Williams shifts, morality still has value, simply not a supreme value. With exo-moral shifts, morality has no value given the prevailing circumstances. Finding yourself in an exo-moral shift does not mean you find morality no longer has supreme value; it may still have supreme value – but only when the circumstances of morality apply. In the present circumstances, however, it has zero value.

For illustration, imagine Heinz steals a drug to save his wife. We may say one of three things: (i) Heinz believed his action was immoral, but he had good reason to violate morality (a Williams shift), or (ii) given the circumstances, Heinz believed himself doing a moral action, all things considered (an endo-moral shift), or (iii) that given the circumstances in which Heinz found himself, morality no longer applied (an exo-moral shift). In all cases, the luck involved in Heinz's circumstance remains the same. Transferring the luck to moral luck, however, occurs only in the Williams shift. Moral luck proponents claim that we are deemed immoral (or moral) by matters of luck. An unlucky morality is easier to dismiss in light of other values we hold. Whereas with either endo-moral or exo-moral shifts, we are not judged as immoral by matters of luck. If we think luck enters the picture, the moral assessment shifts accordingly. Moral luck is a comment about the divide between life and morality. In Williams shifts, morality is seen as an external encroachment on living well; it cannot accommodate the vicissitudes of life, and thus we are entitled to sidestep morality when suitable. As put, to entertain a Williams shift is to conceive of morality as a metaphysical object towards which humans need not attend. This attitude can tolerate luck permeating morality, for morality is seen as too cumbersome a thing to concern itself with the vagaries of human conditions, which is why humans ought not to treat it as supreme.

Return to the intuition that moral luck advocates share and moral luck skeptics dismiss: that we morally blame Bertha (the drunk driver who killed the child) differently than Clarissa (the drunk driver who killed no one). Bertha has blundered into immorality through no fault of her own. To think this is plausible conceives a morality as something independent of human benefit. As put, a Williams shift is sensible. But why conceive of morality in that light? An alternative picture is offered by contractarians. For contractarians, any morality that demands you sacrifice something more important than your autonomous life goals is not a candidate for moral acceptance by rational, self-interested, *ex ante* agents. If so, Williams shifts are not plausible.

5 CONTRACTARIANISM AND MORAL LUCK

Contractarians reject the notion that morality is a thing separate from prudentially based rules governing strategic interaction. To ask whether morality is unfair is to hold morality up to the light of some larger-order morality – but there is no such thing; no *summum bonum* (Hobbes 1651, ch. 11).

The contractarian metaphysic-free picture of morality undermines the worry about moral luck in three ways: by highlighting the *ex ante* justification of morality, by emphasizing the role of self-interest in moral appraisal, and by clarifying the value of reciprocity. The first two clarify how morality must serve the long-term, considered, self-interest of the agents undertaking moral duties, and thereby, cannot be incompatible with other values the way Williams conceives it. The third clarifies the advantage contractarian morality offers over other moral theories; ones where Williams shifts are possible.

5.1 Ex Ante Justification

Enoch and Marmor's talk of *ex ante* justification was insufficient to put moral luck to rest, but only because they did not take their *ex ante* justification back far enough. When contractarians speak of *ex ante* justification, they revert to the thought experiment of a condition where morality does not yet exist. From that point, any moral rule must appease those willing to abide by its mandate. Amoral, self-interested, rational agents would only agree to a rule if the expected net benefit from following that rule (assuming enough others do so as well) comes to the moral agent herself. At the *ex ante* stage, devising moral rules will always have an end goal in mind: to make social life as peaceful as possible while letting individuals pursue their own interests.

Even in games of luck, where outcomes are decided by a roll of the dice or pick of a card, rules are cast at the outset of the game. To that extent, the *rules* are not subject to luck, even while stipulating how luck is part of the game. Something similar is going on with moral rules. The reason we punish drunk drivers is because driving drunk increases the chance of harming others. If you, *in fact*, harm others, so much the worse for you. That rule is not subject to luck. Whether you face that rule may be. Part of the purpose of that rule (including its proclamation) is to get you to avoid putting yourself in a situation where you may face that rule being executed. In other words, don't drink and drive. We morally condemn drunken driving because it increases the odds of causing serious harm to others. That one actually caused harm merely *reaffirms* our evaluation; it does not *alter* the evaluation.

One might object. Comparing Bertha (who is drunk and runs over a child) with Clarissa (who is equally drunk but does not run over anyone), we see that actual harm increases the moral blame over potential harm, and does so whether or not luck is involved. No matter, is the reply. Getting behind the wheel while drunk puts you at risk of being charged with manslaughter even if the cause of death is a matter of luck. Be forewarned. Why would *ex ante* agents agree to such strict rules? Because they do not wish to be struck by drunk drivers.

5.2 *Self-Interest*

Contractarian moral theory's focus is on acts, not personal development. When we dub someone untrustworthy, it is to avoid playing with them in the future. Our "blaming" them is to mark them as defectors. *Ex ante* agents do not care about the personal well-being of those they blame, necessarily; they care about being victimized by them. Being so marked is bad for that person, obviously, and being so marked may have been based on something outside their control. If so, people will be determined to avoid being blamed, if possible, and to apologize and to correct misinformation about the blame, if possible. Adopting certain virtues may help personal relations to that extent, but the character traits we adopt are not themselves of primary relevance; they are of subsidiary importance to help elicit co-operative behaviour with others for one's own long-term interests. Moreover, since my blaming others limits the pool of my collaborators, I have an interest in not blaming recklessly. Tit for two tats, for example, may be beneficial (Axelrod 1984). Or maybe the three-strike rule in baseball. In other words, it may be wise to tolerate the possibility that someone's defection was due to luck ... up to a point, beyond which, self-protection overrides considerations for the well-being of others.[16] Such a fulcrum point may be influenced by degree and scope: how often the infraction occurs and how serious is the infraction.

For an *ex ante* self-interested moral theory, moral blame has something to do with how important our blaming another is to us. Compare our reaction to a fifth-century murder in Mali with our reaction to a murder on our street today.[17] That both murders are identical in badness hardly warrants our treating them the same. That we respond with more blame to faults that concern us more is perfectly apt. It would be shocking if we were indifferent in degrees of blame between the local murder and the historical murder. When we blame people, our concern is with the effect that agent's action has on us. That concern is not subject to luck. Why I am concerned about your action is a matter of situational luck – you may or may not have crossed my path – and my concerns may or may not have been constituted to be what they are, but that I am concerned about what concerns me is not a matter of luck. Nor is it a matter of luck that we have devised moral rules to impede actions of others that impede our pursuit of what concerns us (at the cost of impeding our own behaviours that impede others' like liberty – a necessary offering).

The point of the above is to clarify how moral luck dissolves when we understand the origins of morality to be about protecting the moral agents themselves. Moral luck appears only when morality is construed as having an objective, universal, interest-free, situational-independent status.[18]

5.3 Reciprocity

The benefit of adopting a moral disposition focuses on expected benefits, not actual benefits. Deciding the merit of actions based on results alone is not the picture contractarians endorse (contra Williams 1981a, 23). Contractarians recommend the mixed strategy of reciprocal co-operation; not the pure strategy of unconditional defection, nor the pure strategy of unconditional co-operation. The distinction between pure and mixed strategies is key.

The moral luck debate has always been presented as a clash between two camps: motive camps and action camps (Statman 2019, 202). Motive camps, crediting Kant rightly or wrongly, claim that moral evaluation of agents is to be restricted to their inner will alone (Kant 1785, Ak. 393–4). To the extent that we care about actions is only because actions typically express the will of agents. Action camps "judge people for what they actually do or fail to do, not just for what they would have done if circumstances had been different" (Nagel 1979, 66). A third camp is generally ignored: those who judge actions according to expected net benefit. Contractarians are in this third camp.

A bit of game theory helps illustrate this third camp. In a prisoner's dilemma, the disposition to unilaterally defect (UD) will beat the disposition to unilaterally co-operate (UC). But the disposition to reciprocally co-operate (RC) (co-operate with co-operators and defect with defectors) will beat other dispositions, assuming enough RCs exist.[19] Since only the reciprocally co-operative behaviour is associated with moral behaviour, moral behaviour is shown to be prudent. Some might protest that UC is the moral disposition, not the self-serving RC. But UC will co-operate with other defectors, and this is morally indiscriminate if we think we ought to boycott interactions with abusers. That said, an RC will co-operate with either a UC or another RC, but not with a UD. But if we judge RC as a UD in her interaction with a UD merely on the basis of what RC did (defect), we will get things wrong. Nagel's camp, in other words cannot distinguish between an RC and a UD, or for that matter an RC from a UC. This is a serious lack of discriminating power. On the other hand, the lure of being an RC has nothing to do with the intrinsic "jewel" of a good will (Kant 1785, Ak. 394). We adopt the RC strategy – our moral disposition – for purely prudential, self-interested reasons. Morality is prudential, for contractarians, whereas Williams shifts presuppose morality and prudence can go separate ways.

SUMMARY

Moral luck occurs in the clash between what befalls us in life and what we imagine a higher-order, metaphysical morality proclaims ought to befall us. If we deny there is a higher-order morality, and we see morality simply as an instrumental tool to help regulate human social behaviour, we leave no room for moral luck.

5

The Moral Dilemma Dilemma

A moral dilemma occurs whenever someone is faced with at least two moral obligations in which the satisfaction of one entails the non-satisfaction of the other and vice versa. Moral dilemmas cast aspersions on moral theory for two independent reasons: if in a dilemma, no moral advice is possible; and any moral theory that admits dilemmas is inconsistent. If moral theory cannot generate consistent guidance to action, one answer is because moral theories have given us false hope. No one theory can pretend to make consistent a morality that is inherently messy (Williams 1973a; Mothersill 1996).

I argue that moral dilemmas do not exist – with two pseudo-exceptions: (i) terrorist demands and (ii) competing *in personam* duties at least one of which is positive. An *in personam* duty is a duty owed to a particular person, not to everyone (an *in rem* duty). A positive *in personam* duty is one in which you must do something to a specific other, like pay your debt to Martha, in contrast to a negative *in personam* duty, such as having a restraining order against contact with Martha. Neither exception casts aspersions on moral theory, however. In the second case, even if plausible, the dilemma follows from improperly making a promise. The fault is the individual's, not moral theory's. In the terrorist case, we have found ourselves outside the scope of morality. Morality has value only within certain parameters; outside those conditions, moral rules will fail. This is not a blight on morality. It is exactly what we should expect if we understand morality as a tool to serve human interests within the norms of human living. Contractarianism, an approach so far avoided in the literature on moral dilemmas, is better suited than other theories to reject moral dilemmas by stressing the importance of conditionality in moral obligation.

My plan goes as so: 1. Define moral dilemmas, specifically separating moral conflicts from moral dilemmas. 2. Venture briefly into deontic logic to clarify the problem of admitting moral dilemmas, including attempts at objection. 3. Offer a catalogue of possible conflict of duties once we distinguish type (negative and positive) and scope (*in rem* and *in personam*). By examining each category of moral conflicts, and not conflating them, we can more easily see why moral dilemmas are not possible. Two pseudo exceptions remain, but, as I will discuss, have no effect on moral theory. 4. Clarify why conditionality is embedded in contractarian moral theory to ward off complaints that the except-when clauses I invoke to escape moral dilemmas are ad hoc.

1 MORAL DILEMMA, NOT MORAL CONFLICT

A moral *dilemma* occurs when the following four conditions each apply: someone has (i) at least two conflicting duties (ii) that cannot both be satisfied. Furthermore, (iii) neither duty overrides the other, and as a result, (iv) one must necessarily violate a moral obligation.[1] If I must do *A* and I must do *B* yet cannot do both, my doing *A* is a violation of my duty to do *B*, and vice versa. In serving one obligation, I necessarily fail my other.

A moral *conflict* occurs when only the first two conditions are met; namely when someone is faced with (i) two conflicting moral duties that (ii) cannot both be met. In conflicts, one duty overrides the other and a good moral theory tells you which. Admittedly, you may not know which your overriding duty is. Moral conflicts do not become moral dilemmas merely because of epistemic doubt. It is not the phenomenal experience that makes a conflict a dilemma. The difference between moral conflict and moral dilemma concerns conditions (iii) whether overriding principles exist (yes in conflicts, no in dilemmas) and (iv) whether failure of a duty is inevitable (yes in dilemmas, no in conflicts). Moral conflicts occur aplenty.

Moral dilemmas pose a serious problem for moral theory. We imagine moral theory is to be action-guiding. It can offer no advice concerning what you ought to do should you be faced with a dilemma. When faced with moral conflicts, on the other hand, moral theory is able to provide advice: "Choose the overriding obligation!" or "Pay attention to the except-when clause!" Since most moral theories have in place a rule about which duty overrides which, moral conflict is not a problem for morality, merely a problem of life.

Or so I claim. Others disagree. In the following section, I examine and reject the notion that even moral conflicts pose a problem for moral theory.

1.1 Moral Conflicts Pose a Problem

We might wonder whether condition (iv), the inevitable violation of a duty, applies with moral conflicts or not. If an inevitable violation of a duty, even a lesser duty, occurs in moral conflicts, they may pose as much of a problem as moral dilemmas. Two distinct arguments for the problem moral conflicts create for moral theory are common. The first concerns residual guilt. The second concerns the obligation to apologize or make amends.

RESIDUAL GUILT

If my moral theory both obligated me to do *A* and nevertheless makes it the case that another obligation prevents me from doing *A*, we have a problem. Even if there is an overriding principle, the non-chosen duty is not simply dismissed. As Williams (1973b, 173) remarks, after I have chosen one duty to obey, the moral pressure on me to have chosen the other duty still lingers. To suggest that all moral conflicts have a correct solution suggests that one of the "duties" is, in fact, not a duty. Failure to do a non-duty hardly ought to evoke grief or guilt. When we are confronted with a moral conflict, however, lingering anguish is inevitable and appropriate. Absent such grief would be alarming. After telling the truth to the Nazis about the whereabouts of the Jewish family you were hiding, we cannot imagine standing over the corpses saying, "I did the right thing. Three cheers for me" (Varden 2010). This helps highlight, for Williams, that by obeying one horn of a moral conflict, we are not released from the obligation to do the other. Even Mill, the paradigmatic utilitarian, agrees: "[H]e who betrays the friend that trusts him, is guilty of a crime, even if his object be to serve another friend to whom he is under greater obligations" (Mill 1863, ch. 2). This is an odd admission for a utilitarian if choosing the action that produces overall net happiness given the alternatives is still deemed "wrong." Moral conflict condemns us to be immoral, and not even utilitarianism can accommodate this peculiar fact (Norcross 1995).

APOLOGY

When we find ourselves unable to honour our promises, we owe an apology to the one we wronged, and, if possible, make amends. Such a need does not vanish when neglect of our duty is due to obeying a trumping duty. To give credence to that secondary duty of apology is a worry for moral theory. The obligation not fulfilled does not simply go away. If it did, we would not have to apologize for failing to fulfill it. You do not have to apologize for not meeting me for tea if you never had a duty to meet me for tea. If one of the duties in a moral conflict dissolves by recognition of an overriding obligation, you would think the need to apologize about it dissolves as well. It does not. The duty not done still exists. That seems to be an admission that even moral conflicts pose a problem for moral theory.

1.2 Moral Conflicts Do Not Pose a Problem

While I admit that any moral dilemma would pose a problem for moral theory, if they exist, moral conflicts do not pose any problem for moral theory. Neither the residual guilt nor the apology arguments are as strong as supporters imagine.

RESIDUAL GUILT

That we would have residual grief over doing the right thing in a moral conflict, as Williams tells us, does not show that moral principles are problematic. Nor does it mean our guilt is unfounded or unreasonable. Sometimes it may be. After renouncing his religion, one that called going to movies a sin, a man still felt guilt at the movies (Rawls 1971, 481–3). More often, however, misplaced guilt seems fine. McConnell (1996, 39) gives a case of a motorist who, despite obeying the rules of the road, runs over a child tobogganing into the car's path and, understandably, feels extreme grief.[2] That the driver did nothing wrong yet grieves hardly shows a problem with moral theory.[3] Residual grief – even call it guilt – is no more sufficient to show the reality of a duty than fear of God shows the reality of God.

APOLOGY

Nor does the need to apologize for failing a duty – even due to an overriding obligation – reveal a difficulty for moral theory. The need to apologize does not show the lesser duty still holds; it shows that the lesser duty has been supplanted with a secondary duty that *can* be fulfilled (as soon as possible).

When we make promises, we understand they are contingent upon things going as planned. Life often gets in the way of our plans. People who make and people who accept promises need to be cognizant of the conditions under which we expect their fulfillment. Let us say I promised to help you move, but at the time scheduled, my daughter has an accident and I have to take her to the hospital. In attending to my daughter, it is false to say I still have a duty to help you move. During my stay at the hospital, you have already moved. I can no longer help you move. I do owe you an explanation, however, and although I did no wrong, to apologize seems prudent to better ensure continued relations. That these new obligations are upon me for failing to satisfy a duty I *at one point had* does not show the duty still exists. Admitting this has no impact on moral theory. Moral theory, presumably, embeds in its original except-when clause the initiation of secondary duties of apology. If not apology, which assumes wrongdoing, an expression of regret. Thus: At T_1, I have a duty to do *A* at T_2 that gets trumped by a duty to do *B* at T_2. Having to do *B* at T_2 absolves me of my duty to do *A* at T_2 *assuming I take on a secondary duty of making amends, which may include communicating regret,* at T_3. In other words, the except-when clause has its own rider. No blow to moral theory ensues from pointing out an obligation to make amends.

Moral conflicts have overriding principles or except-when clauses to guide us (Donagan 1977, 92–3). Moral dilemmas do not. The next challenge, then, is to explain why moral dilemmas cannot exist – with two pseudo exceptions.

2 DO MORAL DILEMMAS EXIST?

For Kant, moral duty is derived by a priori means. To think a priori logic could generate contradictions is like thinking geometry can churn out square circles. Thus, he says, "[A] conflict of duties and obligations is inconceivable" (Kant 1797a, 6:224). On the other hand, absolutist theories such as his seem most prone to moral dilemmas given their refusal to admit overriding conditions. Two maxims can independently fail to be universally willed (lying and abetting a murderer, for example) yet clash in real life.[4] We need not believe morality is an a priori judgment, however, to use logic against the prospect of moral dilemmas.

Deontic logic is logic applied to normative utterances. A cup's not being on a coaster does not contradict the claim that a cup ought to be on a coaster. In cases of perfect duties (as opposed to imperfect duties) our obligation to do *A* entails that we are not permitted to do ~*A*. Let O(A) stand for having an obligation to do *A*. Let ~P(~A) stand for not being permitted to do ~*A*. Then O(A) is equivalent to ~P(~A), which we may represent as O(A) ≡ ~P(~A) and call the *rule of equivalence*. The same will arise with the second duty, *B*, of a moral dilemma. Along with propositional logic's rules of *simplification* [(A & B)⊃A; B] and *conjunction* [A; B⊃(A & B)],[5] we can show how starting with a moral dilemma deposits us in a logical impasse.

1	O(A) & O(B)	p
2	O(B)	1, simplification
3	~P(~B)	2, equivalence
4	O(~A)	3, equivalence
5	O(A)	1, simplification
6	O(A) & O(~A)	4,5, conjunction

The derivation at line 3 follows, for to do anything other than *B* (such as *A*) is a violation of ~P(~B). If I have an obligation to do *A* at T_1 and I am obligated to do *B* at T_1, and being obligated to do *B* at T_1 means being morally unable to do anything else than *B* at T_1, my doing *A* at T_1 is a violation of my duty to do *B* at T_1. The derivation at line 4 follows, for your not being permitted to do ~*B* entails that you must do *B*. Having to do *B* means you must not do *A*. Both derivations follow the rule of equivalence.[6]

Notice, however, that line 6, O(A) & O(~A), is not a contradiction. It is merely a contrary. While both cannot be true, both can be false. I neither must eat an apple (so O(A) is false), nor must I eat an apple (so O(~A) is false.). The contradiction of O(A) is ~O(A).[7] So after all that work, we have not shown how a moral dilemma entails a contradiction.

Even ~O(A) may not contradict O(A), depending on whether the obligation is categorical or hypothetical (Wright 1951, 15). When I say a chicken is a farm animal without hooves, I am defeating the universal statement that all farm animals are hoofed. But when I say it is sometimes permissible to lie, I am not defeating the claim that lying is immoral; I am only defeating the claim that lying is categorically immoral.

Nevertheless, since moral dilemmas yield the proposition, O(A) & O(~A), we have enough to show the *impossibility* of moral dilemmas. While O(A) & O(~A) can both be false, they cannot both be true, whereas moral dilemmas claim that both duties are, and remain, true in the sense that they each obligate you whether you act on them or not. Since deontic logic shows the impossibility of moral dilemmas, proponents of moral dilemmas need to reject one or more principles of deontic logic. One principle normally challenged is the rule of conjunction.[8]

2.1 *Conjunction*

Deontic logic may be unable to tolerate the rule of conjunction,[9] which states that if you ought to do *A* and you ought to do *B*, then you ought to do both *A* and *B*. Hence: O(A) & O(B) ≡ O(A&B). The reason for dispensing with a rule that makes perfect sense in modal logic, Williams (1973b, 181–3) tells us, is because people do not *intend* the rule of conjunction when in a moral dilemma. Assume an agent is confronted with having to fulfill two obligations when filling one precludes the filling of the other. Williams says, "[N]o agent, conscious of the situation of conflict, in fact thinks that he ought to do both of the things. What he thinks is that he ought to do each of them; and this is properly paralleled at the level of 'can' by the fact that while he cannot do both of the things, it is true of each of the things, taken separately, that he can do it" (Williams 1973b, 181). Whether I *intend* a logical derivation, the logical derivation still applies. If you owe Jane five dollars, and unbeknown to you, Jane is the best pole-vaulter in Saskatchewan, then you owe the best pole-vaulter in Saskatchewan five dollars. "But I don't *mean* that!" you might say. Who cares, says Logic.[10]

Williams (1973b, 182) offers the following non-moral case where the rule of conjunction, he claims, does not apply: Tom wants to marry Susan and Tom wants to marry Joan, but Tom does not want to marry both Susan and Joan. This is not a great example. Tom may not mind marrying both Susan and Joan if it were possible. To include Tom's desire for monogamy would be to claim, instead, "Tom wants to marry only Susan and Tom wants to marry only Joan, but Tom does not want to marry both only Susan and only Joan." With the inclusion of "only," application of the rule of conjunction is not a problem; it rather highlights the incompatible desires of Tom: Tom wants to marry only Susan and only Joan. That is his problem, not a problem with the rule of conjunction. Presumably, what is really going on is not Tom's desire to marry Joan *and* Susan, but Tom's desire to marry Joan *or* Susan and he cannot decide which. To derive "and" from "or" is not permitted in any logical system. Nothing violates the rule of conjunction in saying that.

Other examples may be better. I offer two. "You are permitted to drive. You are permitted to drink. You are not permitted to drink and drive."[11] "Food safety permits you to have one ant (*A*) in the kitchen, and food safety permits you to have a different ant (*B*) in the kitchen, but food safety does not permit you to have two ants in the kitchen." Even these cases, however, do not show a failure of the rule of conjunction. Being permitted to drive is a rule with qualifications: namely the one about needing to be sober. Thus, we get, "You are permitted to drive if and only if sober," and that is all that is required to derive the rule that you cannot drink and drive. We could assert this as "~P(Drive) | Drunk," which translates to you are not permitted to drive given that you are drunk. Similarly, we might say, "You are permitted to not do *A* given that you must do *B*," or "~P(A) | O(B)." The case of ants in the kitchen is a kind of Sorites paradox. A conjunction of separate propositions may be fine up to a point, but we are not clear where that point is. Presumably a clean kitchen is one with no ants. That we may tolerate one but not two does not run afoul of the rule of conjunction if we understand the single-ant rule as claiming we will permit a single ant, but not more. Thus, we get the revised version: "Food safety permits you to have one ant only in the kitchen (be it ant *A*), and food safety permits you to have one ant only in the kitchen (be it ant *B*), but food safety does not permit you to have two ants in the kitchen." No violation of the rule of conjunction occurs when the intended propositions are spelled out more clearly.

2.2 *Checkmate*

Holbo (2002) compares moral dilemmas to checkmate. In chess, the king must move out of check and, when moving, cannot move into check. When in checkmate, these two rules collide: a player cannot move the king out of check without moving into check. A dilemma, but not a dilemma invoking a problem for chess. Similarly, in moral dilemmas, we find ourselves bound to break one or another moral rule. But so what? We are in a moralmate. In chess, we may find ourselves unable to move our king while being told to move our king. In morality, we may find ourselves unable to move morally, at the same time as being told to move. In either case, we simply find ourselves unable to avoid losing a game – a moral game or a chess game. Resolution of the checkmate dilemma is loss of game. Resolution of the moral dilemma is the admission of moral defeat. Holbo's idea is that deontic logic need not exclude the possibility of moral dilemmas any more than chess rules need to exclude the possibility of checkmate.

If dilemmas can occur due to poor play by moral players, as opposed to dilemmas driven by the rules of morality, then Holbo is correct: those moral dilemmas would pose no difficulty for moral theory. I shall discuss one such (remote) possibility in section 3, but for now, let me suggest a few disanalogies. Rules of chess determine what constitutes checkmate. Rules of morality do not determine what constitutes a moral dilemma. Does this difference matter? I think so because our worry about a moral dilemma is because it reveals a problem of inconsistency in our moral rules. Whereas falling into checkmate has no such implication.

A second disanalogy is that in chess, falling into checkmate ends the game. The players may play again, the pieces return to their original positions without battle scar. In the moral game, we continue playing as is, broken and bruised from our moral dilemma. Does this difference matter? Again, I believe so. In checkmate, I cannot do anything. In a moral dilemma, I can still continue playing by picking one option and accepting my fate. To find a parallel to a moral dilemma in chess we would need to find two rules colliding that would neither end the game, nor offer guidance as to which rule to follow. We do not currently have such a dilemma in chess, although the legal chess moves we have today were not the legal chess moves they once were. Pawns could move only one square. Allowing pawns to jump two squares on their first move led, eventually, to the invention of en passant. Queens used to move only one square diagonally. Bishops could move up to two squares diagonally, to show that the church was more powerful than royalty, perhaps. Kings were able to move two squares, including leaping over any other piece. The rule of castling, once it was invented, had more flexibility than a jig. In the interim years of shifting rules, dilemmas were possible, at which point, the players would muddle through somehow. Are we not thankful that we kept tinkering with chess rules to avoid dilemmas? And if so, why not fix, or rid, those moral rules that cause dilemmas? To think we cannot go about fixing morality makes sense if we imagine morality to be a hidden force of physics, like dark energy, or some metaphysical imprint of a god. If we conceive morality to be a human invention aimed at helping humans navigate among humans, the thought of tweaking our current moral notions is sensible.

In sum, moral dilemmas are inconsistent with principles of deontic logic. But this does not show that moral dilemmas are impossible. It may show that morality is not logical. Whether that would be a good thing or a bad thing will depend on what one takes morality (and logic) to be. Contractarianism offers an alternative way to dismiss the possibility of moral dilemmas. To that I now turn.

3 TYPE AND SCOPE OF DUTIES

Support for moral dilemmas comes from the idea that they are so pervasive that almost any case will do. Common examples include Plato's return of a borrowed weapon to someone intent on murder, Kant's worry about whether we ought to lie to prevent abetting a murder, Sartre's student having to choose between taking care of his ailing mother or joining the French Resistance, and Sophie's choice between which of her children will be killed by a Nazi, lest he kill both (Plato, 331c; Kant 1797b, 8:427; Sartre 1946; Styron 1980). We would do better cataloguing all possible duty collisions by distinguishing type of duties (positive and negative) and scope of duties (*in rem* [to everyone] from *in personam* [to a specific individual]). Doing so, I argue, makes clear why moral dilemmas cannot exist.

A negative duty is to refrain from doing something specific. Its correlating right is the liberty to not have something done to you without your consent. A positive duty is to provide something, aid, typically, to one who has a right to such aid. The duty not to kill anyone is negative. The duty to provide welfare is positive.

Negative duties are easy to satisfy. I have not murdered anyone, yet, and do not feel thereby deprived. We can satisfy all our negative duties by doing nothing. This may seem false. Imagine a weak-bladdered traveller visiting a town that, due to a pandemic, closed all public and patron washrooms. Despite the absence of any available washroom for this traveller, posted signs proclaim: No urinating on city property. Assuming these signs speak a moral truth, and assume also the unwritten rule not to urinate on anyone's private property, this traveller has a negative obligation not to urinate at all within the city limits. That is not an option, however. He is going to urinate within the city limits and in doing so will violate a negative obligation. Rather than showing that it is possible to be unable to satisfy a negative duty, however, the urination case highlights how a "duty" cannot be moral given one's inability to satisfy it. Ought implies can.

Positive oughts are less easily satisfied than negative oughts. Since this is known ahead of time, however, positive duties typically have an "if you can" clause built into them (Vallentyne 1989). Save someone from drowning, *if you can*. Give to charity, *if you can*.

An *in rem* duty, meanwhile, is an obligation you owe everyone equally. When I opt not to steal your money, I am obliging an *in rem* duty I owe to everyone, not just you. An *in personam* duty is one in which you owe a very specific person (or persons) a very specific consideration. When I borrow money from you, I have to pay you, and only you, back the money – an *in personam* duty I have voluntarily taken on. Positive *in personam* duties can be had without promising, but rather by nature of one's position, or authority. For example, parents have positive *in personam* duties to their children and pilots to flying safely.

By distinguishing type and scope of duties, we get ten possible duty collisions. Obligations may conflict between (i) two negative *in rem* duties (nr,nr), (ii) negative *in rem* and negative *in personam* duties (nr,np), (iii) negative *in rem* and positive *in rem* duties (nr,pr), (iv) negative *in rem* and positive *in personam* duties (nr,pp), (v) two negative *in personam* duties (np,np), (vi) negative *in personam* and positive *in rem* duties (np,pr), (vii) two positive *in rem* duties (pr,pr), (viii) positive *in rem* and positive *in personam* duties (pr,pp), (ix) negative *in personam* and positive *in personam* duties (np,pp), and (x) two positive *in personam* duties (pp,pp).

A clash between two *in personam* duties involving at least one being positive (ix and x) opens the possibility, however implausible, of an exception to my claim that moral dilemmas can never exist. Such an exception – even if possible – would not undermine moral theory, however. The prospect of terrorist intervention makes another pseudo exception to the claim that moral dilemmas do not exist. To this objection, contractarianism is well suited to disagree.

(i) *nr,nr*. Conflicting negative *in rem* duties cannot arise. A negative duty is to refrain from taking or harming. By doing nothing, one typically satisfies all one's negative duties (both *in rem* and *in personam*). One may violate a positive duty, either *in rem* or *in personam*, by doing nothing, but never a negative duty. I can satisfy all my negative duties by taking a nap.[12]

Goldilocks naps in Baby Bear's bed without Baby Bear's consent. To that extent, Goldilocks fails a negative *in rem* duty by napping. Fair enough, but the napping is not the violation, it is the being in someone's bed uninvited. Possibly Goldilocks fails two negative duties at once: she sleeps in Baby Bear's bed and wears Baby Bear's pyjamas. Since the prevention to negative rights violations is doing nothing, no moral dilemma can ensue from two (or a thousand) negative obligations arising all at once. For example, Goldilocks neither sleeps in Baby Bear's bed, nor wears Baby Bear's pyjamas. Since refrain satisfies all one's negative duties; one can never be in a situation where failing a negative duty is inevitable.

Consider two seeming counter cases. First, Kant's case: a monkey-wrench-wielding neighbour asks if you know where his spouse is because he wants to kill her. You know, perhaps recommended, that his spouse is hiding in your closet. Do you lie to him or do you answer honestly and thereby abet a murder? Lying and abetting a murder are each a violation of a negative duty. Saying nothing is not a case of lying, however. If one opts to speak, one has a positive obligation to tell the truth (or what one takes to be the truth), but (except in special circumstances in law) we are not obligated to speak. While the rule not to lie is a negative duty, not saying anything is not a violation of that negative duty. To the extent that not saying anything is a live option, we are not faced with competing negative *in rem* duties.

Sinnott-Armstrong (1988, 82) disagrees because, supposedly, any positive duty may be redescribed as a negative duty, and vice versa. For example, is not lying a negative duty, or is truth telling a positive duty? To solve his ambiguity, ask yourself whether saying nothing (neither telling the truth nor lying) is morally permissible. If saying nothing is morally permissible, not lying is a negative duty. If saying nothing is not morally permissible, truth telling is a positive duty. The latter view may be maintained in circumscribed cases, such as being subpoenaed, or on the stand (although an accused need not take the stand!), but in the general case, as when being arrested, we have the negative right to remain silent.

Another seeming counterexample: A terrorist gives Goldilocks an ultimatum: kill Baby Bear (a negative *in rem* duty violation), or sleep in Baby Bear's bed (another negative *in rem* duty violation); otherwise be killed herself. As put, she can opt to do nothing and risk death: hence no dilemma. Few may suggest such an option. Let us call this, then, a *practical dilemma*, since although it is not true that she must fail a moral obligation, the recommended action is to violate a moral obligation, and as put, we would suggest the lesser violation: Take a nap in Baby Bear's bed, Goldilocks!

A caveat. We are not allowed to violate someone's negative right without their consent, but sometimes we add, *or without their* presumed *consent*. My pushing you out of harm's way will likely get your consent after the fact, for example. Once Baby Bear knows of Goldilocks's options, we can imagine Baby Bear's presumed consent to her choosing to nap. If so, Goldilocks has not violated any negative *in rem* rights.[13] No dilemma.

Let me change the scene. "Kill one member of the Bear family," the terrorist says to Goldilocks, "or I'll kill you." The dilemma is now between committing one or another negative *in rem* rights violation (nr,nr). Since she can opt to kill neither Bear and face the consequences, we are not faced with a pure dilemma. Since few would recommend that option, call it again a practical dilemma. Goldilocks is forced to be immoral by killing one of the Bears. Assuming each family member has equal right to remain unkilled, and assuming no family member would offer post-consent (if possible), we seem to be faced with a moral dilemma, whether merely practical or not. Not so. The problem is unique to the immoral circumstance in which Goldilocks finds herself. As Rawls, Hume, or Hobbes might say, Goldilocks has been thrust outside the conditions in which morality applies, where "notions of Right and Wrong, Justice and Injustice have there no place" (Hobbes 1651, ch. 13; Hume 1739, bk iii, pt ii, sect ii; Rawls 1971, 126). Hence no moral dilemma.

(ii) *nr,np*. Negative *in rem* and negative *in personam* duties can also never create a dilemma. At Charlie's bequest, I promise Charlie that I will never more invite Charlie to a checker game with me. I also have an obligation never to harm anyone, including Charlie. Satisfaction of both is simple. Whenever the omission of any action is an option, the satisfaction of a negative duty, *in rem* or *in personam*, is always possible.

A counter: I promise you not to tell Charlie a truth, a negative *in personam* duty I have willingly taken on, but this conflicts with my *in rem* negative duty never to lie to anyone, including Charlie. Keeping quiet is not a lie, however. Thus, my not telling Charlie the truth is consistent with my not telling Charlie anything. A new problem: What if I am subpoenaed to speak the truth to Charlie? Now, my negative *in personam* duty to you cannot be met. But any *in personam* duty must be understood with an except-when rider. I promise you not to tell the truth (about something) to Charlie assuming I am not subpoenaed to speak to Charlie the truth about that particular thing.

What if after promising Charlie to not play checkers with Charlie, I am instructed by a bomb-strapped terrorist to play checkers with Charlie or I kill Charlie. My choosing neither option results in the terrorist blowing us all up. I am faced with another practical moral dilemma. Assuming my doing nothing is not desirable for me, I must either violate a negative *in personam* duty or a negative *in rem* duty. As with the problem Goldilocks faced, creation of moral dilemmas by terrorism backfires: we are no longer within the sphere of morality. Not all moral theories can accept this. Contractarianism can.

For contractarians, any moral rule as well as any condition to any moral rule must be justifiable at the *ex ante* position. An *ex ante* decision is what hypothetical agents would consent to in a pre-moral state. *Ex ante* agents are deemed to be rational, amoral, and self-interested not because contractarians have a dour view of human psychology, but because they wish to avoid begging the question when it comes to endorsing moral principles. Such agents, contractarians claim, would invent moral rules in order to live as well as possible given their social and environmental circumstances. Such rules, however, will be conditional upon others doing so as well. The conditionality embedded at the root of morality is what distinguishes contractarianism from all other moral theories. To say a moral rule binds you whether or not the other plays along, as in terrorist scenarios, is not something *ex ante* agents could stomach.

(iii) *nr,pr.* Nor can a dilemma arise between a negative *in rem* duty and a positive *in rem* duty. This is not because negative *in rem* duties always trump positive *in rem* duties. Contractarians can adopt the position that positive *in rem* duties ought to, under certain conditions, trump negative rights. For that to occur, however, at least two conditions need to be in place: (a) the cost to the helper is expected to be minimal,[14] and (b) the duties are evenly distributed.[15] Assuming the two conditions are satisfied, no moral dilemma can occur. I may be morally obligated to help save you from drowning (positive *in rem*) at cost to my liberty to lounge on the beach, but not to risk my own drowning. When the cost to the self is too great, the priority rule switches back to the default where negative rights trump positive *in rem* rights, and we presume the rescuer is the best judge of that cost. We are dealing with imperfect duties, after all.

Foot's (1967) Rescue case gets traction here. To save *A*, an ambulance has to run over *B*. We are faced with a conflict between a positive *in rem* duty (saving *A*) and a negative *in rem* duty (not running over people, including *B*). We cannot satisfy both. Different moral theories may differ as to which duty takes precedence, or when numbers of people being saved versus being run over matter, but no moral theory is stymied. Contractarianism, for example, is clear: positive *in rem* rights of people can trump negative rights of people – except when the cost to the duty upholder is too great and the duties not evenly distributed between all persons capable of taking on that particular duty. Slavery is an example of an unevenly distributed duty. Being run over is too great a cost.

A counterexample. The terrorist tells Goldilocks to kill Baby Bear, or the terrorist will kill the entire Bear family.[16] Such a case is certainly a conflict between Goldilocks's negative *in rem* duty not to kill anyone, and her positive *in rem* duty to do what she can to limit deaths. She can avoid one moral violation, but not the other. Or so it may appear. By doing nothing Goldilocks can avoid committing any rights infraction. That she does not kill anyone satisfies her negative *in rem* duty. The positive *in rem* duty, meanwhile, applies *only if she can* satisfy it. *Can* is not a physical restriction, only. It may be psychological, and, in this case, it may also be a moral restriction. Save others *if doing so harms no one else*. Since this condition is not met in the terrorist scenario, Goldilocks is not in a moral dilemma. Utilitarians may disagree; not so contractarians. Compare: a surgeon can *physically* give a blood transfusion to a Jehovah's Witness patient, but cannot *morally* do so, given the patient's non-consent. Such a scenario is not a moral dilemma.

(iv) *nr,pp*. Nor is it possible for a moral dilemma to occur between negative *in rem* duties and positive *in personam* duties. Imagine Armin and Bernd agreeing for Armin to eat Bernd.[17] After the agreement, Armin has an *in personam* positive obligation to eat Bernd, but, presumably, Armin also has a negative *in rem* obligation not to eat anyone, including Bernd. Such a conflict for Armin would be a moral dilemma if no overriding principle can be found. Moral philosophers may disagree on what that overriding principle might be, but for contractarians, at least, consent trumps all – assuming the consent was voluntary and the consenters competent and informed. The case at hand might make one doubt the competency of Bernd to so agree, but even those who think the rule against cannibalism trumps consent think a trumping principle is at hand. Hence, again, no moral dilemma.

A collision of negative *in rem* and positive *in personam* duties may also occur if *A* promises *B* to violate *C*'s negative right. Since violating *C*'s negative right is not an action *A* is allowed to do, *A*'s promising *B* to do that is itself a violation. Hired assassins, for example, do not find themselves in a moral dilemma; they are immoral for taking on the *in personam* duty in the first place.

Is it possible to take on a positive *in personam* duty to violate someone's negative *in rem* right without knowing about that violation until later? Possibly. If so, it looks like we have a dilemma: I made a mistake, but here I am in this mess. What ought I to do: keep my promise or violate this person's negative right? Perhaps Confucianism might put greater weight on the fiduciary relations I have with the person to whom I promised (assuming the other person has less relational connections to me), but every other moral theory will be clear: *A*'s negative *in rem* duties to *C* trump *A*'s positive *in personam* duties to *B*. Thus we have entered a moral conflict, not a moral dilemma.[18]

(v) *np,np*. An *in personam* negative duty, perhaps uncommon, is when person *A* promises person *B* that *A* will not do something. Perhaps *B* will come to *A*'s party only if *C* is not invited. So *A* promises *B* that *A* will not invite *C* to the party. After having promised *B*, *A* now has a negative *in personam* duty to *B*. Meanwhile, *A* promises *D* that *A* will not invite *E* to the party. *A* can satisfy both her negative *in personam* duties to both *B* and *D*. No confluence of negative *in personam* duties can ever create a dilemma. Promise specific people all you want to refrain from doing something (assuming the not doing the thing is within your power), refraining from doing those things is always possible.

(vi) *np,pr*. Any dilemma between a negative *in personam* duty and a positive *in rem* duty is also impossible. My promise to you that I will not rescue Charlie when Charlie is drowning and I am capable of rescuing Charlie is to promise to violate an overriding duty owed to everyone, including Charlie: thus the *in personam* obligation I take upon myself with you is not mine to promise. As a result, the conflict is impossible. But what if, somehow, I find myself in the situation of needing to rescue Charlie and my having promised you that I would not rescue Charlie? I am in a conflict of obligations, but not a moral dilemma, since all moral theories, one would imagine, have a priority rule about such situations: abandon your *in personam* promise and save Charlie!

(vii) *pr,pr*. Dilemmas between two positive *in rem* duties are also not possible. Imagine a fire trapping two people. You, a bystander, have time and ability to save one, but only one. To ask, "Which one?" seems wrongheaded. The important point is to do what we can. After you saved one while the other died, we would not accuse you of intentionally failing to save the other. It is not an obligation we hold you to. We would blame you if you failed to save either while you could have saved one, assuming no psychological, physical, or epistemological impediment.[19] This follows from our thinking you have a positive *in rem* obligation to save someone from burning when you can, all else equal. But saving one satisfies the positive *in rem* duty in this case (because the saving of one makes impossible the saving of the other), despite lingering anguish about not saving the other as well.

(viii) *pr,pp*. We have the prospect of a dilemma between *in rem* and *in personam* positive duties. It may look like these exist all the time. I promised to meet you for tea, but on the way, I witness an accident and in staying to help, I miss our engagement for tea. My positive obligation to you is *in personam*; my positive obligation to help an accident victim is *in rem*. We may say attending tea is the lesser duty, but it is still a duty given my promise. Have we found a moral dilemma such that (a) there is no overriding duty and (b) it is inevitable to break one duty? Few would imagine that our *in personam* obligations do not have implicit except-when clauses when we make them. I will meet you for tea *assuming no greater obligation or accident gets in the way*. When life intercedes, a secondary duty kicks in – to make amends as soon as possible. Since that replacement duty is not impossible to fulfill (at some point), no moral dilemma.

Sartre's example may be thought of as discovering a collision between a positive *in rem* duty (fight for your nation) and a positive *in personam* duty (take care of your mother). Sartre's student may have difficulty choosing, but it hardly counts as a *moral* dilemma (contra Sinnott-Armstrong 1988, 208–10). Four actions are possible – fight, do not fight, help, do not help – each of which are morally permissible. To think one morally ought to join the resistance, for example, would mean we ought to morally blame non-resisting citizens of conquered countries for not doing their part. If the student's choice was between taking care of the mother or killing her, or fighting with or against the Nazis, then we would have a moral question, but hardly a moral dilemma. (We would also wonder how useful Sartre's advice, "Just choose!" would be.)

(ix) *np,pp*. Under plausible conditions, no dilemma involving negative *in personam* and positive *in personam* duties is possible. This may seem false. *A* promises *B* not to help *C* at the same time as *A* promises *D* to help *C*. In such a situation, ought *A* to help *C* or not? Part of this scenario depends on whether or not helping *C* is an *in rem* positive duty (saving *C* from drowning, for example) or not (helping *C* with homework, for example). If the former, the negative *in personam* promise is not *A*'s to make: thus is void. If the latter, whichever promise occurred first (the negative or the positive) would make invalid the second.

But what if, somehow, perhaps an attack of split personality disorder combined with amnesia, *A* is in the position of having promised two actions (not helping *C* and helping *C*) to different people (*B* and *D*) that, combined, cannot both be met? The simultaneity of the promises prevents our giving priority to the first promise. That *A* ought not to be in this mess in the first place does not invalidate that *A* *is* in this mess. *A* is faced with a moral dilemma and no moral theory can offer advice as to what *A* ought to do now.

An individual uttering simultaneous and conflicting promises is not something I can imagine happening. Should it occur, I admit we are faced with a bona fide moral dilemma. It would not be the sort of moral dilemma that would cast aspersions on moral theory, however, because the circumstance does not arise due to the structure of moral theory, but rather by the agent's own doing. To make a promise is to commit to not placing obstacles to satisfying that promise, such as making other, even if simultaneous, conflicting promises.

(x) *pp,pp*. Sophie's Choice is a case of conflicting positive *in personam* duties. Being a mother, Sophie has a positive *in personam* obligation to take care of each of her children, but she is faced with a situation in which only one of those duties can be satisfied. A difficulty with the Sophie's Choice example is that the culprit is the evil Nazi. That people can force you to choose between two immoral options is hardly a slight against moral theory. Moral theory of any brand tells people not to be so cruel. When we are confronted with such cruelty, we are outside the bonds of morality. Outside morality, moral dilemmas cannot exist.

We can imagine a Sophie's Choice situation without wrongdoing, however. Imagine a mother hiking in the woods with her two children. A grizzly bear attacks. The mother has time to throw one child safely off a cliff into a lake, but not both. Even still, not a dilemma. First, we do imagine an overriding rule here: All else equal, saving one is better than saving none. True, it does not tell you which child to save (Sinnott-Armstrong 1988, 56), but nor does a duty to be charitable tell you into which non-fraudulent charity bucket to drop your donation. To think "Which child?" and "Which bucket?" are *moral* questions can only invoke utilitarian-like calculations: which option does more for society? Alice is good at math, but has a lame leg; Bobby is poor academically, but is kind to the elderly. One bucket helps the blind. Another the deaf. Second, in the grizzly case, we imagine that it is morally *permissible* to save one child while letting the other die in cases where saving both is not possible (contra Sinnott-Armstrong 1988, 83). Hence, it is not inevitable that when in a grizzly case, Sophie will violate a moral obligation. Not all tragedies that people face are moral tragedies.

Apart from Sophie's Choice scenarios, dilemmas between two *in personam* positive duties seem to arise all the time. I promise *A* to go to the nine o'clock movie on Saturday and later promise *B* to go to the nine o'clock concert on Saturday. Both promises cannot be met. Since the second promise cannot be filled without violating the first promise, the act of promising *B* is already a violation of the promise to *A*. There is no conflict, because the second promise is void.

B may not be aware of the void agreement I made with *B*. Since I ought to have known that my second agreement is void, I have misled *B*: a negative rights violation. But this shows only that a person may violate an ethical more, not that a person can be put into a position where they must *necessarily* violate an ethical more. In the above scenario, my obligation was to not make a false promise to *B*, given my prior obligation to *A*. The right thing to do now is to apologize to *B* and keep my agreement with *A*, even if I prefer *B* and would not have promised to meet with *A* had *B* asked me first. That we often find ourselves in positions where we would prefer the immoral choice is not a mark against moral theory – assuming our attending to moral rules is, in general, beneficial.

Sometimes competing positive *in personam* duties arise without implicating the one who promised, however. You promised to attend two weddings, *A* and *B*, that were, at the time of promising, not in conflict. Things change. Wedding *A* gets moved to overlap with wedding *B*. Now you cannot attend both, but we cannot blame that on sloppy promising. Once you discover the conflict, you now have a duty to inform the relevant party about your non-attendance. Since promises come with an all-things-equal clause, abrogating your promise is permitted, assuming you inform the ones you let down as soon as possible. This secondary duty is not impossible to fulfill, typically.

But what if at T_1, I somehow simultaneously promise to meet *A* at T_2 at place *x* and promise to meet *B* at T_2 at place *y*. The dilemma I have is my own doing. That I promised *A* and *B* simultaneously (somehow) makes useless any appeal to the rule that I ought to honour my first obligation. Assume the importance of both meetings is incommensurable. As put, no obvious rider can tell us which of the obligations I should meet. Whichever overriding or except-when principle we choose can apply equally to both duties, so no moral advice on how to proceed is forthcoming.

A dilemma of two simultaneously made positive *in personam* duties strikes me as implausible, but should it occur, the dilemma is predicated purely on agents voluntary undertaking those positive *in personam* duties, and thereby, poses no trouble for moral theory. Moral theory tells us not to get ourselves in moral trouble, and the simultaneous promising of incompatible actions was what got us into this mess. The fault lies with moral agents, not moral rules.

SUMMARY

By disambiguating type and scope of moral duties, we more clearly see why we can never be in a position where we *must* violate a moral obligation. A logically possible exception occurs when two *in personam* duties, at least one of which is positive, are somehow simultaneously made and yet conflict. Such a circumstance, even if it could ever occur in reality, would not bother moral theory, however, because moral theory already tells us not to make conflicting promises. Another pseudo exception occurs whenever we bring terrorists into the picture who force us to choose between two immoral options, lest we ourselves be killed. Doing so places us outside the scope of morality. Morality is geared for humans interacting with other humans who are prone to reciprocal co-operation. Terrorists revert us back to the state of nature.

4 CONTRACTARIAN BACKING

Excluding the positive *in personam* exception, no dilemma can occur because moral theory has always a built-in except-when clause to settle matters. My defence also resorts to the claim that sometimes we are not even in the moral game anymore. Are such manoeuvres arbitrary, as Mothersill (1996, 71) claims? The advantage contractarianism has over other mainline moral theories is that contractarianism (i) banishes any metaphysical assumption concerning the origin of morality, which (ii) enables contractarians to build conditionality into its moral foundation, not as an afterthought. Such conditionality also explains the rejection of terrorist-like examples from the discussion of moral dilemmas.

Lurking in the belief about moral dilemmas are meta-ethical assumptions that contractarianism, at least, rejects outright. You can see the metaphysical backing in Marcus (1980, 135) when she suggests we treat moral dilemmas as teachable moments. Given the angst that occurs to participants of moral dilemmas, we learn to organize our world so as to avoid them as much as possible.[20] She used the example of abortion (131). A moral dilemma occurs in the case of abortion because we have two competing rights (one the woman's, the other the fetus's) and we cannot satisfy both. The solution: learn to avoid the situation, presumably by abstinence. Whether abortion counts as a moral dilemma (or even conflict) depends on whether we think crediting a first-term fetus with rights (at all, or sufficient to trump the rights of the pregnant woman) is plausible. That it will feel like a moral dilemma to any woman struggling with the decision to have an abortion is different from saying abortion is a moral dilemma. But whatever example Marcus uses, our learning from experience is hardly relevant. Imagine a kitchen theory that says broken glassware that falls on the floor must remain on the floor. From such a theory you can learn to wear heavy-soled boots in your kitchen after having stepped once on broken glass in your bare feet, but I am not clear why you would not simply alter your kitchen theory to permit sweeping up broken glass. Besides, a sure way to arrange your life to avoid moral dilemmas is to become a shut-in. Another good way: become a moral nihilist (Mothersill 1996, 84).

Thinking that dilemmas provide teachable moments is similar to theodicy. Telling us that our suffering is God's way of teaching us moral lessons gets the relation between morality and suffering backwards. Contractarians think morality is a tool to lessen suffering. We invent morality *because* suffering exists. Others think suffering is invented to enhance moral development (Hick 1966; Swinburne 1996). Similarly, to think we need to arrange our lives to avoid moral dilemmas makes sense only if we understand morality as something real, objective, and authoritative, not to be toyed with, as if disseminated from supernatural agency.

Williams is not much different. To think the overridden duty in a moral conflict still *exists* offers a picture of morality that is independent of human agency. Although both Williams (1973a) and Marcus (1980, 121) claim that moral dilemmas counter moral realism, I think Wiggins (1980, 216) captures their perspective better when he claims "powerful phenomenological support for realism" comes from how competing claims in moral dilemmas "present themselves as objective and real."[21] For Williams's (1973b) belief that no theory can hope to make consistent a morality that is inherently messy assumes a picture of morality as being objectively real in a way that human cognition may fail to grasp – a meta-ethical conception that contractarianism, at least, abhors.

Moral realism conceives of morality as an objective, real, mind-independent thing.[22] For contractarianism, on the other hand, morality is real (enough) only at the *ex post* stage, conditions in which morality applies, but not at the *ex ante* stage, conditions in which morality is forged. Once moral rules have been fashioned, they apply (*ex post*) independently of interests. But the inception of morality (*ex ante*) depends on the overall interests of those willing to adopt moral constraints (Gauthier 1986). To think that moral dilemmas exist and are problematic for moral theory assumes that morality is a real thing at the *ex ante* stage, something we discover and to which we are bound to obey, a concept well critiqued by Mackie (1977, 38–42).

Conditionality is embedded at the root conception of morality for contractarians. Contractarianism conceives of morality as a reciprocal arrangement for the instrumental ends of peaceful cohabitation and enterprise. This reciprocity condition is ever-present. To say a moral rule binds you whether or not the other plays along, as in terrorist scenarios, would be rejected by *ex ante* agents. *Ex ante* agents will ensure conditions apply to prevent the overall cost of a duty to be greater than the overall gain from a right. A right is granted only after *ex ante* agents would expect to benefit despite the overall cost of honouring their duty to uphold that right. Conceptually, duty comes before right. Moral duties will be sanctioned only so long as the general conditions for benefiting duty-holders remain. Outside those conditions, the *ex ante* endorsement of the unconstrained duty dissolves, and with them, the duty itself.

To be clear, contractarians can say terrorist acts are immoral, since terrorists violate the consent principle, but should we be confronted by so-called moral dilemmas produced within terrorist scenarios, morality no longer applies.

6

Blackmail: Immoral or Imprudent?

Blackmail, at least typically, is a case of asking for a fee to refrain from doing something. The puzzle about blackmail comes when both the doing and the not doing of that something is independently morally permissible, as is asking for a fee. Can two rights make a wrong? After dismissing attempts to explain the wrongness of blackmail, I offer an error theory. Acquiescing to blackmail is decidedly imprudent. A complication: for contractarians, morality is a subset of prudence. Thus, I need to explain when prudential advice counts as moral advice and when it does not. For that, I rely on the concept of one's status quo.

1 THE STRUCTURE OF BLACKMAIL

People typically assume that blackmail is not a moral negotiation. To explain why, however, is puzzling. Consider the following two cases:

> *Case 1*: Jones claims Jones will let Smith's spouse take a painting if Smith pays Jones $10,000.
> *Case 2*: Jones claims Jones will not inform Smith's spouse of Smith's infidelities if Smith pays Jones $10,000.

Everything else being equal, Case 1 is a straightforward moral transaction in structure identical to any common business deal. Smith's spouse praises the painting and exits. The curator approaches Smith to make a sale. Consider Case 2. Jones is free to tell Smith's spouse about Smith's infidelities. Likewise, Jones is free to tell Smith that Jones will tell Smith's spouse about Smith's infidelity. For that matter, Jones is free not to tell Smith's spouse about Smith's infidelity and Jones is also free to tell Smith that Jones will not tell Smith's spouse about Smith's infidelity. By implication, then, Jones is free to tell Smith that Jones might or might not tell Smith's spouse about Smith's affair. Typically, if we are free to do something, we are also free to ask for a fee for our doing that thing (Block 1997, 235). Meanwhile, others are free to accept our offers or not, and if they accept our offers, we assume they do so because they believe they stand to benefit from it. If Smith pays the money in Case 2, we assume Smith prefers paying the $10,000 to having Smith's secret revealed to Smith's spouse. Likewise with Case 1. If Smith accepts Jones's offer, we assume Smith prefers Smith's spouse having the painting to Smith having $10,000. In both cases, then, Jones makes an offer that Smith is free to accept or decline. In both cases, the principal parties stand to benefit from the transaction. On what grounds, then, can we say Case 2 is wrong while Case 1 is morally permissible?[1]

The puzzle about blackmail occurs only when all component actions of the transaction are independently morally permissible.[2] For the following, the structure of blackmail is so:

> *A* blackmails *B* whenever *A* informs *B* that *A* will do, or forbear doing, action *x* unless *B* does, or forebears doing, action *y*, while doing, or not doing, *x* and *y* are independently morally permissible actions.[3]

When a particular component of a blackmail proposal is immoral, we have no difficulty calling that case of blackmail immoral. In such cases, however, the immorality is for reasons independent of being blackmail. For example, Jones claims Jones will go public with intentionally fabricated information that will harm Smith's reputation, unless Smith pays Jones $10,000. Or Jones claims Jones will inform Smith's spouse of Smith's infidelities unless Smith lets Jones's daughter into law school. No one should find it puzzling that an immoral component of an action makes the whole action immoral, just as the truth value of a conjunction requires both terms to be true. It is not the blackmail that makes the component wrong, but the component that makes that case of blackmail wrong. Such cases would not show blackmail itself to be wrong, any more than lying in a business transaction makes business transactions wrong. The wrongness is not found in the formal structure of blackmail, but in other sorts of moral violations, lying or misuse of authority, for example.

To return to the paradigmatic blackmail case (case 2), all else being equal, it is morally permissible for Jones to tell or not to tell Smith's spouse of Smith's infidelities.[4] All else being equal, it is morally permissible to ask and receive $10,000. The problem, if there is a problem, comes when we conjoin the two. The puzzle about blackmail comes from precisely this conjoining of two independently moral actions. True, what Smith does may be immoral, but if blackmail is wrong, we are to say that the blackmailer is doing something wrong; not the blackmailee. Normally, when we conjoin two independently moral components of an action, we get a morally permissible action, as in case 1.

We know two wrong acts cannot make a right act.[5] Can two right acts make a wrong act? True, I like peanut butter and I like watermelon, but not combined, and drinking is fine and driving is fine, but not drinking and driving. To think two things that are fine by themselves are thereby fine together is to commit the fallacy of composition, where we assume what is true of the parts carries over to what is true of the whole. On the other hand, many things that are fine independently are also fine together. If blackmail is wrong despite consisting of two morally fine acts, it cannot be shown to be wrong merely by telling us about the fallacy of composition. Besides, the most relevant analogy, the drinking and driving example, is wrong for the damage the combination may do to unconsulted third parties. No unconsulted third parties need be involved in blackmail (see 2.3.1).

The definition of blackmail captures both informational and non-informational cases.[6] The typical case of blackmail has it that x is a withholding of information, but it may also entail withholding actions. "Give me money or I shall give your reckless daughter a motorcycle" (Katz 1996, 134). For that matter, y need not be money. "Give me that cookie and I won't tell Mom you had a cigarette."

My definition also ignores whether the component acts in blackmail are commissions or omissions. The typical blackmail case involves payment for omissions, such as Jones's refraining from telling Smith's spouse something. Business transactions typically pay for acts of commission. Something somebody does is typically worth more to buyers than something somebody does not do. Despite such norms, the commission–omission distinction is morally irrelevant, at least concerning business or blackmail. For example, many meals are more valuable to me with certain ingredients omitted. Or imagine viewing an unfinished painting in an artist's studio. The way it is now may be worth more in the eyes of a buyer than if the painter continues working on it, judging by the finished works in the gallery. If buyers wish to pay for the painter not to do anything else to the painting, that is an offer they can legitimately make. "I'll give you $500 for it." "No, it's not finished yet." "Ok, I'll give you $700 for it if I can take it away right now." Value is found in an act of omission.

While I maintain that blackmail, in itself, is not morally problematic, I do believe our intuitions capture something unsettling about blackmail. As Berman says, blackmail just "smells nasty" (Berman 2011, 90). Whether smelly or not, it is certainly the case that responding to blackmail is imprudent. Before I examine its imprudence, and what implications fall from that, I will review the reasons scholars offer for why blackmail is immoral, and what makes those reasons unconvincing.

2 WHAT IS WRONG WITH BLACKMAIL?

I partition arguments against the morality of blackmail into five: 1. harms; 2. motives; 3. externalities; 4. rights violations; and 5. duty omissions.[7] Each type may be further subdivided, and no category is mutually exclusive of another, admitting the defence that while none are sufficient in themselves, "the aggregate collection" makes a formidable argument (Levy 2007, 1090).[8]

2.1 *Harms*

A common explanation of an immoral action is that it causes harm to others, or the harm to others outweighs the benefit to the one harming. For contractarians, the issue of harm is less the point than that consent is missing. Typically, people do not consent to being harmed (hence the conflation), but not always. Getting an inoculation is not immoral, for example, despite the harm of the pin prick. The question about blackmail being harmful, then, needs to be cast as whether blackmail causes non-consensual harm. Ways that blackmail has been said to harm without consent include coercion, exploitation, and harassment.

2.1.1 COERCION

According to Gorr (1992, 53–4), blackmail is a kind of theft. "Give me $10,000 or I will shoot you," is similar in form to, "Give me $10,000 or I will tell your spouse about your affair." When the blackmail victim opts to pay, the payment is deemed worth the service of withholding the information. That the blackmail target willingly consents to the blackmail proposal makes blackmail unlike theft, one might think. We can say the same in the mugging case, however: the mugging victim deems the payment worth the service of not being shot. The voluntary submission of the victim is coerced, and this coercion is what makes both blackmail (and theft) wrong (Altman 1993, 1642; Gorr 1992, 53–4; Katz 1996, 163–4). If Smith declines in blackmail (case 2) and mugging, bad things will happen to Smith. Not so in business transactions (case 1). Hence Smith's action is not voluntary in case 2; it is voluntary in case 1.

Threat of assault is wrong for contractarians because remaining at your status quo is not an option.[9] The status quo is the state one was in before the offer (Gauthier 1986, 204). Contractarians call any act "voluntary" if at least one option is to remain at one's status quo baseline. In a mugging, for example, your options are to be killed or to lose your money; your status quo is neither. With blackmail, however, the status quo is a live option. The blackmail victim has the option of declining the blackmailer's offer to withhold sensitive information. We cannot count Smith's status quo baseline as simply what Smith *believes* it to be. Some beliefs might be false. My believing incorrectly that my aunt left me $1,000,000 in her will does not make it the case that my aunt's estate owes me $1,000,000. Despite my belief, my real baseline is not being assigned anything in my aunt's will. If she did bequeath me anything, great. If not, no loss. Likewise, in case 2, Smith's real baseline is a marriage in jeopardy of Jones (or anyone) telling Smith's spouse about Smith's affair. Jones allows this option: hence Smith's choice is voluntary.

One might object to this assessment of where to draw the baseline. The duty of beneficence, for example, places the baseline above the status quo in cases where the status quo is already below par. Surely in the blackmail case (case 2), Smith is better off without Jones's offer.[10] If Smith refuses Jones's proposal in case 2, Smith is out of a marriage (or at least the marriage is in peril), whereas if Smith refuses Jones's offer in case 1, Smith remains at the status quo. Hence only in case 1 is Smith's action voluntary. Blackmail, then, violates the contractarian credo of not doing to others without their voluntary consent. Many cases exist, however, where Smith would be better off without the existence of an offer by Jones without making Jones's offer coercive. As a welcoming gesture, Jones offers Smith a bowl of monkey brain. To refuse would be rude, to eat it even worse. Smith would be better off without Jones's offer, but that does not mean Jones's offer is coercive. Altman (1993, 1642) suggests a counterfactual baseline. Would the blackmailer have done the threatened action without the payment not to? If no, then fine; if yes, then not fine. By such thinking, yard sales would be immoral assuming owners would take unsold items to the dump.[11] Berman is more direct: "Nonmoral baselines cannot do the moral work required of them" (Berman 2011, 66). It is not whether a person can remain at her status quo that makes the act right; the *pressure* to not remain at one's status quo is what makes the threat immoral (Wertheimer 1987). This will not do, either. Upon seeing you carting your old lawnmower to the dump, I offer you ten times its original value. The pressure to abandon your status quo (and simply cart the lawnmower to the dump) is enormous. Few would be able to decline. My offer is stupid, admittedly, but not immoral.

2.1.2 EXPLOITATION

To exploit people is to take advantage of their vulnerability. Blackmailers do take advantage of their victim's vulnerability, so blackmail is exploitive (Altman 1993; Daly and Giertz 1978; Fletcher 1993; Lindgren 1993b; Murphy 1980). Whether that makes blackmail (or exploitation) immoral, however, requires a closer look. Chess players, for example, exploit their opponents' weaknesses without being immoral. Consider another example. Smith is stuck on the Coquihalla highway during a snowstorm and Jones arrives in a tow truck. For $300.00, far above market price, Jones offers to pull Smith to the top of the desolate pass.[12] Smith's relief is short-lived, since Smith is still at risk of becoming stuck. Jones may keep watch for just that possibility and charge another fee for another partial rescue. Does Jones exploit Smith? We assume nothing is wrong with tow trucks charging for their services. When is charging too much wrong? In economical terms, charging too much is the point where no one buys. One charges as much as one can. One pays as little as one can. Under normal conditions, with competition and lack of urgency to purchase certain wares, prices will be much lower. One ought not to compare tow-truck fees on mountain passes in a snowstorm to tow-truck fees under normal conditions in a city. Since the conditions are significantly different between the two cases, demanding comparable market prices is illegitimate. Of course, some say that while the Coquihalla tow-truck driver can legally get away with an exorbitant fee, the driver is still immoral for doing so, precisely because Jones exploits Smith's unfortunate predicament. On the other hand, we can say Smith is lucky Jones is present. The tow-truck driver is offering Smith a service given Smith's situation, a service that costs Jones. It is a risk on Jones's part and surely Jones has a right to try to recoup any losses. If Jones were forbidden to do that, Jones would not be out there and Smith would suffer more – perhaps suffer hypothermia. While Smith would have preferred a lower fee, Smith would prefer the high fee to Jones not being there at all. We present a mixed message to say both that we are happy about the tow-truck's arrival and that we morally condemn the tow-truck driver.

In the tow-truck case, notice, Jones did not cause it to snow and nor did Jones cause Smith to become stuck in the snow. Being stuck was due to Smith's being insufficiently prepared for mountain weather. The situation Smith was in before Jones's arrival was being stuck, and Jones left that option available to Smith. Smith's accepting Jones's exorbitant fee is therefore voluntary. Blackmail takes the same pattern as the tow-truck scenario. The blackmailer did not cause Smith to have an affair any more than the tow-truck driver caused Smith to become stuck in the snow. Smith had the affair voluntarily. The blackmailer is not the cause of jeopardizing Smith's marriage. This is due to Smith's being insufficiently prepared for the consequences of extramarital sex. In essence, the blackmailer is offering Smith a service – the service of protecting the secrecy of the affair. In any event, Smith's accepting Jones's terms is strictly voluntary on Smith's part because the situation Smith was in before Jones presented Smith with the blackmail option was being at risk of someone's reporting the affair to Smith's spouse.

Does it matter that Smith's protector is also the person from whom Smith needs protection? Paying a private security to protect damage to my property is one thing. Paying a fee to the Mafia to "protect" my property from the Mafia itself, another. Damaging my property, however, is an immoral act. Telling my spouse a truth is not, especially a truth that my spouse may deem important to hear. What matters is that someone was going to tell Smith's spouse, and a service to prevent that from happening is worth the fee or it is not. If we understand exploitation as causing a disservice, blackmail is not exploitive. To the extent that the blackmailer and tow-truck driver are exploitive speaks to their character, not the morality of their actions. We may not wish to befriend them, but that is a different matter (to be discussed in 2.2).

2.1.3 HARASSMENT

For Levy (2007, 1081–3), blackmail is immoral in the same way as stalking and harassment are immoral. They upset the status quo of enjoying life without the contaminant of stalkers and harassers. Stalkers and harassers induce, often with intent, great fear and anxiety in the target. Since blackmail causes, and often is intended to cause, anxiety and fear in their targets, it, too, should be rightly deemed immoral. The types of threats are different, admittedly. Blackmail threatens one's reputation; harassment one's safety; but both are supremely valued interests we hold.[13]

Lindgren (1989, 604–5) and Block (1999b, 23) point out that countless legal activities may cause fear and anxiety, for example, roller coasters. In response, Levy offers the *reductio ad absurdum* that we should then not criminalize harassment and stalking (Levy 2007, 1086). This will not work. The worry is not about what we ought to criminalize, but what reasons we offer for criminalizing. In any event, we condemn stalking and harassment not because they induce (and often intend to induce) fear and anxiety. They do cause fear and anxiety, but it is not the causing of fear and anxiety that makes them immoral. The problem is that stalkers and harassers do not take no for an answer. As put, the target's status quo is not a live option. In the case of blackmail, however, not paying ransom and being vulnerable to sensitive information being leaked is one's status quo, and that remains a live option. Blackmailers may become harassers if they also do not take no for an answer, but that would not make blackmail immoral any more than we would deem date requests to be immoral due to impertinent date-askers refusing to take no for an answer.

2.2 *Bad Motives*

The adultery blackmail case (Case 2) has bad motives: personal gain at the expense of another's vulnerability (Katz 1996, 160; Berman 1998, 797–8). Even Walter Block (1999, n. 1), while defending the legal right to blackmail, admits that he is not speaking about the *morality* of it. By that, he seems to imply some unethical motivation. While the motive in blackmail is self-gain, self-gain motivates all business transactions.[14] Of course, in business transactions, we expect the interaction to be mutually beneficial. While some deny that blackmail offers mutual advantage (Altman 1993; Smilansky 1995), mutual advantage need not be equal advantage, let alone similarly scaled advantage, like money. If the blackmailee accepts the offer voluntarily (which we questioned in 2.1.2), that presupposes the blackmailee finds accepting the offer more advantageous than not. As put, the blackmailee benefits as well as the blackmailer. Moreover, I can have bad motives and commit perfectly moral acts. Perhaps I am mad at my roommate and, for retaliation, buy a brand of toothpaste my roommate hates. My spiteful action may be blameworthy, but the blameworthiness would not transfer to the purchase of toothpaste. But wait! Purchase of toothpaste is not typically done with malice, whereas blackmail always has bad motives. Alas, one may blackmail for nice motives. Jones claims Jones will go on a hunger strike and alert the media about it unless Smith improves prison conditions. Or Jones tells Smith that Jones will reveal to Smith's spouse Smith's prostitute visits unless Smith gives $10,000 to a homeless shelter. These have the same blackmail structure as Case 2, but the blackmailers' motives seem morally praiseworthy. If something is wrong with blackmail, it cannot be due to the bad motive of the blackmailer.

I have highlighted how a good motive may be achieved by blackmail and thereby conclude that motives cannot be the thing that makes blackmail wrong. We may wonder about this in three ways. (i) Can we not complain about the motive to use blackmail to achieve our good ends? Would that not be a case of doing bad to achieve good, precisely the kind of utilitarian calculus that contractarianism rejects? My answer is, Yes, as long as we agree that blackmail is a bad. The concern has not demonstrated that blackmail is bad; it has merely presumed it is. (ii) Is it not enough to show that blackmail is wrong when motivated by a bad motive? My answer: No. It may be enough to show that the act is immoral, but not that blackmail itself is immoral. Compare, *A* marries *B* for a bad motive (money, e.g.). *A* may be morally criticized without our criticizing marriage. (iii) But what if, unlike marriage, blackmail is always, or typically, driven by a bad motive? Is it sufficient now to say that blackmail is immoral? My answer: Ignoring that my good-motive blackmail case was trying to stymie such a response, other things have bad motives, like assault and theft. Assault and theft are not deemed bad because the motives are bad; they are bad because they rob another of their status quo. Blackmail, so I claim, at least in its prototypical case, does not do that.

An available response is to claim non-prototypical cases of blackmail are bad because of bad motives, and when no bad motives can be found, as in the prototypical case, we stop calling it "blackmail." We call it, instead, a morally permissible transaction. Similarly, not all cases of killing humans are cases of murder. But many actions done with bad motives are neither given a new name nor deemed immoral. If we admit the act is morally fine, only the motive is bad, we are speaking no longer about the act but the character. "The toothpaste purchaser was spiteful!" "The blackmailer was insensitive!" This captures, I think, Katz's claim that blackmail will always involve, if not moral infractions, at least petty motives (Katz 1996, 163). Even if we agree that having bad motives is immoral (although I believe a conflation occurs between morality and well-being), it would not show that blackmail is immoral; it would show only that things we do with bad motives are, or tend to be, immoral.

2.3 *Externalities*

Externalities concern uncompensated adverse affects to those not part of the agreement. In Case 2, other concerned parties to the agreement may include the spouse, the paramour, and the adulterer's children. If the blackmail victim resorts to crime to pay the blackmail ransom, the victims of these crimes count as externalities. Society, abstractly conceived, may also count as being adversely affected should we imagine the particular act being universally generalized. Conversely, vigilantism, with all its obstructions to justice, may increase.

2.3.1 CONCERNED PARTIES

Smith's spouse was a concerned party when Smith decided to have the affair, and to the extent that Smith's spouse was not consulted about it, the affair is immoral for contractarians. Smith's spouse is not obviously a concerned party in the transaction between Smith and Jones, however – at least no more than Smith's spouse is a concerned party in Smith's buying the painting in case 1. Stores may sell merchandise to customers who are buying gifts for someone else. The fact that the purchase will affect someone else is a concern between the purchaser and that other person, not between the merchant and the consumer. Likewise, case 2 concerns Smith and Jones only. If Smith pays Jones, Smith's spouse remains at the status quo: the circumstances of being ignorant of Smith's infidelity. If Smith does not purchase Jones's service, then Jones tells something true to Smith's spouse, and telling something true to someone is not forbidden on contractarian grounds. Whatever Smith decides to do, Jones has not done anything wrong to Smith's spouse.

It may seem a different matter concerning Smith's paramour. If Smith's spouse finds out, this may adversely affect the relations between Smith and the paramour. In this sense, we may think of the paramour as being an uninformed concerned party concerning the interaction between Jones and Smith's spouse. Not all people whom third-party agreements affect count as a concerned party, however. Imagine Jones and Smith competing for a job. Smith would not agree that the company hire Jones rather than Smith. Jones's getting the job adversely affects Smith, who remains unemployed as a result. Nevertheless, Jones's being hired is not up to Smith to decide, and thus, despite Smith's being an uninformed and adversely affected party, Smith is not a concerned party in the contractarian sense. Similarly, the fact that the paramour may be negatively affected is not sufficient to call the paramour a neglected concerned party.

The above aside, blackmail can occur when we have no third party to worry about. Imagine if Smith is an independently wealthy, unattached homosexual with no living relations, and Jones threatens to publicize Smith's sexual orientation, unless Smith pays Jones $10,000. It looks like a typical blackmail scenario, but without any unconsulted third parties. This is sufficient to show that if something makes blackmail wrong, it cannot be the existence of unconsulted third parties.

2.3.2

Like drug addicts, blackmail victims may resort to crime to pay off their ransom. In this sense, blackmail is "the handmaiden to corruption and deceit" (Epstein 1983, 566). When a jeweller asks a fee for an engagement ring and the fiancé resorts to crime to pay it, we do not blame the jeweller (Berman 2011, 49). Admittedly, jewellers' clients tend not to have to resort to crime to pay the fee, unlike the clients of illicit drug dealers. I do not know the evidence to support the notion that blackmail targets are more like drug addicts than jewellery shoppers, but one would sensibly expect blackmailers to target only those who could afford the fee. At any rate, upscale blackmailers could not be deemed immoral by this sort of reasoning, and, presumably, Epstein wishes not to exclude this group.

2.3.3
Epstein (1983) suggests bad social consequences would occur if we permit blackmail. Large organizations would emerge and trade in dirty information about people's private lives. Like paparazzi swarming famous people to sell photos to gossip magazines, blackmail sleuths will swarm the wealthy to dig out blackmailable grime. If the information the blackmail paparazzi gleans is not itself an invasion of privacy (see 2.4.1), we cannot say that the increase of a thing already moral is immoral. We cannot show something to be wrong by pointing out that, if we permit it, more of those things will come about. That more violinists will emerge if we permit violin playing (and violin schools and violinist associations) is hardly a justification to outlaw violin playing. If something is immoral, it must be so on its own terms, not merely because more of it will come about if allowed. True, I may not mind a few ants in my kitchen, yet mind a horde of ants in my kitchen. Sometimes, then, a little bit is acceptable, and a lot, not. With morality, however, we do not think a few murders are fine, but draw the line at a lot of murders.[15] If murder is bad, it is bad independently of how often it occurs. The same with blackmail.

2.4 *Rights Violations*

Some actions are wrong due to violations of principles, and they are wrong even if no harm accrues to anyone. I glance at your driver's licence and see what date you were born. I trespass across a bit of your lawn. I lie to you about my age. None of these actions have much, if any, harm potential, but are violations of moral principles concerning privacy, property, and fraud.

2.4.1 PRIVACY
For Murphy (1980) and Posner (1993), blackmail is wrong for being an invasion of privacy. Blackmail uses someone's private information against them. Should Jones gain information on Smith through

invading Smith's privacy – by wiretapping, computer hacking, or home burglary – we can complain. When Jones stumbles on the relevant information by simply being at the right place at the right time, however, Jones's possession of the information concerning Smith is not an invasion of privacy. Imagine Jones repeatedly saw Smith enter a motel room with a person who was not Smith's spouse. If Jones were the motel clerk, one could say Jones has moral constraints concerning confidentiality. If Jones were a patron of the motel, however, or happened to be passing, the knowledge Jones has is public information – at least it is information any passerby could glean. That is, any passerby who can recognize Smith and Smith's spouse and realize Smith's motel companion is not Smith's spouse. As such, the information is not in this sense private anymore.

Those who argue that blackmail entails privacy invasion need to show that Jones cannot use the information concerning Smith's private life without invading Smith's privacy. Sissela Bok (1982), however, argues that we can only understand privacy rights in terms of access. In any event, we can blackmail people without invading their privacy. Smith, a former nude model, is running for political office. Jones tells Smith that Jones will tell the press about Smith's past life, unless Smith pays Jones $10,000. If Smith willingly posed nude in a magazine, we can hardly say that anyone who buys the magazine is invading Smith's privacy. Nor can we say that anyone who discusses what is available in that magazine is invading Smith's privacy. Nor do we suppose that this fact changes after a few months, years, or decades go by. To point out to the world the existence of this magazine is not an invasion of Smith's privacy, since Smith willingly consented to its publication. Nevertheless, threatening to publicize a politician's past nude modelling career is still a case of blackmail. Smith may regret posing nude given Smith's current political career and may be motivated to keep the information private, but that hardly makes it a privacy invasion. We do not count as private merely that information we would not want made public. For that matter, if Case 2 is wrong for being an invasion of privacy, we would be immoral to warn spouses of their cheating mates – a throwback to the days of not reporting spousal abuse for its being an invasion of privacy.

2.4.2 OWNERSHIP

Perhaps the worry about privacy is better expressed as a worry about ownership. As Lindgren says, blackmailers are parasites, using someone else's bargaining chips for personal gain (Lindgren 1984, 702). In this sense, the wrong is akin to a quid pro quo case. For example, a lecherous professor threatens an F to a student unless that student acquiesces to have sex with him. In doing so, the professor abrogates his authority. He is using the university's bargaining chips, not his own. In Shakespeare's *Measure for Measure*, Angelo blackmails Isabella to have sex with him for Angelo to halt the execution of Isabella's brother. Angelo is usurping the state's authority: he is using the state's bargaining chip for his own ends. A worker on a ladder inadvertently sees a clergyman having sex with a parishioner. At threat of divulging the information, the worker demands money from the clergyman. The information (the bargaining chip), however, belongs to the clergyman's superior and flock (Lindgren 1984, 706). In adultery blackmail (case 2), the immorality is found in the blackmailer's use of a bargaining chip that rightfully belongs to the spouse. The blackmailer may possess the information, but not the right to use it for personal gain without consultation with the real owner: the spouse. As Lindgren says, understanding blackmail as use of someone else's bargaining chips explains the seeming paradox of two independently moral actions becoming immoral when combined. Actions are fine when the right people do them; not necessarily fine when someone else does them (Lindgren 1984, 717).

While Lindgren claims to have identified a descriptive feature that all blackmail cases have (Lindgren 1993a), this feature (use of someone else's bargaining chips) cannot be the explanation of the immorality of blackmail for five reasons. The first concerns morally mandatory actions. The second concerns a sufficiency condition. The third concerns contractual obligations. The fourth concerns the difference between information belonging to and information about someone. The fifth concerns gossip.

(i) The idea is that blackmailers *use* information to which others have proprietorship, but in the clergyman case, neither the superior nor the congregation have that information, so it is difficult to maintain an abuse of information that someone does not even have, unless we claim that they morally *ought* to have that information. If so, the worker on the ladder has a moral obligation to report his findings. Asking money to forbear doing a moral requirement is, of course, immoral. Whether one morally ought to report a clergyman's consensual sexual affairs is not obvious, however. (If the sex were non-consensual, for example sex with a child, that is a different matter.) The same worry applies to the adultery case. Reporting adultery is not obviously mandatory.

(ii) Imagine Jones owns a painting that Jones loves very much. Unbeknown to Jones, the artist is a child molester. Should Jones discover this fact, Jones would get rid of the painting immediately. Smith possesses the information about the artist's background, but opts to not divulge it to Jones because he does not wish to upset Jones. This is not a case of blackmail, nor is it a case of moral wrongdoing (by Jones or Smith), but it is a case of Smith withholding information that counts as a bargaining chip belonging more to Jones than to Smith. It is up to Jones to decide what to do given the information, not Smith. But saying this means neither that Jones is the sole proprietor of the information, nor that Smith has no right to do with the information as Smith sees fit. Mere use of someone else's bargaining chip seems, then, insufficient to account for its wrongness.

(iii) Lindrgen admits that his idea is clearer where a formal agency exists, for example a union leader threatens to cause a strike unless personally paid off (Lindgren 1984, 702). Quid pro quo cases are wrong for an abuse of their authority for personal gain, but neither the blackmailer in Case 2 nor the worker on the ladder, are abusing *their* authority. A professor has been granted authority to assign grades. The lecherous professor abuses that contractual privilege. The worker on the ladder has not been given authority to pass information onto parishioners: therefore no contractual privilege has been abrogated by the worker on the ladder. While Smith, the adulterer, has a contractual obligation toward Smith's spouse, Jones, Smith's blackmailer, has no contractual obligation toward either of the Smiths and thus cannot abuse his authority over them since he has no authority over them. Lindgren's ownership argument may work well in showing why quid pro quo cases are wrong, but it does not help show why blackmail is wrong.

(iv) A difference exists between information *belonging to* someone and information *about* someone. Whether it is parasitic or not, using information about other people is not necessarily immoral. Scouting an opponent goalie's weaknesses and passing the information to one's team is morally fine, I assume, despite using information about an opposing team. If a member of Team A offers Team B the secret weakness of Team A's goalie for money, this is blackmail as well as a case of using information about someone else. The scout is a loyal teammate; the blackmailer a traitor. But what makes the blackmail case not simply selling information about someone else, as opposed to using information that belongs to someone else? In the traitor case, the blackmailer is part of a team to which the information belongs, just as the lecherous professor is part of an institution to which he belongs, an institution that has a stake in how grades are regulated, something the professor ignores for his own ends: a traitor. In the scouting case, the benefit accrues to the team to which the scout belongs. The scout benefits his own team by extracting and using information on someone else. The traitor does not benefit his own team; he benefits only himself. But this analysis misses the fact that the scout uses information for his team's benefit that could rightfully be said belongs to the opposing team. If blackmail is wrong for use of information that does not belong to the blackmailer, the scouting case is as bad as the traitor case.

(v) The above aside, blackmail can occur without bargaining-chip abuse problems. Smith is an independently wealthy, self-employed, unattached homosexual with no living relations. We have met him before. Jones threatens to publicize Smith's sexual orientation, unless Smith pays Jones $10,000. Lindgren might say that the bargaining chip in this case is the victim's, not the blackmailer's, to use. That would make gossip wrong, however. If Lindgren does not want to go as far as saying gossip is immoral (as I read him in Lindgren 1993a, 1984), the only difference is the asking for money for the conveying of someone else's information, something that (a) would make gossip columns immoral; and (b) is unfounded in any event: something does not become immoral by the mere attachment of a fee.

A counter may be offered. Asking for money to save a drowning person is immoral, whereas saving a drowning person is not immoral. Ignoring our paying lifeguards, the cases are different. We feel that we have a moral duty to save drowning people if we can. Asking for money to do what we are morally obligated to do anyway is a problem. But the mere asking for money for doing something we are not morally obligated to do does not make the action immoral.

2.4.3 FRAUD

According to Galoob (2016), blackmail is wrong because it is fraudulent. You fraud someone when you knowingly pass off as valuable that which is valueless, such as a counterfeit bill, or a cheque that will bounce. Blackmail is fraudulent for the blackmailer offers non-disclosure (typically) without any guarantee (Galoob 2016, 35).

Consequently, a blackmail victim remains in the blackmailer's grip indefinitely (Coase 1988, 675), making the blackmailer's offer valueless – hence fraudulent (Galoob 2016, 39).

As I will make clear in section 3, I agree that blackmail offers nothing of guaranteed value, but whether we can accuse the blackmailer of fraud is a different matter. With fraud, not only is the intent deceit, but the act also. When someone gives me a counterfeit twenty for two tens, the act is fraudulent if (i) the one giving the fake bill knew it was a fake bill, and (ii) it is, in fact, a fake bill. Neither condition need apply in blackmail. The silence blackmailers offer may well be legitimate. They need not be offering a fake silence and nor need they intend to offer merely a fake silence. Whether we can trust blackmailers to keep their word is another matter, but that is not sufficient to call blackmail fraudulent.

2.5 *Duty Omissions*

Our last grouping of reasons against the morality of blackmail concerns omissions of prior duty. Three types of omissions have been raised in the literature: the failure to report an immorality, a failure of beneficence, and a failure of acting according to one's own moral beliefs.

2.5.1 FAILURE TO REPORT

We are all supposed to uphold morality, and that includes a duty to rat on immoral agents, a kind of social policing.[16] We like to imagine blackmail requires someone to have something to hide. Otherwise, no leverage exists. Typically, we want hidden that which would harm our reputation. Being engaged in immoral activities would be good things to hide. From this, we infer that anyone hiding something is involved in immoral activity. From this, we think blackmail is a case of benefiting from someone's immoral activity, and from this we condemn blackmail (Katz 1996, 193). The blackmailer is asking for a fee to forbear doing something the blackmailer morally ought to do. Even if we have no moral obligation to report immorality, we have a moral obligation not to collude with immorality. Assuming infidelity is immoral, the blackmailer violates that in Case 2. By offering to forgo what the blackmailer morally ought to do, the blackmailer becomes an accomplice to the original crime (Altman 1993). Threatening not to do one's moral obligations is wrong.

One may attract blackmailers for reasons other than by being engaged in immoral activity, however. Embarrassment can suffice. At any rate, we cannot simply say that informing Smith's spouse of Smith's affair is morally permissible. We need also to assert that we have a moral obligation to inform Smith's spouse about Smith's affair. To convince someone of that seems a harder task than convincing someone that blackmail is wrong.[17]

The problem of infidelity for contractarians involves a violation of the marriage contract. Whether explicitly stated or merely implied, most marriages begin with the idea that the parties involved will be faithful to each other. Nevertheless, we almost expect infidelity. Not that that makes infidelity morally permissible, though one might suggest the demand for lifelong fidelity to one person is too much to ask (Firestone 1970). Such vows seem as sensible as promising to love someone's next poem. Heartfelt, yet hollow. Still, marriages do not necessarily crumble from revelations of infidelity. Infidelity is often a symptom, as opposed to the cause, of a failing marriage. The problem of marriage is that people change. Predicting how my future self will feel about your future self because of how my present self feels about your present self is hardly a sound inference (Halwani 1988; hooks 1989). Nevertheless, marriages are more likely to blossom from revealed infidelities if it is the unfaithful who confesses; not a third party. Thus, if we are focusing on what Jones morally ought to do, it is not clear that Jones ought to rat on Smith. If we discover a friend is a thief, our moral obligation to society may permit us to first talk to our friend, rather than simply rat on the friend. In fact, the threat of ostracization may be too onerous on a would-be informant for us to insist on their having a moral obligation to rat on friends. So, at best, Jones ought to encourage Smith to confess to Smith's spouse voluntarily. Only in that way can the Smiths rebuild the trust and intimacy upon which a good marriage is based. One creative way of encouraging Smith to confess is to blackmail Smith.

If Smith were an unrepentant child abuser, and Jones knows this, then we might say that Jones has an obligation to rat on Smith. If Jones suggests to Smith that Jones will refrain from ratting on Smith's abuse if Smith gives Jones $10,000, then we can complain about Jones's action. To say this is what is wrong with blackmail, however, would be misleading. Blackmail can occur without either failing to report a crime, or abetting a crime. Smith is running for political office. Jones decides to falsely accuse Smith of having an affair unless

Smith pays Jones $10,000. Since the accusation is false, there is no moral obligation on Jones's part to tell the world about the affair. The immorality concerns the false accusation, not the blackmail. Of course, if all blackmail has immoral components, then we could say all blackmail is wrong for violating some moral code. Even still, it would not show that blackmail itself is wrong; only anything with immoral components is wrong. Ignoring all that, the case about the politician who once posed nude has no immoral components. Posing nude in non-public spaces is morally permissible. Telling someone a public-domain truth is morally permissible. To say Jones *ought* to inform the public about Smith's past life would be hard to maintain. If blackmail were wrong *because* one ought to inform, we could not say that blackmailing a politician over a nude photo was wrong.

2.5.2 NON-BENEFICENCE

Shaw (2012, 170) and Galoob (2016, 27) argue that blackmailers fail the moral obligation of beneficence. Smith is drowning. Jones offers to save Smith for a fee of $10,000. Otherwise, Jones will do nothing. The difficulty, presumably, is that we believe that Jones has a moral obligation to rescue Smith from drowning, all else being equal. Call this a duty of beneficence. If Jones has a moral obligation to save Smith, Jones's asking for money from Smith for Jones to do Jones's moral duty will be problematic. Saying, "Pay me $10,000 to refrain from killing you," is the same sort of violation. Asking for payment to do that which I morally ought to do anyway (refrain from killing you) is wrong, and contractarians would agree. The duty of beneficence does not stop at saving people from drowning, however. When I exploit your vulnerability – even if this does not count as harming you, since your status quo remains a live option – I am certainly not benefiting you. Even if (contra Singer 1972) the duty of beneficence is not so great as to help relieve world famine, the least it can do is forbid exploiting people's vulnerability.

To return to the Coquihalla Highway mid-snowstorm, to forbid exploitation is to prevent the tow truck from looking for prey. The result: snowbound drivers are much worse off. To say that tow-truck drivers are morally obliged to help these people would put a too hefty price on tow-truck drivers. Conversely, every citizen pitches in through increased taxation to place tow trucks at the ready on every remote highway. In the meantime, however, leave it to the entrepreneur's discretion: how much they would be willing to make to take the risk. That those stuck believe they have no choice is false. They can decline and remain at their status quo. That we wish people would bail us out at their expense whenever we need help is only an ideal status quo, not the baseline from which contractarians, at least, determine non-consensual harm.

2.5.3 BELIEFS

Berman (1998, 2011) and Shaw (2012) devised a cunning explanation of the wrongness of blackmail: blackmailers necessarily believe that one of their threatened actions is immoral. A blackmailer offers a conditional threat to disclose sensitive information unless paid. To disclose the information is either wrong or right. If right, to withhold that disclosure for money is wrong. If wrong, then to threaten to disclose that information is wrong. In either case, the blackmailer is willing to do that which the blackmailer deems to be wrongful. Shaw's argument is simpler. In the case of adultery blackmail, if it is good to tell the spouse about the affair, then the information holder should tell without compensation. If it is not good to tell the spouse, then the information holder should not tell period. Either way, asking for compensation involves the withholding of doing a good.

The main problem for both Shaw and Berman is a false dichotomy, but a preliminary problem exists. A stated assumption in Berman's argument (2011, 68) is that we have a moral duty to do that which we believe to be moral and a moral duty to avoid doing that which we believe to be immoral.[18] This assumption seems innocuous, since it concerns merely the subject's own beliefs. Two issues confront it. One concerns the tension between a true belief and a false belief. If I wrongly believe x is moral, do I really have a *moral* obligation to do x? This seems unlikely. Another worry is double counting. If x is moral, and I believe x is moral, then I have a moral obligation to do x. This makes sense, but it does not make sense that I have the moral obligation to do x *because* I believe x is moral. That gives me a rational obligation to do x – to do that which I believe I ought to do.

As mentioned, the main worry is an excluded middle. Both Berman and Shaw assume disclosing adultery is either morally obligatory or morally forbidden in a given case. Another option is that disclosure is morally permitted and the blackmailer believes that to be so. If morally permitted, it is also morally permitted to not disclose. Such is the logic of moral permissibility. If so, whichever the blackmailer does, disclose or not, it is morally permissible.

2.6 *Summary*

When no arguments succeed in forbidding certain actions, the default should be permission. On top of that, contractarians call something morally fine when all concerned parties have sufficient information, are competent, and enter the agreement voluntarily. Since this is what occurs with typical transactions of blackmail, contractarians can find nothing immoral with blackmail.

3 PRUDENCE AND MORALITY

3.1 *Prudence*

Cases of blackmail that are immoral are immoral for independent reasons than for having the structure of blackmail. When we cannot morally fault any of the components of a case of blackmail, at least concerning the blackmailer's doings, contractarians are committed to calling the action morally fine. While we cannot find *moral* fault with blackmail, my concluding suggestion is to say that we can, nevertheless, find *prudential* fault with succumbing to blackmail.

We frown upon blackmail because it is a bad deal. No right-thinking person ought (prudentially) to accept the blackmailer's services for five reasons. (i) There is little guarantee that the payment will secure the intended service,[19] especially when the blackmailer's offer is to forbear doing something. If Jones, the blackmailer, forbears telling your spouse this week, is Jones's obligation to you satisfied? Can Jones tell your spouse next week? Do you have to pay Jones off again in a year's time? To calm yourself of these fears, you will need a contract with the blackmailer, which, of course, would be useless. Any legally sanctioned contract is a public document – precisely the thing you are motivated to avoid if you were susceptible to being blackmailed (Coase 1988, 675; Kipnis 1999, 22). Going to the police about a breach of contract with a blackmailer is tantamount to just going to your spouse about it.[20] The prudent choice for any deal the success of which we cannot sufficiently guarantee is not to accept it. You risk having your secret exposed and paying $10,000. Such a consideration makes acquiescing to blackmail imprudent; it does not make blackmail immoral, however. Many business transactions are endless in this way (Berman 1998, 824–5), for example, the insurance industry. (ii) The service is for one person to do or to forbear doing x. The payment cannot prevent others from doing or not doing x. How many others know about the affair? Will others come to you and charge for the same service? Assuming you cannot afford to pay off blackmailers indefinitely, your secret will be divulged despite your previous payments.[21] (iii) Consider your spouse. It is likely that your spouse would prefer to know about the affair than be out $10,000 on top of your having an affair. For that matter, once the bank account is down $10,000, and you have no ready answer, the marriage you wanted protected is at risk anyway.[22] (iv) Any behaviourist would say your infidelity shows that you are not concerned about protecting the marriage. So why would you choose to pay $10,000 for something you do not even want? What is the big deal about failed marriages, these days? Presumably the benefit of an affair is partly to avoid the hassles of divorce. Whether hassle avoidance is still worth it after blackmail payments, however, one can decide for oneself.[23] (v) Lastly, if you call the blackmailer's bluff, what motivation has the blackmailer to carry through with the threat? Failing to sell a painting to Smith's spouse does not rob the art merchant of the ability to sell the painting to someone else. Without the money, however, Jones's telling Smith's spouse about Smith's affair has no benefit to Jones,[24] other than spite (Altman 1993; Berman 2011, 43).[25] Moreover, to tell dissolves the bargaining chip that might have use in future. Overall, the prudent choice is to call the blackmailer's bluff.

That we find acquiescing to blackmail imprudent counts as an error theory, if you will. It helps explain why we have the intuition that blackmail smells nasty without the need to call it immoral.

A caveat: when I say it is imprudent to abide by the blackmailer's threat, I speak only of those cases of blackmail when each component is morally permissible taken by itself. When a component of blackmail (the threat to you or others for non-compliance, or the action you need to do to avoid the threat) is immoral, it may well be prudent (and possibly morally permissible [McConnell, 1981]) to acquiesce.[26] Similarly when faced by a mugger, the prudent move may be compliance.

3.2 Morals

Succumbing to blackmail is decidedly imprudent. A new question confronts us: since contractarians believe morality is a subset of prudence (Gauthier 1991, 20), might the imprudent nature of succumbing to blackmail be sufficient grounds to deem it immoral? For example, when contractarians say, "Murder is wrong: so do not do it," they mean, at least from a state-of-nature standpoint, "Those who murder are likely to be set upon by the rest of us who do not like to be murdered: so, all things considered, it is not in your self-interest to do it, so do not do it." Only by viewing morality as a subset of prudence can contractarians offer a non-question-begging grounding for morality. If murder is immoral for being imprudent, and blackmail is imprudent, are contractarians not committed to say that blackmail is also immoral for being imprudent?

Paternalistic interests try to prevent people from being suckered into bad deals. If our society wants to be paternalistic, blackmail would be one of the forbidden exchanges, but so would playing the lottery be immoral, and smoking. Contractarians restrict moral concerns only to prudence connected with strategic social behaviours, rather than merely parametric (typically asocial) choices (Gauthier 1986, 21). When your decision options are the sole variables in a fixed environment, your choice is parametric. When your decision options involve interacting with others, you must take into account your expectations of how those others will respond, responses themselves largely based on their expectations of how you will respond. This makes your decision strategic. Apart from identifying the domain of morality within strategic prudence, moral advice concerns the status quo. Of the set of prudential strategic choices, contractarians call acts "immoral" only when the status quo is not a live option for one of the players. In the case of blackmail, blackmailees can remain at their status quo.

To demonstrate with a bit of game theory, we need first to clarify the preferences of the blackmailer and blackmailee. A typical blackmail case occurs when *A* (blackmailer) asks for a fee from *B* (blackmailee) to keep a secret from *C*. The blackmailee's preference to pay or not to pay will be largely influenced by the recognition that *A* can only guarantee that *A* does not reveal the secret to *C*. *A* cannot guarantee that C will never learn of the secret. Besides, since one person (*A*) already knows the secret, we cannot rule out the possibility that others know the secret. The secret being kept from C is, therefore, not something that *A* can guarantee. Moreover, even when *A* does keep the secret from C at time T_1, does *B* know that *A* will keep the secret from C at T_2? Will more money need to be paid

Table 6.1 | Ordinal ranking of blackmail

	Blackmailee's ranking		*Blackmailer's ranking*
1st	don't pay, secret kept	1st	get money, keep secret
2nd	don't pay, secret not kept	2nd	get money, not keep secret
3rd	pay, secret kept	3rd	no money, keep secret
4th	pay, secret not kept	4th	no money, not keep secret

for that promise? Given these worries, the blackmailee would prefer not paying and risk the secret being revealed to paying and have the secret kept (by the blackmailer). Concerning the preferences of the blackmailer, we assume divulging the secret is a cost to the blackmailer. Should the bluff be called, the benefit to the blackmailer is nil, and we assume a cost of divulging the secret, at least in effort and time. Barring the motive of revenge for non-payment, blackmailers would rather not divulge whether they get the money or not. Given these assumptions, we may rank the order of preferences for the blackmailer and blackmailee as depicted in table 6.1.

In this game, the status quo is the condition where the blackmailee does not pay while the secret is not kept. I base this on the fact that we are now in a situation where someone knows the secret, so to that extent, the plausibility of C knowing the secret is already positive with or without the blackmailer's intervention. In other words, the secret may get out whether the blackmailer exists or not.

If we reverse the ordinal ranking such that the first choice gets the most points, and calibrate the payoffs to zero for the status quo, we get the matrix shown in table 6.2.

Notice how the blackmailer cannot lose in this game.[27] The blackmailer's worst outcome is the status quo. Not so the blackmailee. The blackmailee can be made worse off than the blackmailee's current status quo. The status quo is a live option for the blackmailee,

Table 6.2 | Blackmail dilemma

		Blackmailer	
Blackmailee		Keep	Tell
	Pay	−1, 3	−2, 2
	Don't pay	1, 1	0, 0

however, and this is the important feature of the argument for why blackmail is morally permissible.

Consider the blackmailee's options: to pay or not to pay. Whether the secret is kept is out of the blackmailee's hands. If the blackmailer tells, the blackmailee does better not paying (0 > −2). If the blackmailer does not tell, the blackmailee does better not paying (1 > −1). So, no matter what the blackmailer does, the blackmailee ought not to pay. Since not paying is both the prudential choice and the status quo, we cannot call the blackmailer's offer immoral.

PART TWO

7

The Is-Ought Problem and Moral Dubbing

Ulysses needed to steer his ship between two very different but equally appalling monsters, Scylla and Charybdis. Similarly, any moral theory trying to derive moral principles from nature needs to steer between two appalling errors, begging the question and the is-ought problem. To beg the question is to defend our moral mandates by appeal to morality itself. To commit the is-ought problem is to move from factual states of nature alone to normative dictums of morality. We might say that burning cats is immoral because it is immoral to harm sentient creatures, but if we have nothing to back up our notion that it is wrong to harm sentient creatures other than an appeal to what morality demands, we have begged the question. To say, without further ado, that burning cats is immoral because cats feel pain is to commit the is-ought fallacy. The puzzle: to avoid the is-ought problem, begging the question seems inevitable. To avoid begging the question, the is-ought gap seems necessarily breached.

My goal here is to explain how to safely navigate between the two monsters, at least as safely as possible. Ulysses lost a few crew members. Similarly, we will lose a few pet notions of morality, specifically those parts of morality we think beyond the scope of mere prudence.

1 THE IS-OUGHT PROBLEM

The is-ought problem (or fact-value problem) claims we cannot move from ises (descriptive statements, or facts) to oughts (normative statements, or values). If any is-ought move is a fallacy, then all moral reductions are fallacies. A moral reduction occurs when we try to explain morality in terms of non-moral utterances. To explain morality in terms of moral utterances would be a case of begging the question. If we start from a completely amoral initial position (an is), we will forever be unable to get to a morality (an ought) without committing the is-ought gaffe. As David Hume says,

> In every system of morality, which I have hitherto met with, I have always remarked, that the author proceeds for some time in the ordinary way of reasoning, and … makes observations concerning human affairs; when of a sudden I am surprised to find, that instead of the usual copulations of propositions, is, and is not, I meet with no proposition that is not connected with an ought, or an ought not. This change is imperceptible; but is, however, of the last consequence. For as this ought, or ought not, expresses some new relation or affirmation, 'tis necessary that it should be observed and explained; and at the same time that a reason should be given, for what seems altogether inconceivable, how this new relation can be a deduction from others, which are entirely different from it. (Hume 1739, bk iii, pt i, sect i)

Sometimes the is-ought problem is confused with Moore's (1903, ch. 1, sect. 10) "naturalistic fallacy." The naturalistic fallacy occurs when one defines a non-natural property in terms of a natural property. It is true that if *A* is non-natural, it cannot be reduced to something natural. That is a subset of the general error of claiming one thing is like a totally different thing. Admitting that naturalistic fallacies are fallacies, however, does not mean moral reductions are naturalistic fallacies, since it has not been established that morality is non-natural (Frankena 1939; Geach 1956).

Moore also gives us a lesson about definitions. He thinks reductionists cannot distinguish ises of identity from ises of attribution (Moore 1903, ch. 1, sect. 12). Because of that, reductions fail the "open question test." Take the contractarian claim that a moral action is one which is strategically prudential. If this is a full reduction of morality, whenever we find the term "moral" in a proposition, we can replace it without loss of meaning with "strategically prudential," and most will find such translations non-equivalent. If they are non-equivalent, the translation has not been successful. The objection, however, relies on an agreed convention of the meaning of specific concepts. To complain that the conventional meaning is flawed will, by definition, fail Moore's open question test. Lightning does not mean electromagnetic energy. A bunch of functional brain states is not what we mean by mind. We do not mean by God a mere fiction.

The is-ought problem is not so easily dismissed. If the utterance, "You ought not to murder," is reduced to a bunch of non-moral ises, say *x*, *y*, and *z*, then, in reverse, the descriptive facts of the world, *x*, *y*, and *z*, magically give us an "ought." But no is can yield an ought. Values are what we project onto certain facts; they are not peeled off the facts. When we see Harman (1977, 6) burn a cat, all of the ises that we see do not add up to the value that we ascribe to the fact of Harman's burning a cat.

2 THREE OPTIONS

Three avenues to solve the is-ought gap are possible. 1. Happily insert a moral ought in the premises. 2. Deny that there is a gap, that we bridge ises and oughts routinely. 3. Bridge the is-ought gap by inserting a non-moral ought in the premises. Although an ought appears in a premise, it is a non-moral ought. Since it is a non-moral ought, the derivation, if successful, avoids any question begging.

2.1 *Beg the Question*

Moral oughts may appear in the premises in three ways: in the objective world itself, in the minds of moral agents, or in the sentiments of moral agents. Concerning the first, properly sensitive people will automatically recognize that certain value projections are merited by the facts of the case (Gibbard 1990; McDowell 1998; Wiggins 1987). The idea is not that from the facts, certain ought inferences are sound; rather values are in, or on, the facts themselves. Such a view is deemed a "realist" position, rather than, as D'Arms and Jacobson (2006) suggest, a conflation with projectivism.

The second appeals to intuitionism (Butler 1726). The idea here is that moral values are disseminated to us via an authoritative, presumably supernatural, source via a faculty we each have called intuition. A less godly approach is offered by Moore (1903), Gass (1957), and Huemer (2005). We all know that burning a cat is immoral and there is not anything more to it. To ask *why* it is immoral is to demand a premise more certain than that burning a cat is immoral: an impossible task, supposedly.

The third, Hume's (1739) solution to the is-ought problem, suggests that we are naturally endowed with various sentiments toward helping conspecifics, an idea taken up by Prinz (2011). Of interest, however, is why humans would have developed such sentiments, and also whether some of those internal sentiments may misfire. For example, we used to have negative sentiments toward homosexuality. Does that mean homosexuality is immoral, or is it that once we realized, despite our sentiments, that homosexuality is morally permissible, we then adjusted our sentiments to match our moral outlook? I suspect the latter. If so, the moral concepts have the ability of controlling moral sentiments, not the reverse.

2.2 *Routine Is-Ought Leaps*

Anscombe (1958, 124) gives an example of leaving a grocery store without paying for eggs. The clerk yells that the cost of eggs *is* \$3.25: therefore she *ought* to pay him \$3.25. Anscombe cannot hope to respond, "Sir, you are making an error of induction. Good day." According to Searle (1964), similar havoc would occur to baseball. The ball *has* touched the runner between bases: therefore the runner *ought* to be "out." Does it matter that the umpire has proceeded to the normative verdict of the player's being "out" solely on the description that the player was touched by the ball between bases? Surely not, for if we cannot go from an is to an ought, the umpire's verdict is useless. Since we take the umpire's verdict as not being useless, we can go from an is to an ought.

What the egg and baseball examples are intended to show is that we do routinely move from an is to an ought without further ado. In this sense, the is-ought problem is like Zeno's argument against motion. On paper it looks fine; in the real world it is defeated. But Searle and Anscombe are mistaken. Their cases presuppose conventional norms.

Conventional norms are a bit ambiguous. On the one hand, a conventional norm may be viewed as an is. "People around these here parts view abortion as immoral." On the other hand, a conventional norm may be understood as normative. "If you're in these here parts, don't have an abortion!" If you take the convention as purely descriptive, you cannot get to a moral ought without equivocating. If you take the convention as normative, you are not moving from an is to an ought, but an ought and an is to an ought. Take Anscombe's eggs. There is a market convention that you ought to pay the merchant her asking price if you want her wares. Given that convention, you ought to pay the merchant her asking price if you want her wares. Without this assumed ought, we cannot get to the conclusion. Consider the following is-ought manoeuvre:

P1. Poison ivy causes rashes.
C1. Therefore you ought not to touch poison ivy.

What is missing is:

P2. You ought not to touch things that cause rashes.

Hence, the derivation moves from an is and an ought enthymeme to an ought, and no one complains about that any more than moving from a universal and a particular to a particular.

Searle (1964) resists such an objection. For him, the appeal is to institutional norms that have within them two sorts of rules: constitutive and regulative ones. Constitutive rules define the game itself. "A bishop moves on the diagonal," is not merely a rule within chess, but a rule that partially constitutes chess. Moving the bishop laterally is a case of not playing chess. A regulative rule, on the other hand, is independent of the constitutive rules of the game but which help control play. A rule of etiquette at the dinner table is independent of eating, but helps make eating more enjoyable (Searle 1964, 55). To agree to play baseball, for example, is to agree to the constitutive rules about baseball, such as being out when touched by the ball in the right circumstance. Similarly, when we make a promise, we agree to be bound by the promise made, all things equal. That is, the rules governing promise making and baseball are constitutive rules. By entering the game (the is) you take on its rules (the ought). When our choice is between a rule of etiquette and a constitutive rule, morality seems more like the latter. If so, oughts are embedded in the institution, and to enter the arena is to take them on. A third type of rule is available, however, and morality is more like this third rule than Searle's constitutive rule.

Along with constitutive rules, we may distinguish two types of regulative rules, that between etiquette and that between prudence, or rules of counsel. In chess, the constitutive rules concern how to set up the pieces and how each piece moves and such. To violate constitutive rules is to no longer play chess. To follow the constitutive rules of chess is what it means to play chess. But playing chess and playing chess well are different things. Prudential rules are rules of counsel to help a player play chess well. These may be further divided into strategy ("Gain control of the four centre squares") and tactic ("Fork your opponents' pieces, when possible," "Don't move your queen out too early," and "Don't double up your pawns"). Good tactics help to achieve one's strategy. Poor tactics do not. Rules of etiquette, meanwhile, focus on behaviour outside the game itself. You are to say, "En guarde," for example, when you threaten the opponent's queen, and it is deemed impolite to distract your opponent with noises. General lifestyle advice may also be applied under etiquette, such as, "Don't be a sore loser." One can violate rules of etiquette and still play chess well, where "well" is defined in the prudential sense. When we define "well" in the etiquette sense, one can win yet play poorly.

Of course, rules of etiquette are themselves prudential to meta-games. Following rules of etiquette better enhances future prospect for more chess games. But if you fail to abide by the prudential rules of chess itself, i.e., lose all the time, the meta-benefit of future chess may not be motivating to you. Morality for evolutionary reductionists is a set of prudential rules governing interpersonal play, and in that sense, it is comparable to prudential rules of chess. In both cases, the contextual purpose of restraint is to reap overall, or long-term, personal advantage.

It is mutual advantage, not unilateral advantage, that is sought from moral rules, whereas the goal in chess is unilateral, not mutual, but this difference is unimportant to my comparison. Moral reductionists insist that the benefit from moral action has to be reduced to the benefit to the actor (not just the acted-upon), and *that* is what motivates the individual to be moral. That said, the purpose of morality is *not* specifically mutual benefit. The aim for mutual benefit is more of a tactic to assist one's overall strategy, a compromise individuals ought to be willing to accept in order to reap individual advantage. So, in the specific context, I offer mutual advantage as my goal. In chess, my goal is to beat you, and your goal is to beat me. If we did not each have these zero-sum goals, there would be no point to play. In context of the desire to play, however, mutual advantage has to be reaped. To get that mutual advantage, we each have to pursue a unilateral victory. With morality, things are reversed. To reap individual advantage, we each have to pursue mutual advantage.

Apart from that difference, morality, then, like prudential rules of chess, is a set of prudential rules of counsel to solve interpersonal conflicts within strategic co-operative interactions. They are prudential like the prudential rules of chess. That is, adhering to them increases the chances of overall success. In chess, you are more likely to win (or at least last longer) if you follow the prudential rules compared to not following the prudential rules. With morality, you are more likely to increase overall net utility if you follow the moral advice compared to not following the advice.

In both cases, exceptions to the rules exist. Someone might recognize that bringing the queen out early (against *this* player, for example) might enhance winning. Similarly, one might increase overall net utility by violating certain moral rules (in *this* situation). But even then, we would not likely imagine one can win at chess by violating *all* the prudential rules, or violating them in *all* circumstances, or against *all* players. Similarly, we cannot expect to increase our overall net utility by violating *all* the moral rules, nor violate them in *all* circumstances, nor against *all* agents. So this counts as a similarity.

My point is that morality is more like prudential rules of life than the constitutive rules of baseball and chess. If so, the move from an is to an ought is not yet explained. Searle leaves unanswered why we would accept the prudential rules of morality, like the rule, "You ought to live as peacefully with others as possible."

2.3 Non-Moral Oughts to Moral Oughts

The third option inserts a non-moral ought into the premises – typically what one rationally ought to do (Gauthier 1986). The command, "You ought to be moral," is predicated on, "You ought to be rational." If successful, we have avoided both monsters: we do not beg the question because we base our moral ought on a non-moral ought, and we avoid the is-ought problem because we rely on an ought in the premises: a prudential ought.

Smith (1994) makes a similar case. We can say giving to famine relief under suitable circumstances is the right thing to do (the normative utterance) when coupled with a second premise, "Giving to famine relief in circumstance C is the feature that we would want acts to have in circumstance C if we were fully rational" (Smith 1994, 191). That we ought to be fully rational is not a moral ought; merely a rational ought. The second premise relies on a special component: what is rational to want. If it were merely what we wanted, it would be an is statement. That it is what we *would* want *were* we rational embeds some oughts. But it is difficult to conceive how those oughts, specifically positive oughts, are *rational* oughts. It is difficult to support the claim that "we ought to want to give to famine relief" in purely rational terms. Something about its being the moral thing to do is what seems to be driving our ought to want to do it.

With negative rights claims, things are easier. We can rely on the non-moral normative claim that you ought not to like a knife in your back and thereby derive the moral imperative that you ought not to put a knife in someone else's back via suitable descriptive facts, including resource availability, what happens to the body when a knife is stuck into it, typical preferences and goals of people not to like harms to their bodies, and facts governing strategic interaction among human agents. This last bit captures the fact that people hate knives in their backs so much that they will retaliate against back-stabbers for their own protection. That is, my seeing Jones put a knife in Smith's back makes me wary of Jones. My wariness of Jones is not a moral concept – or need not be so called. If a boa constrictor eats a neighbouring baby, the boa constrictor is not immoral, but we will kill that boa constrictor nonetheless to protect our other babies. If that boa constrictor knew the outcome of its eating the baby, it might have acted differently. Similarly, we may say that potential stabbers ought to be aware of retaliation from others. While such retaliation may develop into a moral convention (and morals may do well to constrain the type and extent of retaliation), the expectation of retaliation is rooted in the bare fact that people will retaliate against actions that endanger them. The convention of warning would-be stabbers helps lessen stabbing: a benefit to us non-stabbers.

Is there a moral ought enthymeme lurking? Not obviously. The derivation rests on the normative claim, "You ought not to want a knife in your back," but that it has an "ought" should not by itself qualify it for being a *moral* ought. We may even deny it to be a normative claim at all. Rather it is a predictive or probabilistic claim.

When I say, "He ought to be in pain," after witnessing someone fall, I am not speaking normatively. I am making a prediction. Similarly, when I say, "People ought to not want a knife in their back," I am not making a noramitve claim, but a prediction based on evidence. True, it may be normative. Telling someone that they should not like a knife in their back may be a kind of corrective to their being so indifferent, but that would be rare. At any rate, a moral claim may follow: "Don't put knives in people's backs!" This cannot follow directly. That I do not want a knife in my back is not a reason on its own to not wish to put a knife in your back any more than my not wanting mushrooms on my plate is a reason to prevent mushrooms from being on your plate. But it can follow from the prediction that, since people do not like being stabbed, they will do what they can to retaliate against stabbers, so if you do not like being retaliated upon, avoid retaliation prods, such as stabbing. More needs to be put into the derivation, otherwise moral advice is to simply go with the crowd, but the root idea suffices.

A problem. While we may agree that no moral ought appears in the premises, we may now be dubious that any moral ought appears in the conclusion, either. Moore's open-question test re-emerges: "You've derived prudence, not morality!"

3 A FOURTH OPTION: MORAL DUBBING

Inserting prudential oughts in the premises seem to yield only prudential oughts in the conclusion. We had wanted to derive moral oughts. Consider the following argument:

P1. You do not like someone assaulting you.
P2. If you assault others, this increases the chances that you will be assaulted in return.
P3. The utility you derive from assaulting others does not outweigh the disutility of others assaulting you.
C. Therefore you ought not to assault others.

But for an ought to be in the conclusion, we need one in the premises. Hence:

P4. You ought to prefer higher utility than lower. Preferring more to less utility is part of what it means to be rational.

But the contractarian derivation is not really suggesting one *ought to be rational*. Rather, they assume it. And by assuming it, it is not the case that finding counter cases upsets their derivation. The assumption is a recognized limitation. If you are not rational, the rational reduction is not going to work for you. But that means "you ought to be rational" is not properly a normative claim: it, too, is a probabilistic claim. It means, chances are, you are the sort of person who *is* rational, where being rational means you prefer more utility to less, and, hence, prefer the action that secures greater net utility than less. Hence P4 can get converted to:

> P4'. You are probably one of those persons who prefer greater utility to less.

And this means we can convert the conclusion to

> C'. You are probably one of those persons who – all things considered – do not want to assault others.

C' is a descriptive statement, not a normative statement. We have gone from an is to an is, not even an is to a prudential ought.

Kraus (1993), among others, has raised half of this objection against Gauthier-like derivations. Starting from non-moral premises can only yield non-moral conclusions. The objection is correct. I do not think this ends the reductionist project, mind you. Rather than try to argue that moral conclusions really do fall out of the derivation, it is time to look closer at what people think they mean when they speak of moral utterances. Reductions must get rid of moral talk entirely such that a successful reduction is precisely one where someone says, "Hey, where did the moral talk go?" We have to stop treating that as an objection.

That some is-ought inferences can be made simply by removing the ought does not mean all is-ought inferences are valid; any more than noting that since some arguments are valid, all arguments are valid. "I have no coat, therefore you ought to give me one" is not likely to be an allowable inference, but its problem is not simply moving from ises to oughts: it is that there is no obvious connection to strategic prudence.

Differentiating prudential warnings from moral invocations can be handled simply in terms of interpersonal and intrapersonal matters. The injuction against touching poison ivy concerns yourself alone. That is, it is a rule applied to you whether you are alone or not. Injunctions against theft and assault, on the other hand, require another person (or their property). So in *that* sense, we can call the poison ivy rule prudential. If you touch it, it is only you who will suffer. Whereas with moral dictums, your doing the act causes harm (typically) to others. That is all that we need to differentiate moral oughts from non-moral oughts. The reductionist justification for non-moral oughts is that you probably will not like it. To the extent that you like it is the extent to which the argument does not apply to you. If moral oughts are a subset of prudential oughts, then this line of reasoning should apply as well. Hence the basic appeal to what will likely happen to *you* when you cause harm to others.

Gauthier (1986) tends to speak as if he has derived morality from prudence. Since "*X* is prudent," seems to be a different kind of thing from "*X* is moral," something else is required. This is the crux of the open question test. The solution is to speak more clearly. We ought to say, instead, "The thing we dub as moral is a subset of prudence."

Let *ought*^{P} refer to prudence. Let *ought*^{M} refer to moral advice. Gauthier avoids the is-ought problem by deriving ought^{M} from ought^{P}. That is, he derives an ought from an ought. The question, however, is whether ought^{M} is significantly different from ought^{P}. If yes, then Gauthier's reduction is flawed, for it would leave out the explanation for the shift in normativities. If no – that is, Gauthier believes normativity is normativity whether ought^{P} or ought^{M} – then his derivation of morality appears to be a case of equivocation. This is certainly the non-reductionists' charge. They conceive ought^{M} to be significantly different from ought^{P}, and so pointing out a reductionist derivation from ought^{P} to ought^{P} is hardly satisfactory to them. Even if morality is a subset of prudence, we still need something that distinguishes that subset. In other words, saying "*X* is prudent" does not equal "*X* is moral." Using a dictionary may be prudent, but not a moral imperative.

If we are to successfully reduce moral oughts, we mean that moral oughts fully belong to a subset of prudential oughts – the subset we dub "moral." Contractarian reductionism identifies the subset of morality in terms of prudence concerning strategic interaction (Gauthier 1986, 4–5; Rawls 1971, 16). Non-moral prudence concerns parametric choice. (Actually, morality will be a subset of prudence concerning strategic interaction. Advice on how to play chess well may be strategically prudent, but not moral.) This means that, before the dubbing, the two normativities, ought^{P} and ought^{M}, should be indistinguishable in kind. The difference between the two sets is purely contextual. If so, we do not actually have a distinction between prudent oughts (ought^{P}) and moral oughts (ought^{M}), other than contextually. We dub as "moral" that subset of prudential advice concerning long-term strategic interpersonal interaction. If "morality" is a mere dubbing of a subset of prudential advice, then moral advice is not anything above prudential advice. If moral advice is merely a subset of prudential advice, then saying we have moved from one kind of ought to another kind of ought is not accurate. If morality is a subset of rational prudence, then what is true of rational prudence must also be true of morality.

Non-reductionists will disagree. They assume a different picture. Consider two diagrams, figure 7.1 and figure 7.2 below. Both display how two sets, prudence and morality, intersect. In figure 7.1, morality and prudence partially overlap. Some bits of morality are prudent, and other bits of morality are not. In figure 7.2, the set of morality is entirely within the set of prudence.

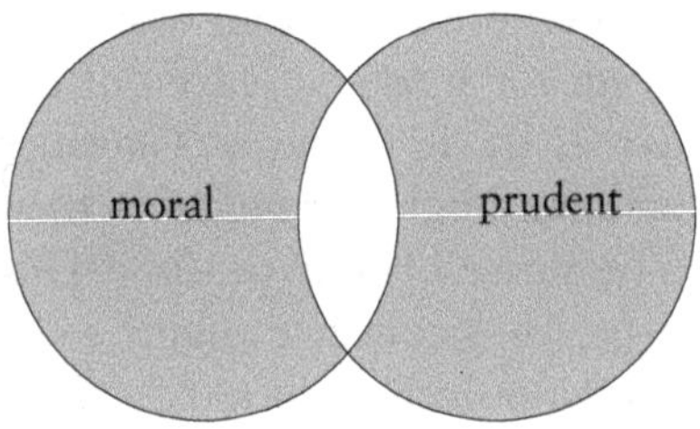

Figure 7.1
Partially overlapping subsets

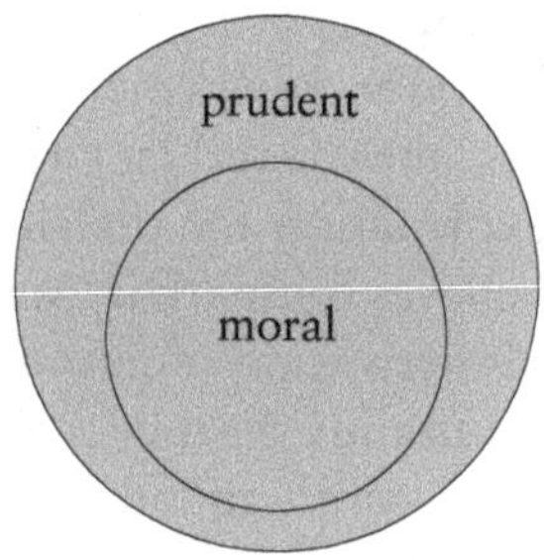

Figure 7.2
Embedded sets

While lots of prudential advice may not be moral, all moral advice will be prudential advice. Non-reductionists believe figure 7.1 captures the relation between prudence and morality. They think something of morality exists independently of self-interested, hypothetical prudence. Reductionists, such as contractarians, believe figure 7.2 captures the relation between morality and prudence. What is true of prudence will also be true of morality.

Those who believe figure 7.2 captures the relation between prudence and morality – i.e., that morality is fully embedded within prudence – if prudence has no special categorical force, morality will not either. This (seemingly) allows non-reductionists to complain that whatever derivation has occurred, it is not a derivation of moral normativity. The complaint is based on their belief that morality, "properly speaking," is some categorical property that cannot be reduced to mere rational prudence.

For illustration, we say an elm tree is a subset of trees. There are distinct features about elm trees that other types of trees lack, but since it is a subset of trees in general, we do not feel we are amiss to call an elm tree just a kind of tree. We think it would be weird to say, "No, an elm tree is *more* than just a kind of tree." In one sense, that is true, the sense that we have not, by such a statement, distinguished elm trees from other sorts of trees. In the other sense, it is a strange thing to say, for whatever we add to distinguish elm trees from other sorts of trees, it is still a tree, and nothing but a tree. When people speak of morality, however, they do not think it weird to say that morality is something more than prudential advice. They feel that we lose something when we say morality is just a kind of prudential advice. For them, morality is its own set, not a mere subset. While we can dismiss such talk, as we dismiss talk of deities, their complaint should force us to speak more clearly. When we say that we have moved from ought^{P} to ought^{M}, we mean it only *nominally*.

I am not saying we should get rid of moral language. Moral terms are useful, as with any delimiting terminology, soberly applied. Simply, reducing moral discourse to prudential statements is not problematic because there is no extra magic in moral statements compared with prudential statements to begin with. Moral talk is simply a subset of prudential advice, the subset that contends with social interactions.

SUMMARY

Moral normativity is simply a kind of prudential normativity (within strategic interactions), and that prudential normativity means no more than the tautology that one ought to endorse those actions that tend to do one well in the end given one's considered preferences. "Morality" concerns the sphere of constraining one's interactions with others in order to reciprocate others' co-operation. Prudential rules cover both interpersonal and intrapersonal relations, both strategic and parametric games, and both co-operative and non-cooperative games. Moral rules concern only strategic, interpersonal, co-operative games. In evolutionary terms, the ability to constrain such interactions is a phenotypic trait that confers advantage on its hosts compared with those who fail to have this trait. Given that, we can predict more agents having this trait over time, which further adds to the merit of any newcomer also having this moral trait.[1] The only normativity missing would be the metaphysically suspect kind.

4 LOST SAILORS

One of the sailors plucked off the contractarian ship of morals is categoricity.[2] Deriving moral oughts from prudential oughts depends too much on contingent facts, whereas morality is supposed to be non-contingent, or categorical.[3] If the ought in the conclusion does not have this categorical nature, it is not properly a moral ought: it is simply another non-moral ought. As Pritchard (1912) laments, a contractarian reduction will show only that we may *want* to be moral, not that we *ought* to be moral, whether we want to or not. That is, if we plug in a non-moral ought in the premises, we can claim another non-moral ought (a mere prudential ought) only in the conclusion. It misses the line of thought that you ought not to assault others *even if you would gain a net benefit.*

This subject is taken up more fully in the following chapter, but we may say four things in brief. First, I admit that if morality is categorical, necessary, and intrinsic, then the is-ought gap is unbridgeable. We cannot go from contingent oughts to necessary oughts. Admitting as much is not a defeat, since I deny the existence of categorical, necessary oughts. Consider, once again, the poison ivy case.

P1. Poison ivy causes rashes.
C1. Therefore, you ought not to touch poison ivy.

Certainly, we do not say, "You ought not to touch poison ivy *even if it didn't cause a rash.*" That would be odd. We would never deem the ought in the conclusion to be a categorical rather than a hypothetical, but it would not lose its motivational force for all that. So the first step in the argument is to recognize that hypothetical imperatives can be every bit as motivating as so-called categorical imperatives.

Second, consider counterfactuals. It is common to test moral principles and such by considering how we would react to counterfactuals. Torturing children for fun is immoral. But what if it were not? Is that even possible? Our failure to see how this could be possible (without being committed to moral nihilism), lends (or is often seen to lend) support to the claim that moral rules are transconventional, that they are real in some way independent of our thoughts, beliefs, interests, goals (Sayre-McCord 1992, 148). They are, in sum, categorical. But really no such inference is warranted. The counterfactual assumes the circumstances remain the same, while the rule changes. But reductionists are the ones who say the rules make sense *because* of the circumstances, not independent of the circumstances. So the counterfactual needs to show that altering *any* circumstance would leave unchanged our moral ascription about torturing children for fun. But this seems implausible. If it seems plausible, it is only when – via a Kantian sleight of hand – we define torture as *wrongful* infliction of pain. Then we might concede that torture would be always, exceptionlessly, categorically wrong. Nothing shows categoricity from this, however. All it shows is the tautology that wrong is wrong. Without such definitional trickery, appeal to categoricity fades. We are free to consider a case where torture was a kind of amusement to children. In such a case, torturing them for fun would be morally permitted. We would probably switch the term to "tickling." Similarly, stabbing people in the back is immoral not for its own sake, but because of the damage to the body. But if the body were so constituted that stabbing was a form of pleasure, then stabbing would not be so bad (though we would insist on consent). This highlights that when we say, "X is immoral," we are necessarily referring to something about the way the world is.

Third, we *can* understand categoricity within contingent boundaries (Foot 1972). If we lose a bet, we *must* pay. Simply, the agreement on that categorical commitment is not itself categorical. When playing chess, for example, you must categorically abide by the rule, "The bishop moves on the diagonal." While the first-order rule concerning bishop movement is categorical, we do not imagine a second-order proclamation about diagonal bishop movement is itself categorical. The *origin* of the categorical rule is not itself categorical; it is purely contingent, perhaps arbitrary. As with Mackie's (1977, 25–6) sheepdog contest: it is an objective fact which dog wins the contest by aptly fitting the objective facts to the standard (if the standard is distinct enough, like length of tail); but what standard we ought to settle on is not itself objective or categorical: it will vary according to our interests. Ditto with morality. Call it first-order objectivity to decide whether murder occurred; call it second-order objectivity that murder is wrong. Similarly, we can distinguish first-order categoricity when rules demand you not murder anyone, no matter your desires, from second-order categoricity that believes one ought never to murder no matter the social and environmental circumstances. Contractarians can accept first-order categoricity, but not second-order categoricity. Admittedly, when murder is approved, we would no longer call it murder.

Fourth, using categoricity as an argument against prudential (hypothetical) morality begs the question. To reduce morality to natural non-moral prudence is to admit that there may be circumstances in which it is more prudent to be immoral (or technically to do actions that for the rest of us would be deemed immoral), and this cannot be shown to be wrongheaded by stipulating that morality must be exceptionless for all for all time. That contractarianism fails to accommodate standard views of morality cannot be used as a critique any more than saying atheism is wrong since it leaves God out of the picture. At any rate, closer inspection of the concept will reveal that categoricity is indefensible and needs to be eradicated. That is the subject of the following chapter.

5 SUMMING UP

No one can bridge the is-ought gap. This is not a problem for contractarianism as we may have once believed. Contractarianism, as I conceive it, explains our moral language in terms of prudential advice concerning strategic interaction. This is shy of what many people think of as morality proper, missing, among other things, the notion of categoricity. While I have offered four hints as to why categoricity ought to be excised, a fuller account awaits us in chapter 8.

8

The Puzzle about Categoricity

When speaking morally, we want to say, "Don't torture people," not, "Don't torture people if you don't want to be cruel." If for whatever reason one prefers the latter way of speaking, we would be obliged to add, "Then don't want to be cruel!" That is, it is hard to understand how morality can be anything but categorical. The categoricity of morality precludes morality's being conditional on anything. It is not a fully moral utterance to say, "If *x* obtains, don't be cruel." Morality wants to demand, "Don't be cruel whether *x* obtains or not." For if ~*x* obtains, what then? Who but terrorists want to say the prohibitions against cruelty may be waived if the right conditions obtain, and then point out the existence of those conditions. To put it bluntly, those who maintain that morality is not properly speaking categorical are not merely misguided, but immoral. All fine sentiments, but for one problem: categoricity is nonsensical.

1 KANT'S CATEGORICAL IMPERATIVE

For Kant (1785), morality's being categorical means that our moral demands are unconditional, inescapable, non-arbitrary, not interest-based, and a priori. As he says,

> [A]ll imperatives command either hypothetically or categorically. The former respect the practical necessity of a possible action as a means for attaining something else that one wants (or may possibly want). The categorical imperative would be one which represented an action as objectively necessary in itself, without reference to another end … [I]f the action would be good merely as a means to something else, so is the imperative hypothetical. But if the action is represented as good in itself, and hence as

> necessary in a will which of itself conforms to reason as the principle of the will, then the imperative is categorical. (Ak. 414) … [The categorical imperative] is not concerned with the matter of the action and its intended result … let the consequences be what they may. (Ak. 416) … The reason for this is that whatever is necessary merely in order to attain some arbitrary purpose can be regarded as in itself contingent, and the precept can always be ignored once the purpose is abandoned. Contrariwise, an unconditional command does not leave free the will to choose the opposite at its own liking. Consequently, only such a command carries with it that necessity which is demanded from a law. (Ak. 420)

Any moral theory, like contractarianism, that supposes moral obedience benefits the moral agents themselves will appeal to merely *hypothetical* imperatives, imperatives that are conditional upon the interests of the moral actors, conditions which may not be in place. If morality is properly categorical, instrumental accounts of morality, such as contractarianism, are incorrect.

In response, two things may be said. 1. Categoricity flounders in senselessness. 2. A system of hypothetical imperatives can do all the work we need.

2 SENSELESSNESS

Each of the components of categoricity, its unconditionality, its inescapability, its non-arbitrariness, its disconnection to interests, and its being a priori, may be challenged.

2.1 Unconditionality

We like to think of love, at least true love, as being unconditional. If we can link morality with love, morality will be in good company. For anyone who has ever been, or is currently being, abused, however, this demand for unconditional love is clearly bad advice. Similarly with morality. Conditions always apply to morality, to love, to life itself.

The success of any evolutionary trait is always conditional. If situations change sufficiently, a currently successful trait may no longer be successful. If we conceive of morality as an evolutionary trait, we can expect that our moral traits are themselves something that has benefited our genes. Evolutionary morality is often misrepresented as thinking that certain moral content is biologically rooted – a clear example of an is-ought fallacy. Rather, the natural trait we identify as moral has nothing to do with content (or strict biology for that matter). The evolved trait has to do with a basic algorithm of reciprocating co-operation with co-operation and defection with defection.[1] If morality is an evolved trait, and all evolved traits are conditional upon the environment's remaining roughly the same as when that trait found success, then we conceive of morality as being conditional. Given the conditionality of morality, conditions based on circumstances in which one finds oneself, we can always conceive of altered circumstances such that the moral imperative that used to work will no longer work. That these circumstances might never apply in our world is irrelevant to our understanding moral dictums as hypothetical. No one who takes evolution seriously can fathom categoricity. Circumstances always matter for trait selection. If morality is an evolutionary trait along with our other adaptations, circumstances always matter to moral recommendation. To search for a non-conditional, interest-independent, categorical essence of morality reveals a flawed conception of nature.

Foot (1972) takes a different approach in her defence of a hypothetical over a categorical account of morality. She finds the unconditionality feature supposedly reserved for moral imperatives in the unlikely places of etiquette and club rules. Following her cue, we may say something similar with golf. The rules of golf are many and varied and complex and most golfers do not know even a small fraction of them, and even those rules that are known are not generally honoured by the average golfer.[2] For example, it is common that golfers adjust their lies, take gimmes, take mulligans, and ignore lost ball rules, not to mention their oblivion concerning golf etiquette ("Don't walk on someone's putting line," "Replace your divots"). Perhaps these rule violators do so for reasons that are internal to the game. For example, strict adherence to the rules slows play. More likely, however, is that the rules seem excessively penal for an already overly penal game. After all, one is supposed to be having fun. Take, for example, the rule not to ground one's club in a sand trap. We are allowed to ground our club elsewhere, that is we are allowed to let our club head rest on the ground before we strike the ball, but we are forbidden to do this in a sand trap. To ground one's club in a sand trap constitutes a rule violation and one is supposed to incur a one-shot penalty in stroke play, and a loss of hole in match play. Few seem to know about this rule, let alone care. What is worse, the rule applies even if you accidently grounded your club. Imagine if you stumbled getting into the sand trap where your ball lay, and your club fell out of your hands. The penalty is the same. Few recreational golfers know about this rule, and of those who do, few would penalize themselves for it. It was accidental, after all. But saying this is not to say that the rule about grounding one's club in a sand trap does not apply. The rule is explicit in stating it does apply. Rather, we say, we are not particularly moved to honour the rule.

Admitting that the rule about grounding one's club in a sand trap does not move us is not to say that the rule applies only so long as one is moved by it. The rule applies whether one is moved by it or not. That is the rule, after all. Once we admit this, we can admit that the grounding of the club in a sand-trap rule applies independently of one's interests, or one's desires, or the consequences. That you did not intend to ground the club, that it was an accident, is irrelevant to the application of the rule and the penalty. So long as we understand categorical imperatives to be imperatives that apply independently of one's interests, or one's desires, or the consequences, we can admit that the rules of golf are categorical. If morality is categorical in a way that rules of golf are categorical, some other feature of categoricity than being unconditional must be at issue.

2.2 *Escapability*

We may say that, in golf, it is wrong to ground one's club in a sand trap, or, in baseball, it is wrong for a runner who has been tagged between bases to refuse to go to the bench, or, in chess, it is wrong to move rooks diagonally and bishops horizontally, but in none of these cases do we say it is *categorically* wrong. Rather, we say is it wrong only within the confines of the particular game. The seeming categoricity of the rules are constitutive of the particular game or practice (Searle 1964, 55). Within that practice, the rules are categorical, but there is no second-order categorical rule stipulating one must engage in that practice. When I dust my chessboard, I may move my bishop horizontally, not diagonally. When I am on my way home from a trip to the store and a stray ball rolls up against my heel, I am still allowed to go home. When I am not playing golf, I can ground my club in sand traps all I want. Whereas morality is not supposed to have any such escape (Kant 1785, Ak. 420). While there are plenty of occasions of not playing chess, of not playing baseball, of not playing golf, there is not supposed to be any occasion where one is not playing the moral game. Morality applies always. Not only are moral rules categorical within the practice of morality, there is also supposed to be a second-order categorical rule stipulating you engage in that moral practice. We will excuse those who do not play golf; whereas we cannot excuse those who do not play the moral game. In that sense, no one is free from moral rules (Kant 1785, Ak 420), whereas few are bound by the rules of golf. With the rules of golf, one may elect to be bound by them (an implicit agreement, if you will, by teeing up the ball). With morality, there is no comparable option. In other words, moral rules are not like rules of golf. It adds nothing new to say of moral rules that they operate, "only so long as you're playing the moral game." There is no case of not playing the moral game.[3] But there are cases of not playing baseball, of not playing chess, of not playing golf. Morality is inescapable. Thus, the definition of categoricity must not be merely its non-predication on interests and consequences, but its inescapability.

The claim that morality is inescapable is overstated, however. Morality may not apply to us in three ways: what I call endo-moral shifts, exo-moral shifts, and, for lack of a better name, Williams shifts. As I discussed in chapter 4, *endo-moral shifts* occur when one feels authoritative enough to alter the rules of the moral game. For example, when conditions warrant, golfers may invoke the lift-clean-and-place rule, a rule that violates the play-the-ball-where-it-lies rule. That would be an endo-shift in golf. In the case of morality, we might say that the rule not to push people is no longer applicable when doing so is an act of saving the person from a falling anvil. With endo-moral shifts, morality as a whole still applies, simply specific moral rules may be waived. *Exo-moral shifts* are cases where morality itself no longer applies. Hume (1751, sec iii, pt i) offered five conditions where morality is absent. The value of charity, for example, applies only in a world of limited resources held unequally. In a world of pure abundance, the value of charity would be nil. Apart from utopias, dystopias can also make morality useless. Conditions may be so harsh that a basic ingredient for moral behaviour is missing. Under such conditions, morality has no value, its clutch on us is released. *Williams shifts* occur when we believe morality is merely one of a number of competing values for us, by no means a supreme value (Williams 1981a, 38). When morality demands of you to sacrifice some other value you deem more important, perhaps relationships, abiding by morality no longer takes precedence. As Williams (37) says, we are often grateful "that morality does not always prevail."

For illustration, imagine Heinz steals a drug to save his wife. We may say one of three things: (i) Heinz believed his action was immoral, but he had good reason to violate morality (a Williams shift), or (ii) given the circumstances, Heinz believed himself doing a moral action, all things considered (an endo-moral shift), or (iii) that given the circumstances in which Heinz found himself, morality no longer applied (an exo-moral shift). In each case, understanding morality as inescapable is rejected.

2.3 *Arbitrariness*

Categoricists may argue that morality has a different purpose than the conventions of baseball, chess, golf, social clubs, and etiquette.[4] For example, why is it the case that there are three strikes, but four balls? Why ought we incur a penalty merely for dropping one's club in a sand trap? If en passant is permissible, why can we not capture a rook traversing the knight's home square on a queen-side castle? How we answer these questions are different from how we answer similar questions concerning moral rules. In the case of baseball, golf, chess, and etiquette, we end up answering the questions by repeating that those are the rules.[5] That is, we can admit that the rules of baseball, golf, chess, clubs, and etiquette are fundamentally arbitrary without affecting our participation in those games. If the explanation for moral rules is likewise arbitrary, this would very much impede our adherence to morality.[6]

If the rules of golf or baseball are deemed fundamentally arbitrary, we are not typically bothered, since the reason for playing is found in the game as developed. Its historical making (perhaps interesting) is irrelevant. The game is enjoyed as it is, or it is not. If it is not enjoyed, we would not likely play it.[7] We do not care how the sport originated – we play because it is enjoyable to us now as it is. Nor would we seek a divorce merely on the grounds that the initial meeting of our spouse was an arbitrary fluke. To discover that a moral sanction is based on some arbitrary fluke, however, is a reason to remove the sanction. An exception may exist for moral norms offered as solutions to coordination problems. It may be arbitrary which side of the road you drive on, although not arbitrary that everyone drives in the same direction on the same side. In other words, it should strike us as problematic if we cannot justify the imposition of the moral rule beyond arbitrary whim, or an appeal to the tradition of doing-things-that-way-around-these-here-parts. Those defences, on the other hand, seem both permissible and routine for golf, baseball, chess, etiquette, and club rules. And that is the difference ... at least categoricists may argue.

Two worries with such thinking confront us. 1. Moral rules are not best understood as the pertinent rules of games and clubs. 2. Hypothetical rules are not arbitrary.

2.3.1 NOT PERTINENT

Following Searle (1964, 55), we can distinguish two types of rules: constitutive and regulative. Constitutive rules define the game, regulative rules regulate the playing of the game. To violate a constitutive rule is not to play the game anymore. Moving the golf ball to a preferred lie is to no longer play golf. Moving the bishop as a rook is to not play chess. A regulative rule, according to Searle, concerns "activities whose existence is independent of the rules" (Searle 1964, 55). He gives an example of how rules for polite dinner conversation, while independent of eating, help to regulate eating. The rule forbidding ladies into the club lounge (Foot 1972) is a constitutive rule, assuming the club is a men's only club. If the club permits women, except in the lounge, then it is a regulative rule. Not all rules, regulative or constitutive, are worth keeping. While calling etiquette a regulative rule is fine, we can certainly identify a different type of regulative rule: the rule of prudence. A prudential rule in chess, for example, will focus on how to play well. Gain control of the centre squares in chess is a prudential rule, neither a constitutive rule nor a rule of etiquette. A constitutive rule in chess concerns how to set up the pieces, and how each piece moves, and so forth. To violate constitutive rules is to no longer play chess. To satisfy all constitutive rules is what it means to play chess, but not necessarily what it means to play chess well. Prudential rules are guides to help the player play chess well. By "well" I do not mean morally or civilly, I mean in the sense of increasing one's chances of winning the game. Rules of etiquette, meanwhile, focus on how to play civilly, for example, not to be a sore loser. Rules of etiquette in golf are more varied. At any rate, one can violate rules of etiquette and still play chess well in the prudential sense. When we define "well" in the etiquette sense, one can win yet play poorly.

Searle's idea is that morality is more like constitutive rules than regulative rules. Certainly, when we make a promise we do under the confines of a promise-making institution in which keeping one's promise is constitutive of making a promise. But why would we wish to put ourselves under such constraints? One plausible answer (a contractarian answer) is that we do better in a world where we can bargain with one another in a co-operative fashion, but for bargains to occur, some promise-keeping constraints need be in place. As put, the explanation of this institution of promise keeping is prudential. To think of morality as a set of constitutive rules, on the other hand, is to think of morality as being itself the game. We get enjoyment from playing golf and chess, but few play morality for enjoyment.

2.3.2 NOT ARBITRARY

Morality for contractarians is a set of prudential rules governing interpersonal play, and in that sense, it is comparable to prudential rules found in games. In both cases, the contextual purpose of restraint is to reap overall, or long-term, personal advantage. But few think murder might have been allowed. The non-arbitrariness of morality that categoricists mean, then, is that moral rules could not have been otherwise, whereas rules of golf, etiquette, baseball, chess, clubs, and all social conventions clearly could have been otherwise. The queen may move like a rook or like a bishop, but never like a knight. It might have been the case, however, that the queen could also have been allowed to move like a knight, or like a knight or a rook, but never a bishop.

Categoricists may avail themselves of the Rawlsian-Scanlonian contractualist manoeuvre. For contractualists, any rational agent suitably situated with full knowledge would agree on (or select) the same moral rules. But no one can maintain that agents from a veil of ignorance, say, would come up with the rule about not grounding one's club in a sand trap. Thus contractualists, as would categoricists, must accept a real distinction between social conventions and moral rules, and that this distinction has something to do with the non-arbitrariness of morality. That agents are supposed to arrive at the same moral rules, the same principles of distributive justice, indicates that moral rules cannot be merely arbitrary, but must be a product of reason in some sense; a sense that the rules of golf, chess, and etiquette are not.

It is to no avail if we admit ideally rational agents suitably situated and with full knowledge would agree on a specific moral rule (like murder is wrong) in a way that we could never *ex ante* arrive at the same rules of golf or chess. It would not prove categoricity over hypotheticity. At least, it would not if the reason we would adopt one rule over another is to serve a particular interest that we happen to have, like keeping the peace, or living in a fair society. Such reasons are predicated on circumstances that themselves might not have been, but for the contingent circumstances in which humans find themselves.

If morality is instrumental, it is enjoyed, not for its own sake, but only, or primarily, for what it can get us. Let us say moral rules tend to get us *x*. *X* may stand for well-being, social utility, considered self-interest, or evolutionary fit. If we enjoy *x*, and morality does indeed serve *x*, then we have a reason to adhere to moral rules. To call instrumentally successful rules "arbitrary" on the grounds that the conditions in which such rules may have been otherwise is to confuse first-order arbitrariness with second-order arbitrariness.[8] A rule based on nothing is arbitrary in the first-order. A rule based on conditions that are themselves arbitrary is a second-order arbitrariness. Moral rules have use given the conditions in which we find ourselves. Call the conditions of nature arbitrary. They might have been different than they are, given the vagaries of natural selection. The second-order arbitrary conditions of nature do not carry over to decreeing that a morality based on those conditions is arbitrary in the first-order sense. Presumably, Kant's worry concerns first-order arbitrary rules, not second-order arbitrariness.

Prudential rules in chess and golf will not tend to be arbitrary. They tend to be based on experience. Abandon the rule about gaining control of the four centre squares in chess and see what happens. Similarly, we recognize the instrumental value of certain moral rules governing social interaction because following those rules tends to get us more of what we want out of our social interactions than by not following the rules. Our evidence is experiential. Given that the evidence is experiential, it cannot be correct to say it is merely arbitrary. Despite its non-arbitrariness, the prudential rules are purely hypothetical. They depend on our subjective interests and social circumstances. That one needs categoricity to combat arbitrariness is, thereby, false.

2.4 *Not Interest-Based*

What Kant was trying to get at is not hard to understand. When we say you ought not to ground your club in a sand trap, the ought does not carry much weight. Whether you ground your club does not matter to me. Such an indifferent attitude is not proper for moral oughts, however. When we say, "You ought not to torture children," the ought is supposed to matter to all of us. We tolerate non-compliance in mere prudential rules, not in moral rules. That moral rules matter more than mere prudential rules, however, does not make morality categorical. In fact, that they matter so much to us is precisely what undermines their categoricity. For Kant (1785, Ak 416), categoricity means that the normative force remains without agents' desires, and this is weird. The reason we will not tolerate your torturing children has everything to do with our desires concerning children. To remove your strong desire about x will make you more tolerant about non-compliance, not less so. If Kant merely wanted to distinguish non-moral prudent claims from moral claims, a less metaphysically suspect distinction is available. Namely, the subset of prudence we call moral involves advice concerning your actions that can adversely affect others. Advice concerning actions that affect yourself only, we call non-moral prudence. Non-compliance of golf rules in tournament play affects others: hence we will not tolerate non-compliance. Non-compliance of golf rules when golfing for fun does not affect others, and that is why we tolerate non-compliance. The rules against theft and murder, for example, are totally predicated on our interests not to be robbed or killed. To remove our interests in our possessions and our life is to remove the merit of rules protecting our possessions and our life. As put, we can distinguish between moral and non-moral advice without severing individual desire.

2.5 *A Priori Judgment*

For Kant, moral imperatives are derived by *a priori* reasoning. Club rules and game rules and rules of etiquette are not. And the suggestion that morality must be hypothetical since morality must be a product of natural selection is of no consequence if morality is a product of a priori reasoning instead. And certainly, a priori judgments can never be accused of arbitrariness. The attempt at demonstrating this surprising a priori feature of morality involves the supreme categorical imperative, *act only on that maxim by which you can will to be a universal law* (Kant 1785, Ak. 421).

The idea is to imagine a world where our maxim, that is to say, our planned action, can be universalized into a global rule for all to follow. Then we wonder whether we can perform that maxim in such a world. If yes, our maxim is moral; if no, our maxim is immoral. For example, because I covet your toaster, I plan to steal your toaster. Since I want to have your toaster but I also want to be moral, I ask myself what would happen if my current maxim was a universal law. So, I imagine a world where everyone would be permitted to steal toasters. Then I ask myself whether I could steal your toaster in a world where stealing toasters was permitted. If taking toasters is permitted, and we define stealing as taking without permission, I will discover the logical impossibility of my being able to satisfy my maxim of stealing your toaster if my maxim was universalized. Hence, I now see, by a priori means, the immorality of stealing your toaster. Such a derivation stands independently of the vicissitudes of natural selection, interests, or our contingent circumstances.

Two problems exist. First, the categorical imperative does not work to show that suicide is immoral, one of the examples that Kant gave to demonstrate the a priori method. My maxim is I will kill myself. Imagine a world that universally permits people to kill themselves. Can one kill oneself in such a world? The answer is "Yes, of course." Thus, by Kant's own standards, he should have said suicide was as moral as playing a piano. Some insist that suicide cannot be moral according to the categorical imperative because if *everyone* killed themselves, then you would not be here to kill yourself. Fair enough, but when we say playing the piano is permissible, we are not saying everyone must play the piano – only those who want to. We are not asking whether you could play the piano if everyone were playing the piano. The answer may be "No," assuming more people than pianos, or assuming people play piano rather than procreate, in which case you would not be here to contemplate your maxim of playing the piano. Rather, we ask, if everyone were *allowed* to play the piano – whether they do or not – would it be logically possible for us to play the piano, and the answer is "Yes, of course." We should give the same answer to suicide.

An objection: the contradiction comes from a specific maxim, which is not, as I put it, "I'm going to kill myself," but from the following: "[F]rom self-love I make as my principle to shorten my life when its continued duration threatens more evil than it promises satisfaction" (Kant 1785, Ak. 422). To derive suicide from self-love is contradictory, evidently. That it is contradictory is not obvious to me. It would be obvious if one's life is going swimmingly, but this is not the condition in which people contemplating suicide find themselves. Notice, also, the elasticity in maxims. This leads me to my second complaint.

Second, and more serious, the categorical imperative does not even satisfy the stealing example. In the theft case, we deemed our maxim to be, "I want to steal this toaster," or in general form, "I would like to be the kind of person who steals toasters." Is this the right maxim? Is it the *stealing* of the toaster that I want, or the toaster? If you offered to give me the toaster for free, would I decline, preferring to have a stolen toaster than a toaster? Or would I say, "Oh, thanks, now I don't have to steal it." Assuming the latter, then the maxim could just as easily have been, "I want to take this toaster," or "I make as my principle toaster taking whenever convenient." If that is my maxim, it now passes the categorical imperative. Imagine a world where it is universally permissible to take toasters. Is it logically possible for me to take a toaster in such a world? Yes. My taking the toaster is morally permissible. True, a world where toaster taking is the norm is a world where no one produces toasters and, thus, is a world where toasters will be unavailable for taking. If it is toasters I want, such a policy may backfire. The backfiring is a consequence that I would not like. I would have no interest in such a consequence. Such interest-related (i.e., hypothetical) consequences are supposed to be irrelevant to categorical imperatives, however. Should there be toasters in a world where toaster taking is permitted, I could logically take toasters in that world.

This shows that my taking your toaster without your permission is immoral under one maxim and moral under another maxim. What is the difference between maxims? The answer is that the first was morally loaded; not the second. We define "stealing" as a case of immoral taking. We define "murder" as a case of immoral killing. For every morally loaded maxim that fails the categorical test, one can change the maxim to a morally neutral depiction of the same event and find it will now pass the test. Can I murder? No. Can I kill? Yes. Can I steal? No. Can I take? Yes. All Kant has shown is that logic dictates that it is immoral to do immoral things. Noting this does not tell us what things are immoral. Nor does it show how moral imperatives are derived by a priori reasoning.

Outside of philosophy, Kant is better known for his formula: "Never treat people as means only; Always treat them as ends in themselves" (Kant 1785, Ak, 429). To treat people as a means is to use them as an instrument to your benefit. To treat people as ends in themselves is to respect them as autonomous beings with intrinsic worth. It is to respect their dignity. On the merit of people having this intrinsic quality, appropriate respect is mandated. Whatever this intrinsic quality that is supposed to reside in us all equally seems not to be an empirically supported notion. Dig inside cadavers and we find only the stuff they teach in anatomy class. We do not find along with intestines an intrinsic dignity. Saying this does not mean we should not respect people, or grant them some gratuitous notion of dignity. That is supposed to be the *outcome* of a moral theory, however, not a basic premise. We might think of something with intrinsic value as a thing that ought to be protected, but to protect something in such terms means to grant it – or conceive of it as having – a right. As put, then, Kant's argument amounts to saying we ought to be treated with moral respect because we are the sort of things that deserve moral respect: not an interesting argument.

A conception of hypothetical morals can agree with Kantian rules of respect, but not because of some question-begging moral mandate to do so. All we need do is recognize that, given people's autonomy, people will likely reciprocate the actions you do to them. This means that treating persons poorly will likely cause retaliation, something you wish to avoid, presumably. The advice to respect people follows from an instrumentalist account easily.

True, our respect for people is supposed to be genuine, not instrumental. But because our lives go better by respecting others as the default, we do well to internalize the disposition of respect and other such moral attitudes, to behave "as if" morality has intrinsic value and is categorical. Can such trickery do the job?

3 Can Hypothetical Imperatives Suffice?

I have made the case that morality cannot be categorical since categoricity, as claimed by Kant, is senseless. My next task is to make the case that a morality fully comprising hypothetical imperatives is not as hopeless as categoricists imagine.

When Mackie (1977, 25–6) dismisses moral objectivity, he clarifies that he dismisses only second-order objectivity, not first-order objectivity. We may objectively determine that a murder occurred (first-order objectivity), but not that murder is objectively wrong in some person-indifferent, grander sense (second-order objectivity). We can make the same distinction when speaking about categoricity. First-order categoricity seems well-supported. "Don't murder!" is a first-order mandate without exception. But to believe that the rule not to murder is exceptionless at the second-order is where we lose sense.

Among others, Joyce (2007) worries about the slippage that may occur if we focus on the distinction between first- and second-order categoricity. The fear is that we will lose the sense of obligation entirely. Although Joyce rejects the notion that morality can be categorical, he argues that categoricity cannot be jettisoned from moral talk. "Any system of values that leaves out categorical imperatives will lack the authority that we expect of morality, and any set of proscriptions failing to underwrite its authority simply does not count as a 'morality' at all" (Joyce 2007, 176–7). This seemingly contradictory position is resolved by his recommending we adopt (or conversely, we already do adopt) a "fictive" stance concerning morality. When we convince ourselves that we *must* do sit-ups, we know the "must" is not categorical: it is only hypothetical. (Conversely, we know the "must" is first-order only, not second-order). But we also know that should we allow ourselves to dwell on the hypotheticity of the "Must do sit-ups!" rule, we probably will not do sit-ups. The categoricity of morality, as is the categoricity of a self-imposed rule to do sit-ups, is both necessary and false.

The comparison backfires, I believe. When we think we must do sit-ups, we have a specific goal or two in mind, a stronger core, perhaps, and given that goal coupled with the belief that regular sit-ups can achieve that goal, we have a desire to do sit-ups. Given the antecedent (our goal), we have an imperative to do sit-ups. We cannot say, as Joyce seems to think, that if we ignore the antecedent, it will appear to us as categorical. That is trivially true. Moral utterances are the same. "I must not steal," may be an imperative conditional upon a line of reasoning that suggests how not stealing leads to better success in society on the grounds that, since people do not like being the targets of theft, they will retaliate against thieves. Assume also that the odds of getting caught are sufficiently high, the cost of being caught is sufficiently high, and the disvalue of such retaliation outweighs the value of the theft. When these conditions are met, the disincentive to become a thief suffices. It is not categorical. It is more of a statistical claim. Generally speaking, people do better by not stealing. There need be no lie about this.

Joyce demurs. When an error is found in a particular discourse, depending on the kind of error, one may either abandon the discourse entirely, like the discourse on witches and phlogiston, or modify the discourse to rid the error, like discourse on physics once we move from Euclidean to Einsteinian geometry. Joyce thinks ethical discourse is more like the former. The suggestion that we merely revise our theories of morality to accommodate hypotheticity, rather than accept an error theory about morality, would be akin to merely revising one's theories about witches once we remove the bit about supernatural powers. His point is that the bit about supernatural powers is the *essential* bit of witch discourse, and removing that is to remove witch discourse entirely (Joyce 2007, 96, 157). The same goes for morality: removing categoricity is to remove the *essential* bit of morality. There is nothing left to talk about once that is gone. If we do continue to talk about morality, we need to be clear about how our discussions are purely fictitious. We must do sit-ups. Murder is immoral.

The witch analogy is not apt. One can be in error about morality in less fundamental ways – even if the view held in error is deemed fundamental by those holding the erroneous view. Theists hold that God is fundamental to morality, but rejecting belief in God does not mean we must reject belief in morality. That those very theists would think so is not informative. The essential bit of morality is not categoricity, but the hypothetical value based on the evolutionary fit strategy of reciprocal co-operation. Remove its value, and you remove the impetus to being moral.

Joyce contends that "the actual world contains ... nothing to make moral discourse true. In such a world humans will still be disposed to make these judgements (most generally to believe that categorical requirements exist) ... for natural selection will make it so" (Joyce 2007, 193). Such thinking is amiss. An impala's speed has evolutionary fit for the impala because of the existence of certain predators in the impala's environment. We would not imagine the development of speed to that extent if there were no speedy predators. To say the development of speed would have come about (been useful) even if no fast predators existed in the impala's environment is to have a peculiar notion of evolutionary fit.

It is the usefulness of moral rules that makes the development of moral dispositions a successful trait. And the usefulness of them entails that they are not mere fiction. Rather, their use is predicated on something true about the environment in which moral agents live. Of course, our believing morality is useful does not mean that our beliefs about morality are true. That a conventional norm is founded on something true in the environment does not by itself prove the conventional norm itself is true. The norm may comprise unnecessary bits that piggy-back on mis-described useful bits. Malaria, for example, was first thought to be caused by bad air (*mal aria*) arising from decaying matter (Reiter 1999). The prevention for bad air was to shut the window. Shutting the window kept infected mosquitoes out, the real cause of malaria. So here the convention of shutting the window worked, but for reasons different than cultural beliefs. Despite the error, the success of the cultural phenotype of shutting the window was based on something true about the world. Likewise, many of our moral beliefs may be false – categoricity is a prime example – but it does not follow that the success of moral behaviour is due to our false beliefs, let alone due to a specific false belief – like our belief in categoricity. If the key element of a moral belief is its categoricity, I would agree with Joyce that moral beliefs *in toto* are false. Given the evolutionary benefit of moral action (and presumably the belief that generates that action), a better conclusion is to insist that moral judgments have been incorrectly identified as categorical.

For Joyce, the alternative to an error theory is to merely stipulate a hypothetical definition of morality. "[S]ince long-term selfish judgments turn out to favour cooperation, promise-keeping, etc., such judgments just are moral judgments (or, at least, such judgments are a proper subset of judgments of 'enlightened self-interest'). But this strategy unravels when we consider the instances where there can be no serious case made that an agent's ends are served by cooperation, coupled with the observation that moral discourse may still adamantly condemn him" (Joyce 2001, 222). In other words, Joyce is swayed by the ring of Gyges problem, the subject of the next chapter.

9

Ring of Gyges: Glaucon Meets Darwin

The ring of Gyges is a magical ring that can make you invisible. If you possessed such a ring, what would you do? According to Glaucon and Adeimantus, characters in Plato's *Republic*, only a fool would be moral if you can get away with immorality. Can we show that possessors of invisibility rings ought to remain moral?

While magic rings may seem too fantastical to interest us, the question highlights two opposing views of morality. We may conceive of morality as having primarily intrinsic worth or as having primarily instrumental worth. If the value of morality is instrumental only, we are moral for some other gain, typically conceived of in terms of long-term net self-interest. Since the goal is net interest, instrumental morality is a prudential good. Just as sometimes prudence demands we relinquish the pursuit of one type of interest for the satisfaction of another type, proponents of instrumental morality see moral constraint on individual interests as sometimes a beneficial compromise to further other interests the agent endorses. This is the view that the ring of Gyges challenges, for we can always come up with scenarios where instrumental benefit is best achieved by immorality. Anyone endorsing such pure instrumentalism "is a menace, an alien being in the midst of human society" (Verene 2010, 213).

My goal here is to defend the instrumental view, specifically contractarianism, against the ring of Gyges challenge. While I am not alone in the attempt, unlike other defenders I appeal to the evolution of morality. Demanding that one should be moral while armed with the ring of Gyges is like suggesting an adaptation for one environment ought to work in another environment.

1 HISTORICAL CONTEXT

In book 2, chapter 5 of the *Republic*, Glaucon, one of Plato's brothers, explains the going moral theory of Athens during Plato's life (428–348 BCE):

> What people say is that to do wrong is, in itself, a desirable thing; on the other hand, it is not at all desirable to suffer wrong, and the harm to the sufferer outweighs the advantage to the doer. Consequently, when men who have had a taste of both, those who have not the power to seize the advantage and escape the harm decide that they would be better off if they made a compact neither to do wrong nor to suffer it. Hence they began to make laws and covenants with one another; and whatever the law prescribed they called lawful and right. That is what right or justice is and how it came into existence; it stands half-way between the best thing of all – to do wrong with impunity – and the worst, which is to suffer wrong without the power to retaliate. So justice is accepted as a compromise, and valued, not as a good in itself, but for lack of power to do wrong. (Plato 1945, 357a–67e)

The account Glaucon offers is what we would today call contractarianism. It reappears in Epicurus's (342–270 BCE) *Principal Doctrines*:

> The justice which arises from nature is a pledge of mutual advantage to restrain men from harming one another and save them from being harmed ... Justice never is anything in itself, but in the dealings of men with one another in any place whatever and at any time it is a kind of compact not to harm or be harmed ... Injustice is not an evil in itself, but only as a consequence of the fear which attaches to the apprehension of being unable to escape those appointed to punish such actions ... In its general aspect justice is the same for all, for it is a kind of mutual advantage in the dealings of men with one another. (Epicurus 1993, ¶31–6)

After Epicurus, contractarianism seemed to have lain dormant for about two thousand years before it was reawakened by Hobbes in 1651. It strutted about for a bit, fell back asleep for three hundred and thirty-five more years until prodded awake once more by David Gauthier (1986).

For contractarians there is nothing in being moral itself that is good, at least primarily. Rather, the benefit comes to the moral agent in self-interested terms. For example, if there is a moral rule not to stab each other, the benefit to me in following that rule is the lowered chances of my being stabbed. The benefit to me is not in my not stabbing people. The benefit to me is in others not stabbing me. Since this same benefit applies to everyone, we can all benefit by mutual adherence to the rule of non-stabbing. Just as sometimes prudence demands we forgo the pursuit of one type of interest for the satisfaction of another type, proponents of instrumental morality see moral constraint on individual interests as sometimes a beneficial compromise to further other interests the agent endorses. We get moral restrictions on our self-interested behaviour based on our own self-interested ends without appealing to any suspicious metaphysical notion of a human-independent moral reality.

The problem Glaucon raises is that such instrumental accounts of morality miss something – the intrinsic value of morality. The ring of Gyges story shows the problem (Plato, 359d–61d). The story is that a Lydian shepherd found a skeleton, once belonging to Gyges, and on this skeleton a magical ring that, by turning its bezel, gave the ring wearer powers of invisibility. If you have such a ring, you can get away with stabbing and stealing because no one could ever know that you were the culprit. An instrumental morality based in prudence cannot explain why you ought not to steal and stab when you can get away with it. On the instrumentalist view, it is not prudent to stab or steal, since people retaliate when harm is done to them or to those in their group. But who can retaliate against you when no one can possibly know it was you who did the deed? Meanwhile, while you are visible, you can enjoy a fine moral reputation and social life. You have the best of both worlds. In such a case, it would not be instrumentally prudent to give up your duplicitous ways. A theory that tells you morality has merely instrumental benefit – a subset of prudence – cannot call your secret stabbing immoral. Since any moral theory ought to call stabbing – secret or not – immoral, morality cannot be a subset of mere prudence; morality cannot be based solely in instrumental benefit.[1]

Adeimantus, another brother of Plato, adds that the benefits of justice concern only repute, honours, and gifts; and the costs of injustice (punishment) occur only if caught (Plato, 367e). This parallels Glaucon's contrast of two people: one absolutely just but taken by everyone for all time as absolutely unjust, and the other absolutely unjust but taken by everyone for all time as absolutely just (361a–d). Taylor (2000, 88) adds that being taken as unjust would, presumably, entail being tossed into a damp, rat-infested prison and then hanged. Between the two, it is difficult to say the truly just person is happier. The intrinsic value of being good for its own sake would have to be powerful, if such a thing even exists, for us to think the truly good person is better off in this comparison.

The ring of Gyges worry for instrumental morality was not unknown when Hobbes resurrected contractarianism. Even if prudence overlaps with morality generally, we can always find some circumstance where morality and prudence drift apart and the rational agent ought to jump on such opportunities. Hobbes called such opportunists, "Fooles." "The Foole hath sayd in his heart, there is no such thing as Justice; and sometimes also with his tongue; seriously alleging, that every mans conservation, and contentment, being committed to his own care, there could be no reason, why every man might not do what he thought conduced thereunto: and therefore also to make, or not to make: keep or not to keep Covenants, was not against Reason, when it conduced to ones benefit" (Hobbes 1651, ch. 15).

2 RATIONAL DEFENCES

If morality were purely instrumental, as contractarians consider it, we face the ring of Gyges challenge: to show that x is wrong even when an x-er can satisfy her long-term self-interest by x-ing. Beals (1952) suggests that Glaucon and Adeimantus's position is self-defeating. His focus narrows on Adeimantus's claim that people praise the repute being just brings; they do not praise being just itself (Plato, 363a). As put, the instrumental value is found in maintaining merely the appearance of being just, as opposed to actually being just (Plato, 367b). Beals is astounded, for surely we would not praise the appearance of justice over real justice any more than we would praise fake diamonds over real diamonds (Beals 1952, 609). We ascribe value to real diamonds, not to sham diamonds, and the distinction is made clear when found out. Fair enough, but it hardly renders the challenge to instrumentalism self-defeating. The value

I give to *your* being just is a different kind of thing to the value I give to *my* being just. Since your being moral benefits me, whereas your sham morality does not, my praising your morality can be purely instrumental to me.

Another approach is to highlight the implausibility of having the ring of Gyges. Picking up on a line by Glaucon, that with the ring of Gyges, the Lydian shepherd becomes "equal to a god among humans" (Plato, 360c), Gauthier correctly asserts that morality is for humans, not for gods (Gauthier 1990, 147–8), an echo of Hume (1751, sect iii, pt i). Outside the conditions for morality, morality will of course not apply. If the odds are so low of any one of us being in the perfect situation to get away with murder and theft, while the risks so great, and obedience to morals as a general rule has adequate gains, counterfactual worries about invisibility are idle. For this reason, Gauthier (1990) distinguishes Lydian shepherds from Fooles. He thought the Foole challenged Hobbes's third law of nature: to keep your agreements made, whereas the Lydian shepherd, being god-like, lies outside the circumstances of justice and therefore challenges Hobbes's first and second laws: seek peace, and lay down your liberty (Gauthier 1990, 147). Humans may have a reason to do so, but not gods.

But being invisible (metaphorically speaking) need not be a trick restricted to gods.[2] Invisibility ought not to be taken literally. Nor ought it to be taken too narrowly. Being invisible would not make me inaudible. An invisible burglar may still knock plant stands over. Nor does being invisible mean leaving no trace. That you did not see me creep into your house and take your heirloom jewellery would not erase suspicion of me as the culprit if you find your missing heirloom jewellery on my dresser. A god need not worry about such stuff; the Lydian shepherd does. Moreover, humans regularly come across situations where their being immoral would not be found out. You lose your wallet in a mall. Someone who finds it can turn it in or keep it – both anonymously. The ring of Gyges is meant to illustrate only that should it be possible to kill and steal without society's ever knowing about it, the contractarian view, based solely in prudence as it is, not only cannot condemn it – it encourages you to do so!

Epicurus offered the following response: "It is not possible for one who acts in secret contravention of the terms of the compact not to harm or be harmed, to be confident that he will escape detection, even if at present he escapes a thousand times" (Epicurus, ¶35).

Hobbes's answer to the Foole is much like Epicurus's. Getting away with immorality once is not the same as getting away with immorality generally, and once caught, the cost will be greater than the derived benefit. The Foole, Hobbes says, "cannot be received into society, that unite themselves by Peace and Defence, but by the errour of them that receive him; nor where he is received, be retayned in it, without seeing the danger of their errour; which errours a man cannot reasonably reckon upon as the means of his security" (Hobbes 1651, ch. 15). In our language, reputation catches up with people, and the short-term gain from defection comes at a long-term cost from no one playing with you in future. This response obviously fails. Lydian shepherds are not abandoning morality wholesale: only the need to be moral in every situation, particularly those situations where being immoral pays without long-term cost. According to Hobbes, the Foole "does not therein deny, that there be covenants; and that they are sometimes broken, sometimes kept; and that such breach of them may be called Injustice, and the observance of them Justice; but he questioneth, whether Injustice ... may not sometimes stand with that Reason, that dictate to every man his own good" (Hobbes 1651, ch. 15).

Let us, then, distinguish Fooles from fools. A *Foole* is one who correctly believes to be in a situation where defection pays more than co-operation, such as having an invisible ring. By contrast, a *fool* is one who incorrectly believes to be in a situation where defection pays more than co-operation. To say that morality generally pays is relevant to fools, but it is irrelevant to the Foole, since the Foole is not presently in the circumstance in which morality pays. With the ring of Gyges, Fooles are such gifted deceivers that other players continually mistake them for being reciprocal co-operators. In such cases, defection is rationally preferable to reciprocal co-operation. Noting that such cases are rare does not undermine this fact. Having an invisible ring is a rare gift, and allows the Foole to say, "Look, against probability, I happen to be in the circumstance where defection will pay me more than reciprocal co-operation will pay me." Similarly, Hume's knave admits that morality is a good rule, but "liable to many exceptions," and the wise man avails himself of such exceptions (Hume 1751, sect ix, pt ii).

Of course, whether you are a Foole or a fool may be hard to tell. Being invisible and thinking yourself invisible are different things. Prisons are full of fools who thought themselves Fooles. However

Table 9.1 | Prisoner's dilemma

	Co-operate	*Defect*
Co-operate	1,1	−1,2
Defect	2,−1	0,0

sobering this lesson is for the most of us, the ring of Gyges problem presupposes the Foole is really a Foole, and not a fool. Hobbes's answer applies only to fools, not Fooles.

Gauthier (1986) is committed to finding a response to the ring of Gyges challenge since he makes a very bold claim: "To choose rationally, one must choose morally" (4). To make good such boldness, Gauthier offers a friendly amendment to Hobbes's reply, one that endorses the adoption of a co-operative heuristic. The discourse is well illustrated by the Prisoner's dilemma (PD).

In table 9.1, the numbers on the left of the comma represent Row's preference utilities; the number on the right of the comma represents Column's utilities. Given the reverse ordinal ranking (calibrated to zero to represent an agent's status quo),[3] we deem a higher number more preferable to a lower number. Utilities match ordinal preference ranking, and preferences are subjective. Notice two things about the PD. First, we can see that mutual co-operation is better for both parties than the status quo (1,1 instead of 0,0). The second thing to note is that, despite the first observation, no straightforwardly rational individual will co-operate. This is easy to see. If the other co-operates, you would do better defecting (2 instead of 1), and if the other defects, you would do better defecting (0 instead of −1). Thus, no matter what the other does, you should defect. The other agent, meanwhile, will come up with the same reasoning, and so will defect. Thus, despite mutual recognition of the benefit from co-operation, rationality dictates defection. Call this the compliance problem.

Hobbes's solution was to invoke a Sovereign to wave a sword above our heads (Hobbes 1651, ch. 17). Gauthier offered an internal solution to the compliance problem that stems from recognizing a difference between pure and mixed strategies. In a world with pure strategies of unconditionally co-operate (UC) and unconditionally defect (UD), UDs will annihilate UCs. Being a UD is rational; being a

Table 9.2 | Pure strategy payoff

	Unconditionally co-operate	*Unconditionally defect*	*Avg.*
Unconditionally co-operate	1	−1	0
Unconditionally defect	2	0	1

UC is not. Given the payoffs depicted in the PD game (table 9.1), we get results shown in table 9.2.

In table 9.2, the utilities shown in the boxes represent Row's score when played against Column. Since UD is the clear winner here, no UD will be motivated to shift strategies to UC. To change yourself to co-operate in a PD would be irrational, assuming the change is to UC. A third, mixed strategy is available, however, one that is conditional, not pure. Such conditionality is consistent with the riders Hobbes attached to his first three Laws of Nature: "[E]very man ought to endeavour peace as far as he has hope of obtaining it, and, when he cannot obtain it, that he may seek and use all helps and advantages of war" (Hobbes 1651, ch. 14). Given the conditionality evident in Hobbes, Gauthier makes the case that Hobbes offered a mixed strategy – one that co-operates with co-operators yet defects with defectors. We may call such a disposition a Reciprocal Co-operator (RC).[4] Any player using the RC strategy will do at least as well as any UD, and better if more RCs join the party. Table 9.3 depicts the tournament scoring of an RC against a UD.

RC is now a Nash Equilibrium, named after John Nash (1950), where no unilateral movement from the lower right box will pay the unilateral mover.[5] By shifting our focus from what to do in any given situation to what strategy to adopt, co-operators can move from the status quo (0,0) to a mutually beneficial result (1,1). We do better, self-interestedly understood, being moral. What rationality demands under strategic interaction is to constrain oneself from straightforward rationality. Doing so offers the best means to our subjective ends in strategic choice scenarios: hence rational.

Table 9.3 | Birth of reciprocal co-operation

	Unconditionally co-operate	*Reciprocally co-operate*
Unconditionally co-operate	0,0	0,0
Unconditionally co-operate	0,0	1,1

That conditional strategies win in PD tournaments over pure strategies is not questioned (Axelrod 1994, Binmore 1998, Skyrms 1996, Trivers 1971). Becoming an RC, then, seems to be prudent advice to the extent that, should you be able to be an RC among other RCs, you will do better than had you adopted any pure strategy (UD or UC). Saying this is not yet saying that the RC strategy is rational, however, nor whether it is rational to adopt the RC disposition. As Binmore (1998, 27) reminds us, if mutual co-operation pays more in PDs, we are no longer describing a PD. What he means is clear. If RC can be shown to be rational only when we alter our meaning of rationality, then this is a confession that rationality is not what we would normally ascribe to RC.

Let me summarize my worry so far. Gauthier (1986) shows us how reciprocally co-operate (RC) strategies do better than strategies that do not conditionally co-operate. If so, is it rational for someone to adopt – in case they have not adopted it yet – a disposition to reciprocally co-operate? Gauthier's answer: Yes, of course, since the conditionally co-operative strategy does better than other strategies. This answer is no good, however, since the claim about reciprocal co-operators doing better is a statistical claim, not a deductive claim. The possibility is not ruled out that someone sometimes can do better by cheating, especially when wearing the ring of Gyges. Since rationality is defined, per usual, as a tool to maximize utility in strategic circumstances, it cannot be rational to forgo such opportunities when they arise.

Can it be rational to prevent yourself from cheating in cheatable circumstances? A cheatable circumstance is one in which an agent may successfully cheat without repercussion. You are certainly rational to prevent yourself from cheating in non-cheatable circumstances, assuming retaliation, but that does not answer whether it is rational to prevent yourself from cheating in cheatable circumstances. True, it is not nice to cheat, but we are wondering whether being nice in cheatable circumstances is rational.

A caveat. Let us say that fully rational people would cheat in cheatable circumstances. Let us also assume that, in general, we can do better co-operating with others. Then it would be rational for us to try to limit cheatable circumstances from occurring. If successful, the worry about whether it would be rational to cheat in cheatable circumstances becomes moot. Yes, obviously we should cheat whenever we can get away with it, we might say, but precisely for that reason we actively prevent circumstances where people can get away with cheating. If so, we would still not be able to say it is rational to prevent yourself from cheating, but we can say it is rational to prevent cheaters as much as we can. The end effect – the prudence of being moral – remains roughly the same (Murray 2007).

The above aside, Gauthier's point is this: by shifting our focus from what to do in any given situation to what strategy to adopt, we can show why reciprocal co-operation is better than unconditional defection. Assuming RC counts as the moral strategy,[6] we find that we do better, self-interestedly understood, being moral. To constrain ourselves to become RCs is to adopt a heuristic of co-operating when others co-operate and defecting when others defect. Once we take on this heuristic, however, we will have to accept that our heuristic will kick in even when, on those rare occasions, defecting against co-operators would technically pay more in terms of self-interest, such as when one happens to be invisible. Since the overall benefit of being an RC outweighs these small lost opportunities, and the benefit of being a Foole is offset when we mistakenly think we are invisible when we are not, being an RC still pays more in the long run than being a Foole.

Gauthier's argument is akin to recognizing that buying a lottery ticket is generally a bad idea even though the advertisements of happy winners tempt us to think otherwise. That is, those who adopt the heuristic of NEVER-BUY do better in terms of expected utility than those who adopt the heuristic of SOMETIMES-BUY, despite our finding lucky people who did better buying.

Alas, Gauthier's answer is no better than Hobbes's. Agreeing with Gauthier that a conditional strategy pays more than unconditional strategies is harmless. Conditional strategies vary widely. With the magic ring, the Lydian shepherd can adopt a more sensitive disposition than Gauthier's RC. Rather than co-operating with other co-operators, and defecting with other defectors, why not co-operate with other co-operators when defection will cost in the long run, but not otherwise?[7] To say, "Ah, but you'll likely make mistakes that will cost you more than the benefits," is a fine reply to us normal people, us fools prone to make mistakes, but not for those special agents who really do have the capacity to get away with murder and thievery, at least when they have the ring of Gyges (metaphorically speaking).

To return to the lottery example, SOMETIMES-BUY is ambiguous. If when to buy is determined randomly or based on gut feelings, we cannot recommend it. If when to buy is fixed on when the expected utility of a lottery is positive, then SOMETIMES-BUY will do better than NEVER-BUY. Similarly with the moral game. We cannot say that rationality forbids defection, period. It forbids defection when the expected utility is lower for defection than for co-operation, but not when the expected utility is higher for defection than for co-operation. The Foole claims (assume a Foole, not a fool) to be able to recognize the difference. As such, the Foole wishes to keep a more flexible strategy, a more sensitive heuristic. Fooles do not wish to be overly bound to a blunt strategy that would, on occasion, commit them to less than utility maximization. Just as some lotteries might have positive expected utilities, some strategic interactions with a co-operator may rationally demand defection.

Although we may agree that there can be no sociability without morality, and being sociable is still of value to possessors of magical rings, aka Fooles, nothing prevents the prospect of some clever agents exploiting others *and* being received into society. Rational instrumentalism cannot rule this out. Socrates and Aristotle, thereby, provide an alternative reply to Glaucon and Adeimantus's puzzle, one espousing the intrinsic value of being moral.

3 INTRINSICALITY

The ring of Gyges problem is deemed so damaging to instrumentalism that an intrinsic conception of morality is thought to be our only alternative. Imagine for a moment that you love your mother. Being in love with your mother is a good thing in itself; it has intrinsic value. Should you find a ring of Gyges, you can now cheat and lie and steal from your mother and she would never know. Would you do so? The question, I assume, ought to sound appalling. No, you would say, I love her. Whether invisible or not you would not harm someone you love. As put, then, it is incorrect to say that all rational people would be immoral in any situation simply because they are invisible.

Socrates and Aristotle need to say more, of course, for exploiters might agree not to exploit their loved ones while happily exploiting others. Love is just one example of an intrinsic value, however. Being content with what one has is another kind of virtue that has intrinsic value. Being greedy or covetous or jealous are all kinds of character traits that make one worse off in general, even though they may be what motivates exploitation of others. Whether visible or not, it is often only through warped character traits like greed and covetousness that we are propelled to exploit others for our gain. But the gain in objects comes at the loss of a more serene life. As Lily Tomlin explained,[8] the trouble with the rat race is that even if you win, you're still a rat.

Socrates reminds us that instrumental value is useless unless it ultimately ends in some intrinsic value (Plato, 358a). If being moral has intrinsic worth itself, wearing the ring of Gyges is irrelevant. This is the gist of Plato and Aristotle's answer to Glaucon and Adeimantus. Intrinsic value is ambiguous, however; in fact, doubly so. We may think of intrinsicality subjectively or objectively, and each of those concepts has at least two distinct meanings.

If the value is subjective, the focus is on the feeling one gets when behaving morally. Subjective intrinsicality may be further demarcated. If subjective, an intrinsic value may be understood either phenomenally or in terms of overall well-being. The phenomenal value of drinking beer is one thing; the overall value of drinking beer another. Phenomenal intrinsicality may be felt in terms of guilt for being bad and a kind of blessedness for being good. These phenomenal states coincide with moral or immoral actions the way we may experience certain phenomenal intrinsic states when looking at art. The intrinsic value of art is immediately felt at the time of looking at or thinking of art. Similarly, with a phenomenal sense of thinking, moral action has intrinsic value. We feel good for doing good acts; we feel bad for doing bad acts, and these intrinsic phenomena outweigh (or are supposed to outweigh) any instrumental value. In terms of thinking that morality has intrinsic value in the overall well-being sense, when we behave morally, the benefit to us is in being that kind of person, having that kind of disposition, not for what it gets us, not even in any phenomenal sense. The subjective well-being sense of intrinsic value of being moral is understood in the lifelong sense of human flourishing. We see this sense at play in Plato's cumbersome analogy of a psychologically well-balanced human. Such a person will always be ruled by reason, never passion or appetite (Plato, 441e). Psychologically unhealthy individuals will let passion or appetite rule reason and, thereby, find it seemingly worthwhile to steal and murder if they can get away with it. That they can get away with it when invisible does not undermine the fact (if it is one) that they are still psychologically unhealthy. Psychological well-being is not impacted by invisibility (Jacquette 2001).

If the intrinsic value is objective, the value of the act is independent of our inner states and any contingencies of human life. The thing or act is good in itself, not for what it does to anyone. Objective intrinsicality may be further demarcated into natural and supernatural senses. If natural, the intrinsic value resides in the act or thing itself purely in natural terms. The natural constitution of diamonds (combined, perhaps, with the constitution of our sensibilities) makes diamonds pretty, for example, and the natural acts of charity make charity intrinsically good. The natural objective sense places the intrinsic moral value in the act or in the world itself, not, or at least not solely, in the actor's interests or phenomenal states.[9] If supernatural, it is less about the natural constitution of the act or thing than that a god has so decreed the thing or act to be good (or bad) in itself.[10]

One difference between the objective intrinsic sense and the instrumental sense of morality is whether we discover morality in the world or invent it. For objectivists, rights come before duties. Of course, no duties can be understood without rights, and vice versa, but which is recognized first varies between instrumentalists and objectivists. Objectivists recognize rights of others or things in the world, and upon recognizing that right, they recognize their duty to uphold that right. Not so with instrumentalists. If instrumentalists are considering whether something has a right, they look to see how costly the duty is for them to take on. There is no right without its antecedent duty, and duties cost the duty holders. Instrumentalists see what reciprocal duties are prudentially worth taking on, then ascribe rights accordingly. In this sense, you have no intrinsic right not to be harmed. Rather, you and I see that we each would do better in our lives if we each took on the reciprocal duty not to harm each other. Our agreement on this is what accords us our rights. For objective intrinsicalists, rights come first. On the basis of recognizing rights in the world, we adopt our duties. For objective intrinsicalists, duties of non-harm have nothing to do with the benefit accrued to the duty holder; they are due to the fact that a person has intrinsic value that demands respect. For instrumentalists, on the other hand, our duty not to stab people has nothing to do with a supposed intrinsic value that people have. It has only (and everything) to do with how they and their confederates tend to retaliate should they discover whom to blame.

While the well-being sense of the subjective intrinsic nature of morality fits Socrates's and Aristotle's answer (virtue theory) best, the phenomenal and natural objective senses make their appearances with them as well. Nothing is problematic about that, necessarily. The different senses are not mutually exclusive. The viewing of a sunset may be phenomenally intrinsic, its aesthetic contemplation conducive to or constitutive of our well-being, and the beauty of a sunset may have objective value in itself. The problem is that ascribing to morality any of these intrinsic senses is untenable.

Consider the intrinsic phenomenal experience of your not murdering anyone last week. I assume you cannot ascribe any intrinsic sense to that at all. Nevertheless, not murdering anyone last week was a distinctly moral act. Good for you! True, we can imagine the guilt that would wrack our lives if we had murdered someone. This may itself undermine any desire I have to murder. Such a correlation between phenomenon and external wrongness does not tell us anything, however. Presumably, we feel the guilt for murdering because we recognize murder is wrong. As put, the wrongness determines the guilt, not the guilt the wrongness. Even if some of us might feel a subjective intrinsic goodness for being charitable, say, it cannot be that we think charity is good *because* we feel good when being charitable. How good we feel doing an act cannot determine its morality. After all, many people feel good for doing horrendous acts, scalping Mi'kmaq, for example. We wish righteous scalpers did not feel so good. Much of the harm humans have caused humans come from self-righteous people who believe they lead virtuous lives. For instrumentalists, we are supposed to feel good for doing the right thing, not call "right" whatever makes us feel good. If so, whatever internal intrinsic benefit we derive from being moral comes after we determine what morality requires. That means the determination of morality must be independent of, and prior to, any supposed intrinsic benefit.

In the *Nicomachean Ethics*, Aristotle tells us that a lover of morality will find being moral more pleasurable than being immoral independent of any other instrumental gain accruing from immorality (bk 1, sect. 8). An instrumentalist can agree. I would like to eat mushrooms if I enjoyed mushrooms, but such a truism does not convince me that I should like mushrooms. That I would like to be moral even with a ring of Gyges if I liked being moral for its own sake, similarly, does not convince me to learn to like being moral for its own sake. If I find that *x*-ing gives me grief, while I also find myself tempted to *x*, I will motivate myself to internalize a disposition that will help prevent me from *x*-ing. Thus, if after awhile, I find myself liking not-*x*-ing, my liking not-*x*-ing cannot be taken as showing that the intrinsic worth of not-*x*-ing has any relevance to why it is good not to *x*.

The overall well-being sense does not fare better. We need not doubt that being psychologically well balanced is intrinsically beneficial. We may even imagine that persons who have well-being tend toward morality and persons psychologically out of kilter tend toward immorality. For example, why stab someone unless one's psychological balance is not already distorted? But such thinking does not lend favour to the subjective notion of an intrinsic morality. According to Copp (2007), such thinking turns on an equivocation. "It is in one's self-interest to achieve the best for oneself, but it does not follow that it is in one's self-interest to be as good as one can be. It certainly does not follow that it is in one's self-interest to be as morally good as one can be" (287-8). In any event, the wrongness of murder cannot have anything to do with the fact – if it is even a fact – that the murderer was out of sorts. Murderers' dispositional states may explain why they murdered, but not why murder is wrong. Being out of sorts may cause us to do a number of things, not all of them immoral. Aristotle's reply: "But not every action nor every passion admits of a mean; for some have names that already imply badness, e.g. ... adultery, theft, murder: for all of those and suchlike things imply by their names that they are themselves bad" (bk II, sect. 6).

Ultimately, even Aristotle appeals to some form of objective intrinsic notion.

The objective sense of intrinsicality, the sense that morality is a good in itself, succumbs to the queerness objection (Mackie 1977, 38–42). The queerness objection has three converging arguments: metaphysical, epistemological, and motivational.

The metaphysical objection highlights how ontologically weird a moral judgment must be if it is not connected in any way with either our mental states or physical matter, yet, somehow, always, properly connects to actions we call moral and immoral. Imagine coming across someone burning a cat (Harman 1977, 4–5). We would all say such torture is immoral, but how do we know? The natural objective intrinsicalist is committed to seeing two things: the physical facts related to the cat burning, and the moral facts that supervene on that action. When objectivists exclaim "Immoral!" they are not relating their value judgment, they are reporting a fact in the world. For contractarians, however, the immorality of burning a cat is not a thing observed when we observe someone burning a cat. The facts are not themselves values. Instead, we see facts and we ascribe a moral value to those facts. If moral value is something we ascribe to facts, we are not deriving the immorality from natural, objective facts in the world.

I look out my window and see ice atop a puddle. I can assume the world is offering me a proposition: "It's cold outside." Given this descriptive proposition, I can make a normative inference: "Wear mittens!" It would be odd, however, to think the world gave me the normative utterance, itself, let alone a specifically moral utterance such as, "Don't steal your neighbour's mittens!"

When I watch a car speed past, I might say, "That's fast," or "It's crazy to drive that fast," or "It's immoral to drive that fast." While interpretation more obviously seeps into the latter two claims, even the first claim is not a thing I have witnessed. It is a judgment I make based on what I have witnessed. The term "fast" is relative. It is not an absolute fact found in the world. "Fast" is a term that makes sense only when used in relation to something else. If we are appealing to any natural facts, it is not fastness, but rate of motion over distance. That is the natural fact; the normative judgment "fast" is not. If we cannot maintain that "fast" is a natural fact, think of how much more difficult it would be to maintain that morality is a natural fact.

Even if the immorality of burning a cat is a natural fact like the cat's being on fire is a natural fact, even if it is a natural fact to not steal mittens is like the natural fact that a puddle has frozen, by what epistemic channel would we come to experience these peculiar propositions? This question raises the epistemological component of the queerness argument. One answer, perhaps the only answer, is intuitionism. Under intuitionism, value ascription is an internal filter imbued in us. As Aquinas (XCI, 2nd art.) claims, intuitionism is "an imprint on us by the divine light," i.e., "the light of natural reason, whereby we discern what is good and what is evil, which is the function of the natural law." We cannot empirically support such an image. Besides rods and cones, we do not have moral receptors in our eyes. Beyond the unexplained mechanics of intuitionism, other problems exist. For example, we could solve disagreements about the moral status of an event, like abortion, or euthanasia, by pointing out that one of us has the right intuition and the other the wrong intuition. If we both maintain that our views are based on our intuitions, deciding who has the right intuition becomes a problem. We cannot hope to resolve the collision of intuitions, since intuitionism can appeal only to intuition. When all our theory allows us to do is to report our inner voice, we have no recourse but to shout louder as if a decibel gauge can decide moral matters. We might suggest that self-interest has corroded our opponent's intuitions, though how they would have let self-interest override their moral intuition before their intuition became corroded is left unexplained, especially if Aristotle is right: that virtue is better for the agent than vice.[11] Conversely, some of us just happen to have better intuitions, lucky us. Such imperialism is indistinguishable from racist and sexist attitudes. A voice in one's head or a feeling in one's gut more likely has its origins from socialization than from any moral objectivity. If so, intuition would have no more moral authority than that which we cede to cultural heritage. While our intuitions may sometimes latch on to true propositions, we never deem the proposition true *because* of the intuition. We must test the intuition out somehow. That is to say, we need not disparage intuitions if we understand them as hunches as opposed to confirmation.

Even pretending we have solved the metaphysical and epistemological problems, the motivational problem remains. We are to conceive morality as an objective signpost, like product information labels that somehow manage to supervene on our every action. Even assuming this is true and we see what the label tells us, why should we be motivated to abide by what it says? When I see a sign telling me, "Buy Mr. Christie's Cookies," I need not doubt that is what the sign tells me to do to doubt whether I ought to obey its directive. Imagine the objective morality sign tells me that homosexuality is intrinsically wrong. Does that mean I should agree? Even if we grant moral values some kind of objective life that resides in the world out there, independent of humans, we still require a motivating reason to follow those normative directives. The motivation must come from within and must connect to one's interests.[12]

Natural objective intrinsicalists can only point to the putative facts of morality, but pointing to facts is not typically enough to motivate us to do anything about those facts. By placing morality out there, in the objective world, we lose the internal motivation to abide by it. I am not denying that morality, properly conceived, motivates us. I am saying that the usual responses to explain why morality motivates us is unavailable to moral objectivists. Moral motivation concerns our desires and values, and desires and values reside within us, not out there. This lends support to instrumentalism: we do not discover morality in the world, we ascribe our moral values to things we discover in the world. Similarly (following Taylor 2000, 98), when we say it is bad to drink poison, we need not assume that poison is bad in itself. Rather, we call poison bad in relation to our desire to live without pain.

4 ENTER DARWIN

I have made two claims. First, rational contractarians cannot claim that the Lydian shepherd ought to not be immoral when possessing the ring of Gyges. Second, the alternative view, an intrinsic morality, makes no sense. So far, this is only an ad hominem of the *tu quoque* variety. Showing metaphysical difficulties with the intrinsic view does not establish the instrumentalist view. To defend the instrumentalist view, I shall present contractarian moral theory as having an evolutionary backing as opposed to a rationalist backing (Murray 2008). Upon doing so, we see that Plato's complaint against the instrumental view simply begs the question.[13] The ring of Gyges problem highlights merely that the circumstances in which strategic interactions take place are ever changing. Sound strategies will vary according to the circumstances, circumstances that not everyone shares. To say one disposition among all that flux is *the* rational strategy is to miss the lessons learned from evolutionary modelling, where environmental variation is the norm.

Let us assume that the current success of humans has everything to do with evolution. Given evolution, we can expect that our moral traits are themselves something that has benefited our genes. The success of any evolutionary trait is always conditional. If situations change sufficiently, a currently successful trait may no longer be successful. If we conceive of morality as an evolutionary trait, we conceive of morality as being conditional. Given the conditionality of morality, conditions based on circumstances in which one finds oneself, we can *always* come up with scenarios where instrumental prudence dictates that you deviate from actions normally deemed moral. Therefore, if morality is strictly instrumentally self-interested, one would have no reason to be moral should one find oneself in a situation where one can get away with immorality and avoid all the usual costs of immorality. That these circumstances might not apply in a specific case, or might never apply in your world, is irrelevant to what instrumental prudence recommends under such circumstances. Because this allows, even if only in theory, our recommending immorality in a specific case,[14] non-instrumentalists make the mistake in assuming that therefore morality must be something outside the set of instrumental prudence, outside the set of things affected by evolution. They look for a reason to be moral that would apply in *any* circumstance. No one who takes evolution seriously can fathom such a request. Circumstances always matter for trait selection. If morality is an evolutionary trait along with our other adaptations, circumstances always matter to moral recommendation. To search for a non-conditional essence of morality reveals a flawed conception of nature.

An appeal to the evolutionary dynamics of natural selection can explain why the Unconditional Defect (UD) strategy will be limited to a small percentage of the population without appealing to rationality. In brief, UD does well only so long as UD has agents to exploit, those who adopt Unconditional Co-operate (UC) (as well as any poorly tuned RCs, those too quick to co-operate). The better UDs do in one generation, the more UDs will appear in subsequent generations. With a rise of the number of UDs, the number of UCs will become depleted. This trend highlights the paradox of success for exploitive agents. The fewer agents there are to exploit, the less well exploiters do compared with other strategies. Since uds fare poorly against other UDs, over time, the population of UDs will decline. Meanwhile, since Gauthier's RCs play well with one another, and generally avoid predation by UDs, their numbers steadily rise. In time, RCs (or variants of RCs) dominate. Of course, once RCs are dominant, this allows UCs (or lazy RCs) to grow in the population proportion, since too-quick co-operators benefit from RC dominance without paying the cost of conditional restraint. The more UCs, the more UDs come back into the picture. The result is a polymorphism of strategies, but one in which Gauthier's RC (or something akin to it) prevails (Skyrms 1996).

In the above picture, the rise and dominance of moral dispositions comes about by natural selection, not rationality. The reciprocal co-operative strategy generally pays its practitioners better than other kinds of strategies pay their practitioners. Gauthier's analysis remains correct in essence, if not in detail. That is, I agree with Epicurus, Hobbes, and Gauthier that, for the most of us, we do better being an RC than a UD, and this should suffice to end the discussion about whether morality is instrumentally worth endorsing for the most of us. It is. But such an answer cannot satisfy the Lydian shepherd. Unlike the rational defences of Gauthier and Hobbes, an evolutionary contractarianism admits that morality is not, nor can be, universally rational.[15] Given shifts in environment and populations, niches continually exist for rational Fooles.

The Lydian shepherd has no instrumental reason to be moral. Have I thereby conceded that instrumentalism is wrong? Absolutely not. My response is not a reply to the Lydian shepherd or the Foole. I reply to those who think Fooles and Lydian shepherds need a reply. The Foole points out that basing morality on individual prudence is not going to sway those persons who can do better, prudentially speaking, by being immoral than by being moral. Most moral philosophers have thought that if the Foole is right about that, there goes the hope of basing morality on instrumental prudence. The Foole is right (assuming the Foole is an individual who really can reap an overall net gain by immoral behaviour in this particular situation, as opposed to those fools who wrongly think they can so gain), but this hardly unravels the instrumental basis of morality. What would unravel the strictly instrumental value of morality is if the odds favoured the Foole. They do not, at least presently. It would also unravel the prudential basis of morality if morality were supposed to be good for *all* agents, no matter their situations. That is what Glaucon and Adeimantus demanded of Socrates: to show that the Lydian shepherd, armed with the ring of Gyges, still should be moral. It is like suggesting an adaptation for one environment ought to work in another environment. The evolutionary depiction of morality's genealogy makes no such grand claims. Whatever metaphysical backing is required for intrinsic claims runs counter to Darwinian evolution.

When contractarians claim that reciprocal co-operation (a.k.a., "being moral") benefits us, they mean (or ought to mean) it as a statistical claim. It speaks to most agents under most circumstances. That we can find a particular agent outside those circumstances is not a refutation of the statistical claim. An elderly, non-cancerous smoker does not refute the claim that smoking (generally) causes lung cancer. Similarly, although some people may be in a circumstance where immorality is better than morality, the odds are against them. Moreover, when contractarians say being moral benefits the moral agent, they mean in the long run, not necessarily in the short run. A moral agent will not necessarily benefit from any particular moral act. Thus, finding that being moral does not pay in one case (being invisible, say) does not show that being moral does not *generally* pay for that individual.

But many of us feel bad when we have got away with an act deemed immoral. Would a prudential basis for morality not lead us to feel good instead? No. Assuming the fallout of visibly defecting against co-operators is high enough, a propensity to adopt dispositions that will less likely exploit the exploitable than exploit the non-exploitable will rise in the population proportion. This highlights why we often feel bad to steal even in the situation where stealing would have no bad external effects for the thief. We have internalized a generally useful heuristic, but heuristics are such that they may not happen to be useful in a particular situation, for example having a ring of Gyges.

But are evolutionary contractarians not committed to say, "Go ahead and steal if you're invisible"? Well, contractarians would not advise such a message, since they are not fond of being exploited. The point is that morality is a useful trait for most of us most of the time in most of the situations in which we find ourselves. No evolutionary trait is refuted merely by pointing out a condition in which that trait is no longer fit. All evolutionary traits are useful *given a particular environment*. Alter any of those background conditions and the benefits of an adaptative trait may no longer apply. While recognizing this, we understand that the ring of Gyges challenge presupposes something that an evolutionary ethic disallows – namely the very demand that morality not be susceptible to environmental conditions.

5 CONCLUSION

Given the state of human social interaction, you will likely do better in the long run being moral than not. Two types of responses may be given. The first is to complain that, therefore, morality is not always the rational choice, thus defeating rational contractarianism. An evolutionary version of contractarianism, however, is not affected. Adding the word "likely" tolerates ring-of-Gyges exceptions. Pointing out that contractarianism could not complain about the Lydian shepherd's antics is as idle as pointing out that one's uncle smoked all his life without getting lung cancer after someone mentioned that people generally do better not smoking. Similarly, the ring of Gyges objection in no way defeats the evolutionary version of contractarianism that claims only that reciprocal co-operators generally do better than other agents, given stable conditions.

The second response is to complain that any moral theory that cannot show the Lydian shepherd's antics to be immoral is not a moral theory at all. Such an objection stems from a metaphysical stance that contractarians dismiss. Consider the following analogy I heard from Daniel Dennett in a talk on consciousness. Magic is real if we understand magic as a conjurer's trick, not as magic, which is unreal. After our explaining the trick, only a child would say, "But that isn't magic!" To such children, we might say, "Well, it's not magic in *your* sense. In your sense no magic exists. In our sense, we have perfectly explained the reality of magic." To think ring-of-Gyges problems counter contractarianism suffers the same confusion. Invisibility would be a problem for a conditional morality if morality were properly unconditional. The ring-of-Gyges objection does not establish the unconditionality of morality; it merely presumes it.

10

A Toxin for Contractarians

Rational contractarians, those contractarians who base morality on pure rationality, want to explain how it is rational for everyone to be moral in all circumstances. One challenge to this claim comes from the toxin puzzle.[1] The toxin puzzle wonders whether we can intend to do that which we have no rational reason to do. If we cannot, this may be a problem for morality, at least if being moral is a case where we commit ourselves to perform an action that, at the time of execution, we have no rational reason to perform. A moral analogue to the toxin puzzle is the seeming irrationality of paying back a loan. We want money. We get money on the promise of repayment. Come the time to repay, however, rationality breaks from morality.

Although I believe in the basic prudential feature of contractarian morality, I am less sanguine about whether morality is fully rationally motivated. I am willing to argue that morality is *generally* rationally motivating, but not necessarily in all situations for all agents.[2] In this chapter, I examine and reject the standard contractarian reasons for the rationality of drinking the toxin. At the end, I apply my own quasi-rational, or evolutionary response. In doing so, I highlight how, similar to Prisoner's Dilemmas (PDs), sticking to one's intentions is useful only in repeated games, not non-repeated ones.

1 THE TOXIN PUZZLE[3]

Imagine a rich alien mind reader who offers you one million dollars to be deposited in your bank account at T_2 if at T_1 you intend to drink a cup of toxin at T_3. The toxin, while making you extremely sick, will not kill you or have any long-term adverse effects. Being a mind reader, this alien can tell the difference between those people who at T_1 really intend to drink the toxin at T_3 and those who do not earnestly intend. With this in mind, let us agree that at T_1 you earnestly commit yourself to drink the toxin at T_3. Given that commitment, the money is now in your bank account (T_2). Come T_3, will you bother drinking the toxin?

Notice that you did not actually promise the alien to drink the toxin; you merely formed the intention to drink the toxin.[4] Failing to drink the toxin then is no more a failure of either an obligation or promise than failing to do sit-ups after having intended to do sit-ups.[5] Your action is not owed to anyone. Moreover, drinking the toxin at T_3 is not itself a condition of receiving the money; only forming the intention – which at this point (per hypothesis) you did. Had you not successfully formed the intention to drink the toxin at T_1, you would not have any money in the bank and then you surely would not bother drinking the toxin. Given such considerations, it seems you cannot plausibly have any reason to drink the toxin. Either the money is in your bank account or it is not, and neither option necessitates your drinking the toxin.

We have no difficulty imagining unexecuted intentions. The problem is whether you can form an intention to do *x* when you know you will not do *x*. Since at T_1 you know it would be irrational for you to drink the toxin at T_3 for the reasons given above, you cannot form an earnest intention at T_1 to drink the toxin at T_3. It is analytic that we cannot intend to do *x* while predicting that we will not do *x*. But since you cannot intend to drink the toxin given your having no reason to drink the toxin (it is unnecessary) and a good reason not to drink the toxin (sickness-inducing), the alien will not deposit the coveted million dollars in your bank account.

This seems incorrect. Surely you would prefer to be sick for a day for a million dollars than have no million dollars given to you and be not sick for a day. Here is your opportunity. Seize it!

But wait. To be a million dollars richer, you would have to intend to drink the toxin and to intend to drink the toxin you would have to understand that your drinking the toxin is a rational output of your intention. But rationality cannot support you. It can be rational to form an intention only if we believe it is rational to execute the intention. "As our beliefs are constrained by our evidence, so our intentions are constrained by our reasons for action" (Kavka 1983, 36). Since it is not rational to execute the intention to drink the toxin under the alien's stipulated conditions, it is not rational to form the intention to drink the toxin. You cannot win the million-dollar prize.[6]

One response is to accept the adage that if it seems easy to win a million dollars, think again. Since I cannot expect aliens to offer me a million dollars, my failure to form an intention that would make me better off overall in such a peculiar case is of little interest. It is like the joke: How to make a million dollars from a horse? Start with two million dollars. But the toxin puzzle cannot be so easily ignored since it captures a peculiarity of moral commitment. With the toxin puzzle, we are to commit to drinking the toxin even when at the time of drinking it seems no longer rational to do so. Likewise with morality: we are to commit to being moral even when being immoral is the purely rational move. For example, at T_1 you offer a promise to repay a loan at T_3, and on the basis of that promise, you receive the loan at T_2. Come T_3, however, the commitment to repay the money goes against your interest. Your promise at T_1 was to get the money. At T_3, you already have the money. The conditionality of the promise seems no longer to apply. Of course, if lenders knew that borrowers would be thinking about such things come due dates, they would not lend their money. (They may give their money, but do not count on that.) Thus, as with the toxin puzzle, your commitment at T_1 has to extend to your being committed at T_3; the intention has to bypass the irrationality of paying the loan back. To say we *cannot* do that seems patently false. We do it all the time. Since we do follow through with irrational intentions, it appears humans have an ability to turn off their rational monitor. How else could we be moral? Morality, as with the toxin puzzle, appears to be irrational.[7]

Admittedly, not everyone is bothered by the thought that morality is irrational. Rationality is merely a tool to serve one's self-interested ends. That morality may tell you to not serve your own ends on occasion ought not to be surprising. The toxin puzzle's connection to morality is a bother only for those who claim that morality is a subset of rational prudence. Contractarians tend to be such people, so it is not surprising that most (if not all) of the arguments for the rationality of drinking the toxin comes from them.

There is one quick way to solve the puzzle, by the way. Earlier, I mentioned how it is not rational to execute the intention to drink the toxin under the alien's stipulated conditions, and that therefore, it is not rational to form the intention to drink the toxin. One of the stipulated conditions Kavka (1983, 34) gives us is, No gimmickry! My hooking myself up to a kind of machine that will force me to drink the toxin, for example, would show only that I intend to make it so that I drink the toxin, not that I intend to drink the toxin. Forbidding such solutions seems unfair. After all, we invoke such gimmicks in other cases where we wish to follow through with a task despite our recognizing the low probability of execution. Ulysses ties himself to a mast in order to hear the Sirens without succumbing to their call. We should praise his ingenuity, not call him a cheater. We drug ourselves to fly. We make bets with someone that we can manage fifty sit-ups in a row by the end of the month to prompt ourselves against akrasia. Similarly, we can think of formalized punishment as morality's gimmick. It is not that we are moral to avoid punishment, but that we willingly invoke a rule to punish disobedience – even when aimed at ourselves – to help us avoid our penchant to renege. If we rule out such gimmickry, a move from the state of nature to a moral state may be hopeless.

Before we resort to gimmicks, however, it is wise to look at contractarian solutions to the toxin puzzle that are gimmick-free. McClennen (1990) argues for how intentions come with the resolution to execute the intended act. If the intention is rational, the resolution to execute the act is rational. Gauthier (1986; 1994; 1998) argues that rationality ought not to focus on individual acts, but on which dispositions individuals ought to embrace that will, compared with other available dispositions, make one's life go best, all things considered. MacIntosh (1992; 2013) and Harman (1998) argue for changing our desires so that we come to find intrinsic benefit in committing the act, the intrinsic benefit being instrumentally induced. Bratman (1998) argues for a forward-looking regret avoidance account of rationality. Albeit a contractarian, I am dubious of these solutions. After explaining why the rationalist defences fail (I focus on Gauthier's and MacIntosh's), I offer a more Humean version of contractarianism, one founded in evolutionary game theory, as opposed to rational game theory.

2 RATIONAL SOLUTIONS

Our normal understanding of instrumental rationality is as a tool to determine the best means to one's subjective ends. The classic example of rational method is employed in parametric circumstances, not strategic situations. Parametric choice is where one's action influences one's outcome. For strategic choice situations, your

Table 10.1 | Pure strategy payoff

	Unconditionally co-operate	*Unconditionally defect*	*Total*
Unconditionally co-operate	1	−1	0
Unconditionally defect	2	0	2

Table 10.2 | Prisoner's dilemma results

	Unconditionally co-operate 1	*Unconditionally defect 2*	*Reciprocally co-operate 2*	*Avg.*
Unconditionally co-operate	1(1)	−1(2)	1(2)	0.2
Unconditionally defect	2(1)	0(2)	0(2)	0.4
Reciprocally co-operate	1(1)	0(2)	1(2)	0.6

outcome depends on choices other agents make, themselves influenced by what choices you have made or what choices they expect you to make. Under strategic interaction, Gauthier offers a revised account of rationality: "In defending constrained maximization, we have implicitly reinterpreted the utility-maximizing conception of practical rationality" (Gauthier 1986, 182). By altering our concept of rationality, we can rationally comply with what we rationally agree to do.

An account of Gauthier's game theoretic argument is offered in the previous chapter. Here is a summary. In a world with pure strategies of Unconditional Co-operate (UC) and Unconditional Defect (UD), the UDs will annihilate the UCs. Assuming reverse ordinal payoffs of standard PD games, we get the results shown in table 10.1.

The utilities in table 10.1 represent Row's score when played against Column. Since UD is the clear winner here, no UD will be motivated to shift strategies to UC. Gauthier's point is that a third strategy is available, one that is conditional, not pure. If we can co-operate when the other co-operates, but defect when the other defects, we have a new, conditional, strategy. A conditional strategy is consistent with the except-when clauses attached to Hobbes's Laws of Nature (Hobbes 1651, chs 14–15). Call this conditional strategy RC for Reciprocal Co-operate.[8] Any player using the RC strategy will do better, subjectively determined, than by adopting either the UC or UD strategies, assuming enough RCs. Picture a world where the UD and RC strategy have two players each, while UC, being the underdog strategy, has only one player. The results (table 10.2) show how RC gains the advantage over the other strategies.

While I have my doubts that an RC agent is *fully* rational (as discussed in the previous chapter), let us instead wonder whether the arguments used to defend RC's rationality can apply to a defence of drinking the toxin. Just as an RC agent will conditionally co-operate with another co-operator in a PD, an RC agent will, at T_1, commit to drinking non-lethal toxin at T_3 on the condition that the money is in the bank at T_2. Since RCs hard-wire themselves to stick to their commitments, they will not be tempted to deviate from their plan to drink the toxin at T_3 when the money is already deposited at T_2. Such commitment ensures the money will be deposited. An RC, then, will be able to legitimately intend to drink the toxin for the RC has the disposition to constrain herself against the temptation to not drink the toxin at T_3. The alien can trust the RC's intention, and thus an RC will be able to win the million dollars. Those who can dispose themselves to follow through with their intentions in toxin puzzles can do better in terms of overall utility compared with those who cannot commit to their intentions. This does not say that it is rational to so commit to drink the toxin. Why absorb *useless* costs to achieve your ends? Drinking the toxin for money when the money is already in the bank is a useless cost.[9] Of course it is not a *useless* cost to drink the toxin if that is what is needed to intend to drink the toxin, I imagine Gauthier saying. But now we are back at the beginning to try to intend to do something the doing of which is useless (and will make us sick).

Table 10.3 | Prisoner's dilemma after desire adjustment

	Co-operate	*Defect*
Co-operate	2,2	0,2
Defect	2,0	0,0

MacIntosh (2013, 632) points out a reversion problem that Gauthier's reciprocal co-operation disposition faces. Assume a co-operative venture in which *A* acts first (T_1) and *B*'s co-operative move happens afterward (T_2). At T_1, *A*, on the basis of recognizing that *B* is an RC, chooses to co-operate. An action is done. *B* already benefits from *A*'s action. In such a case (assume no future interactions between *A* and *B* and no reputation loss to *B* from third-party observation) it would be patently irrational for *B* to co-operate at T_2. That an agent can switch from UD to RC for self-interested benefits would seem to mean that such an agent ought to be able to revert to UD when doing so maximizes expected utility,[10] as it would in any non-repeated PDs. A potential for rational reversion will impede the ability to sincerely commit to drink the toxin.

To avoid the reversion problem, MacIntosh's (1992; 2013) solution involves a simple shifting of one's desires. It is rational to come to like things the liking of which will get you more of what you originally liked. In the PD, liking reciprocal co-operation will get you more of what you originally liked: increased utility (MacIntosh 2013, 639). What we need to do when faced with PDs, then, is to come to desire to co-operate with others. In doing so, apart from the mutual benefits reaped by co-operation, one comes to derive added utility from the act of co-operation itself. Adjusting one's preferences in this way offers an escape from the prisoner's dilemma. Table 10.1 showed the PD payoffs using a reverse ordinal ranking adjusted to 0. Assuming an extra 1 utile benefit to co-operating, table 10.3 shows the new payoffs after desire adjustment. Co-operation can no longer be seen as irrational. Admittedly, nor is defection irrational, but one thing at a time.

In terms of the toxin puzzle, MacIntosh agents see that they must intend to drink the toxin to get the million dollars.[11] Knowing that one will not drink the toxin at T_3 unless one forms an intrinsic desire to drink the toxin, one sees the instrumental rationality of forming a preference to drink the toxin at T_3. Come T_3, the desire-adjusted agent happily drinks the toxin, despite already being a millionaire.

When I find mushrooms on my plate and I confess that I do not like mushrooms, you can tell me that my desires would be satisfied if I came to like mushrooms. True, but that does not change the fact that I do not like mushrooms. Similarly, telling me that my preferences would be satisfied if I came to prefer co-operation intrinsically does not convince me to prefer co-operation intrinsically. But we can imagine a food shortage such that the only thing left to eat is the dreaded mushroom. Assuming I prefer survival more than I loathe eating mushrooms, why not alter my desires so that I come to like mushrooms? While changing my desires willy-nilly is of no use; changing them when necessary may be. Since we cannot co-operate in PDs unless we undergo a desire adjustment so that we come to like co-operating intrinsically (per the desire-adjustment theory), such desire alteration may well be rationally motivated.

At least two worries present themselves. The first we may call the stoic objection. The call to alter our desires so that we more easily achieve our ends is reminiscent of Epictetus's advice in his *Enchiridion*. Rather than try to change the world to get what we want (a matter too often beyond our control), we should change our wants to only those things that happen to befall us. If that seems like good advice, the call to change our desires so that we come to intrinsically desire to co-operate with others seems sensible. Taking a stoical approach, however, is not going to help the desire-adjustment solution to the compliance problem. Why come to like to co-operate in order to get what one wants; why not simply abandon desire of things one wants (other than the desire for things that happen to befall one)? If we can change our desires to match ends with available means, why not go all the way and join Epictetus? We cannot accuse Epictetus of being irrational, since his outcomes (nothing) fully match his desires (of nothing). But nor can we celebrate such a character as an epitome of contractarian morality.[12] At any rate, Epictetus would not drink the toxin; he would just abandon his desire for a million dollars. While stoicism fails MacIntosh's condition of not losing sight of the original desire, it has all the elements of rationality that MacIntosh endorses, yet derives opposite results.

The second problem is the sucker objection. While my newfound desire to co-operate signals to others that I am trustworthy, it also opens the door for exploitation. My new desire to comply with your request is what got you to co-operate with me. My new desire to comply served its purpose. Bravo, new desire. But if this new desire actually takes root, I will find it rational to further its end by seeing what else I can do for you – shine your shoes, perhaps, mend your jacket elbows, mow your grass. Anything! Once you come to see in me my desire to co-operate with you, you are free to enslave me by my own rational choice.

Or imagine we find ourselves in an Ultimatum Game (UG). UG is a game where the first player offers a division of a ten-piece pie and the second player accepts or rejects the offered division. If the second player rejects the offered division, neither player gets any of the pie.[13] The fear of getting no pie rather than some pie makes offerers wary of seeming too greedy. Certainly an offer of "Ten for me and zero for you" stands to be rejected, leaving zero for them both.[14] But is it rational for the hungry to reject an offer of one piece of pie? If not, it would be rational to offer "Nine for me, one for you," predicting acceptance. Like most people, Skyrms (1996) assumes that the moral move is for the first player to offer a fifty-fifty split, and if so, here is another case where rationality and morality part ways. My question is to what extent the desire-adjustment model can solve the UG, and it looks problematic. If "co-operating" equals "accepting your offer," and you come to like co-operating for its own sake, and I know that about you, I should offer at least a 6-4 split of the pie (6 for me, 4 for you) and you could not complain, as long as the intrinsic value of co-operating with me equals one piece of pie. If the value for co-operating to you equals two pieces of pie, I can offer a 7-3 split. And so on.

In the toxin puzzle, when I come to desire the toxin, I do not lose my desire for money. It is the desire for money that drives my desire for the toxin, but I must be careful not to have my new desire for toxin go unchecked. While one dosage may be non-lethal, more such dosages may not be, in which case my new desire to drink toxin may be fatal. Even if it were not fatal, the alien could now sell toxin to me and soon earn back the million dollars.[15]

To avoid the sucker worry, we need to be very specific in terms of the desires we wish to assume. So, I have a new-formed desire to drink toxin once, and only once, at, and only at, T_3. This is a strange desire to develop. Normally if I like something, it is not a matter of liking it only once. When it is a matter of liking something only once, it is due to some kind of mistake. We thought we would like it more than we did, for example.

The sucker worry is that the new intrinsic value of compliance itself is so valued that we would happily forgo our original interests. If our reason to adopt an intrinsic desire for co-operation is instrumental to our other interests, it would be irrational to take on an intrinsic interest that would have power over our original interests. MacIntosh (2013, 641) claims that "that is a risk one is willing to take in changing one's desires to make intentions possible." I am less certain about that. It is not a case where it *might* happen now and then: it will surely happen. Sometimes things may work out for the better. A boy who desired to play guitar to meet girls becomes so in love with guitar playing that he tells girls to keep away, to stop interrupting his guitar playing. Can he complain? Not from his current interest in guitar playing, but here is a case where the new desire supplants the original. If he knew ahead of time that his interest in playing guitar would not lead to the results he wanted, we cannot say the desire to desire guitar playing was rational – even if things worked out well from his new vantage. What is needed is a restriction placed on our instrumentally assumed desires to never supplant the originating desire. But, and presumably this is MacIntosh's worry, such a restriction is going to succumb to the same reversion problem MacIntosh aimed at Gauthier.

The original desire, call it *A*, is what prompted the development of the new intrinsic desire, call it *B*. We invented *B* to serve *A*'s end. To avoid the sucker problem, *B* must remain supplemental to *A*. *B* cannot supplant *A*. The restriction, however, is too strong. If these additional desires can never supplant the original desire, they will not be strong enough to solve the compliance problem. My new desire to drink the toxin, for example, is rooted in and only in my desire for a million dollars. I already have that, per hypothesis. What propels me now to continue to have a desire for toxin? My new desire for mushrooms may be grounded in having only mushrooms to eat, but after a sudden delivery of foods I actually like, what grounds my new desire for mushrooms – especially if, as in the toxin case, I have not yet consummated my newly willed desire? Nothing.

Summing Up

If the desire to co-operate supplants one's original desire, there is nothing to recommend the new desire, at least from the standpoint of the original desire. As MacIntosh (2013, 641) claims, achieving the new ends will be rational given the new desire, but that is merely tautological. I would enjoy mushrooms if I enjoyed mushrooms. Conversely, we see the desire to co-operate as merely instrumental to our original desire. But such instrumentality is what mires us in the compliance problem. If the desire to co-operate is merely instrumental, we will swap back to our original desires when convenient and, knowing this, our co-players will not bother co-operating with us in their first move. Nor will the alien give us a million dollars. To avoid the sucker problem, we get the reversion problem that MacIntosh aimed at Gauthier's solution.

Other attempts to save the rationality of compliance in PDs and Toxin puzzles exist,[16] but I shall move on to offer my solution that hinges on the distinction between repeated and non-repeated games.

3 REPEATED VS NON-REPEATED GAMES

My earlier account of how the RC strategy beats other strategies in PD games skipped over a small, seemingly unimportant, detail. We need more RCs in the mix before any benefit comes to any RC. Imagine if greater computational skills require more fuel. RC requires greater computational skills than UD. Thus, the net value of a utile may be less to an RC than to a UD. If so, it is false to say that an RC will do as well as a UD when no other RC is in the mix. This would greatly impede the claim that RC is a rational strategy even if there were no other RC agents. If being a lone RC is not rational, it is difficult to see how a bunch of RCs can be a rational outcome. Simply saying, "Hey, I'll be an RC if you will be," will sound to any rational agent like a UD trickster.

An evolutionary story, on the other hand, can explain the appearance of a critical mass of RC agents without resorting to rationality. As long as PDs are indefinitely repeated in the natural environment, and the RC trait a possible trait in the population, then over time, the RC trait will dominate (Alexander 2001; Aumann 1981; Axelrod 1984; Binmore 1998; Danielson 1998; Skyrms 1996; Skyrms 2004). Rationally motivated or not, agents with the RC disposition will do better in terms of offspring than those without the RC trait. Can we say the same about committed toxin drinkers?

The toxin puzzle, at least as presented by Kavka (1983), is very much a single-shot, or one-off game. The rationality of commitment will be as difficult for the toxin puzzle, as presented, as it is to co-operate in a single-shot, or one-off PD. Imagine the toxin puzzle as a repeated game, however. Rich aliens, for some reason, desire humans to form intentions to drink non-lethal toxins, and will pay one million dollars for the service. They are so enamoured by our intention to drink a non-lethal toxin they will continue to pay millions of dollars every time we form such intentions. If so, the intention I form at T_1 to drink the toxin at T_3 can easily carry through to my drinking the toxin at T_3 even when I already have the million dollars at T_2. Why do I need to drink the toxin at T_3? Because if I do not, I will be excluded from future million-dollar transactions. That the toxin game is repeatable gives me incentive to drink the toxin even though the money is already in my bank account.

The alien's desire, by the way, need not be too alien. Parents may offer their adult child a loan only on the condition that the child first describe her repayment plan. Such a detail highlights that the child is taking the loan seriously and intends to pay it back. For some parents, this intention to pay it back may suffice. The parents may, thereafter, waive the debt. They are happy enough that the child had intended to pay it back. A valuable lesson.

Notice a difference between the toxin puzzle and its moral comparator: repaying loans. The alien does not care whether I drink the toxin, only that I intend to drink the toxin. Not so with my lender. She is interested in my intention to repay the loan only to the extent that my intending to repay the loan increases the likeliness of my repaying the loan. And my intention to repay the loan carries through to paying the loan precisely because of the lender's interest in my repaying the loan. Given her interest, she will retaliate if I renege. The prospect of the bank's retaliation is my incentive to repay the loan. With repeated toxin games, this difference lessens. The retaliation I would experience is a loss of opportunity to make future millions of dollars. Without some threat at non-payment no incentive to pay can be worthwhile, rationally or evolutionarily.

An evolutionary lens reveals another distinction between toxin puzzles, PDs, and repayments. Assuming reciprocal co-operation counts as a morality, or a moral beginning, the trend toward a morality has evolutionary pull. But as with all adaptions, moral traits work well only given certain environments. Alter the environment significantly, the value of the previously successful trait will alter as well. The upshot is that a trait may be beneficial for the trait holder in the long run, but not necessarily for any particular trait holder in an alien context. For example, a grey-lag goose retrieves stray eggs from her nest, which seems a perfectly rational gesture. The trait to do so, however, is fooled by any spherical shaped object, like beer cans and light bulbs (Lorenz 1988). The egg-retrieving trait is fine under normal circumstances, not for experimentally manipulated conditions. Naturally occurring fixed-action patterns illustrate how seemingly rational traits may not be rational, yet suffice in the trait holder's natural environment. We can say the same for moral traits. We will stick to our intentions, assuming doing so still serves our original ends. This will satisfy our penchant to be reliable for repeated games in relatively stable environments, not necessarily so for non-repeated games or unstable circumstances.

Certainly, we can run computer simulations to show that committed toxin drinkers will do better in toxin puzzles than non-committed toxin drinkers, but that will hardly do. Adaptations develop under regularly occurring conditions. That we can imagine a trait that would do even better (hence more rational) when faced with unusual circumstances is not the deciding factor in that trait's evolution. Natural selection takes time and requires repeatable circumstances. A difference between PDs and loans and toxin puzzles is that PDs and loans occur regularly enough in our natural environment; not so the toxin puzzle. Evolution of traits requires many generations of that trait offering slight advantage. We could never imagine a strategy to commit to toxin drinking to evolve when the occurrence of being faced with a toxin puzzle is a one-off, non-repeated event.

But if the RC trait has evolved independently of toxin puzzles, might it become activated in the toxin puzzle and win the RC agent a million dollars? Another difference between toxin and PDs games prevents such a thought. Normally, when we form intentions to x, we do so because we recognize a benefit in x-ing that comes either during (if x-ing offers intrinsic value) or after x-ing (if x-ing offers instrumental value). The benefit cannot be *solely* in the past (Bratman 1998). In the toxin case, the sole benefit has already occurred before drinking the toxin. No future or present benefit may be found by drinking non-lethal toxin. In our normal, indefinitely repeated commitment cases, we may still count on future or present benefits. I do not this morning want to do sit-ups despite my intention last night to do sit-ups this morning. But it is not a case that I would this morning receive zero benefit from following through with last night's intention. My abs can still benefit from my doing sit-ups. That instrumental benefit still exists, and the rationale that drove me to make my intention can still drive me to execute my intention. I am not saying it will succeed in my case, but the exercise of the intention would not go against anything other than my current laziness. The reason to have made my intention still applies. When the time to pay my debt comes, I would rather not do so, but I know the likely cost to me will be greater by not paying my debt than by paying my debt, given our social norms and future interactions. Lost opportunities due to a loss in my reputation as a payer of debts can be more costly to me than the benefit I accrue by not paying my debts in the current case. While a benefit has already occurred to me before I execute my intention to pay back the money, future benefits for paying the debt (or future costs for failing to pay the debt) still lie ahead of me. The reasoning that drove me to form the intention to pay my debt still drives me to pay it. Assuming a worry about reputation and future co-operative ventures in PDs, the temptation to defect is defeated by the same reason I had when forming the intention to co-operate. Even when benefits have already been received, future potential benefits are still to come. An evolutionary story will highlight how the value of being an RC that prods compliance with one's intentions can only develop when present or future expected gain comes from executing the intention, not when all expected benefits have already been amassed before executing the intention.[17] This feature is sufficiently present in moral games but missing in any non-repeated games such as the toxin puzzle, at least as presented by Kavka. I can expect neither future benefit from drinking the toxin, nor future loss from not drinking the toxin. Since I have already received all the expected benefit from the alien, my having once formed the intention to drink the toxin cannot itself motivate me to drink the toxin.

Since an RC agent can find no future benefit from drinking the toxin in a non-repeated toxin game, the RC agent cannot be committed to drink the toxin. Thus, an RC agent cannot form an earnest intention to drink the toxin, although she can fully partake in the repeated games of moral life.

While an evolved trait to commit to what we intend benefits us in our moral dealing, the evolved trait does not help us intend to commit to just anything. And that is a good thing! It cannot put intention forming ahead of overall utility. While evolution will predict the rise of RC agents, it cannot make them have desires that, once acted upon, can offer neither present nor future expected utility.

4 CONCLUSION

Forming the intention to drink the alien's offer of non-lethal toxin to receive a million dollars may be rational only if the toxin game is a repeated game. To the extent that it is not a repeated game, at least as Kavka presents it, is the extent to which it would be as irrational to drink the toxin as it would be to intend to co-operate – even conditionally co-operate – in a non-repeated, one-off PD.

On the bright side, morality is instrumentally rational when it involves indefinitely repeated games. Under such conditions, our normal moral world, it can be rational to be moral.

Notes

INTRODUCTION

1 See Kujundzic (2013); Poundstone (1990); Sainsbury (1996); Sorensen (2003).

2 Being invisible may help me avoid being caught while I commit my crime, but it is not going to help me explain my sudden possession of the booty.

3 Hobbes listed seventeen or so. The second law tells us to lay down our "liberty." I switched the term to "freedom," since liberty, a right, did not exist yet, per hypothesis. We derive liberty by accepting mutual constraints on our freedoms.

4 Velleman (2012, 342) suggests the definition of status quo will not do, as put. When I ask a passerby for the time, I have altered the passerby's status quo without her consent. Now she has to consider whether she ought to abide by my request or not, let alone look at her watch, let alone speak; none of these things she needed to do in my absence. If my mere question robs her of her status quo, I have done her a moral wrong. If we think asking a passerby for the time is not a moral wrong, we should refine our definition of the status quo.

5 Yes, pilots, for example, have duties relegated only to a subset of the population, but they undertake those unique duties voluntarily. Not so slaves. I ignore here the problem of indentured slaves.

6 In evolutionary biology, the manoeuvre is called, "exaptation" (Gould and Vrba 1982).

CHAPTER ONE

My thesis supervisor was Jan Narveson, a libertarian. Libertarians like to suggest that enforced charity (a.k.a., a welfare program) is a violation of liberty. Unknown to many, Jan was extremely generous. He was also quick to praise the charitable acts of others. He denied any inconsistency in this because, he said, voluntary charity was permitted by libertarians; not enforced charity. Something always troubled me by this response. This chapter addresses my worry.

1 Supererogation's original home is medieval religion, where practitioners believed they could get closer to God by going beyond orthodox observance, leading to charges of heresy (Dentsoras 2023).
2 For Dorsey (2012) and Williams (1981a, 37–8), if the supererogatory becomes a moral demand, morality's authority would collapse. Baron (1987); Crisp (2013); and Hale (1991) disagree.
3 Guevera (1999); Timmerman (2005); van Ackeren and Sticker (2015); Wolf (1982).
4 This may be obvious to grammarians, but is often missed in critiques of seemingly exploitative practices.
5 Or, as Baron (1987) and Guevara (1999) note, one cannot be more charitable than required.
6 See also Igneski (2008) and Pinheiro Walla (2015).
7 As Dorsey (2013, 381–2) complains about Rawls's (1971, 117) notion of the supererogatory.
8 Richards's (1971) worry about costs of non-enforced rules may apply to suberogation; less so supererogation. A suberogatory act is the doing a bad that is not actually forbidden (Chisholm 1963; Ullmann-Margalit 2011). An asymmetry: the greater the supererogatory act, the further away it is from being obligatory. Not so with suberogatory acts. The greater the bad, the more likely we will say it is morally forbidden (Zimmerman 1996, 238).
9 This parallels Wolf's (1982, 420) distinction between the loving saint and the rational saint.
10 What about the reverse, Duncan MacIntosh once asked me, when A goes out of their way at their expense to punish B, a wrongdoer? Contractarians would disapprove; vigilantism often breaches procedural justice.
11 The designations RC, UC, UD are strategies, but I also use RC, UC, and UD to represent an agent who adopts such strategies.
12 See also Pummer (2016), who argues for "effective altruism."
13 In Murray (2017, 207–18), I apply an overextended heuristic to explain beneficence in general.
14 Danielson (1992, 12–16), although our acronyms differ. My RC is his CC (and Gauthier's CM). His RC has an extra move than my RC. I apologize for the confusion.

15 This response is unavailable for those moral theories demanding that all helping actions be morally required.

CHAPTER TWO

1 Thomson 1976 called this one BYSTANDER AT THE SWITCH to distinguish it from Foot's 1967 version called DRIVER where a driver of a brakeless trolley has the choice of turning the trolley onto a spur.

2 For a way of saying, "Yes, why not," see Fischer (1992).

3 Formerly referred to as Fat Man or Footbridge, hence Edmonds's (2014) *Would You Push the Fat Man?*

4 At least no difference in number of deaths. A consequentialist may point out other differences: in the case of Transplant, an erosion of trust in hospitals (Woodcock 2017). This reminds me of how Williams (1981b, 51) rejects utilitarianism: A kind person would not act unkindly when utilitarian calculations demand it. True, a utilitarian can say, but nor would such a person deem her action to be unkind if she were a utilitarian and followed the right calculations.

5 This assumes what Kagan (1988) denies, that what principle we appeal to in one case ought to be a principle we use in other like cases.

6 A difference: death occurs immediately in active euthanasia; it may not occur for a bit in passive. Whether this time lag matters is worth exploring.

7 I share Thomson's (1985, 1412) hunch that a mayor's promise to the person on the spur that he is safe from trolleys prevents the mayor from pulling the lever to save the five.

8 For a No vote, see Taurek (1977). For a Yes vote, see Kavka (1979); Parfit (1978); Woodcock (2017, 309).

9 Aquinas ii–iii, Q 64, art. 7. See also Anscombe (1961); Costa (1986); Edmonds (2014, 177); Nagel (1986); Quinn (1989).

10 These are the (slightly paraphrased) criteria found in The New Catholic Encyclopedia (1967, 1021).

11 Respondents in psychological experiments agree … unless Loop is given *before* Trolley (Liao et al. 2011).

12 Thomson's account would make letting the trolley go straight and killing the five be a means of saving the one. In this case, since the DDE is defeated in both, choosing an option that commits the least damage may be permissible even for DDE supporters. On the other hand, Costa (1987) gives a loop version where, had the trolley gone straight, it would not loop back to run over the lone person.

13 Although Thomson (2008) changed her mind about pulling the lever in both Loop and Trolley, she did not change her mind about that extra bit of track not making a moral difference. If you think it fine to pull the lever in Trolley, you should also think it fine to pull the lever in Loop (Thomson 2015, 130–1).

14 Foot (1967); Hart (1968); McIntyre (2001); Thomson (1973). Other objections exist. For example, Scanlon (2008, 18) wonders what moral difference can be found in consequences that are intended from those that are merely foreseen.

15 Thomson's (1976) approach appealed to the notion of not using someone. She rejected it in her 1985 paper.

16 Again, contra Kagan (1988). Virtue theorists may also disagree, since the right action for the right person at the right time is deemed by them to be situational.

17 Boorse and Sorensen (1988, n6) mention the 1773 Scott v. Shepherd case in Perkins and Boyce (1982, 809): "Shepherd threw a lighted squib into a crowded marketplace and it fell near Willis who, to protect himself, threw it away and it landed near Ryal who also threw it for his protection. It then fell upon Scott and exploded at that instant putting out one of his eyes. It was held that Shepherd had put out Scott's eye."

18 A similar complaint (though against DDE) is raised by Hanna (1992, 325).

19 And thereby making the "right" (defined as utilitarian!) action. See, for example, Valdesolo and DeSteno (2006). The positive feeling was created by showing Saturday Night Live clips to the experimental group compared to a documentary on a Spanish village for the control group.

20 Greene et al. (2009). To be fair, respondents were still less inclined to open the trap door in Trap Door than pull the lever in Trolley.

21 How people say they will behave and how they behave are not correlated. Some studies, however, have simulated trolley problems using mice. Five real mice will be electrocuted (participants were falsely told) if a participant does not push a button, only one will be electrocuted if the participant does push the button. Eighty-four per cent of participants pressed the button, compared with only 66 per cent who predicted that they would (Bostyn, Sevenhant, and Roets 2018).

22 Hanna (1992, 330) suggests the following: "It is impermissible to force a bystander to become a participant in a moral situation, in particular, to become a victim." Accordingly, the sumo wrestler is a bystander, whereas the lone person on the spur is a participant, although why that is so is left unexplained. Other idle options: omission/commission (but

what counts as omission in one case is commission in another, e.g., pulling the plug of a piece of life-saving equipment may be omission for the attending physician, but commission for a visitor) and negative/positive rights (but the question is when can positive rights trump someone's negative rights, so just pointing out the distinction is not helpful unless one's answer is Never!). For a consequentialist solution that recognizes complexity of utility calculations (although I think that is a problem of its own), see Woodcock (2017). Kamm (2007) offers a blizzard of principles, doctrines, and complications.

23 Graham (2017, 177–8) offers a different critique, one that doubts the principle that it is wrong to get someone else to pay the costs of your good deeds.

24 This premoral state is the State of Nature for Hobbes (1651, ch. 13), the original position for Rawls (1971, 17–22, 118–93), and the initial bargaining position for Gauthier (1986, 14–16, 131–4).

25 This is a closer variant of Foot's (1967) original trolley problem.

26 See also Hanna's dice-throwing variant (1992, 322).

27 We may decide to exonerate someone who pulled the lever in Trolley, but that would be at the level of punishment, not the level of moral responsibility. Exoneration of a trolley track switcher would not mean that switching the track is proper in Trolley. We can see this by recognizing that we would not morally blame the person who did not switch the track (contra Frowe 2018); whereas, absent psychological, physical, or epistemic constraint, we would morally blame someone for not pulling the switch in Empty Spur.

CHAPTER THREE

1 Close family did not partake in the mortuary practices of the Wari': only the family's community (Burley 2016, 497; Conklin 1995, 80–1).

2 Although Barth (1975, 152) claims cannibalizing the enemy (at least for the Baktaman of New Guinea) is done in "lust for revenge."

3 His argument is to support growing lab animal meat to replace the cruelty of keeping and killing animals to eat, assuming veganism is not a global practice. To ward off complaints of putting humans ahead of animals, he advises growing lab human meat, too.

4 Bittles (2004, 51) describes a study showing 18 per cent of females involved with incestuous relations were "mentally disabled" at the time.

5 Accordingly, Meiwes cut off Brandes's penis, flambéed it, and the two of them ate it together. After the meal, Meiwes stabbed Brandes repeatedly in

the neck. After dissecting and freezing the corpse, Miewes ate Brandes at leisure. Predictably, there remains some doubt as to Brandes's mental competency. The courts convicted Meiwes on the grounds that his sexual-cannibalistic appetite would never be satiated, and, thus, the public was at risk. But how could a public be at risk to actions affecting only those who properly consent?

6 Tralau (2013) leaves the reader the option of whether to accept liberalism or condemn incest, but not both. If not a *reductio ad absurdum*, a *reductio ad incommodum* (104).

7 Cannibalism may even help with the homeless problem, adds Swift (1729) satirically.

8 Wisniewski (2014) examines and rejects a virtue theory critique of cannibalism.

9 Whether it would be respectful to oblige such a post-mortem wish is another thing. Max Brod opted not to oblige Kafka's post-mortem request to burn Kafka's stories, though, apparently, having alerted Kafka ahead of time.

10 Or "purity" violations. Another category: "Divinity" violations (Rozin et al. 1999).

11 After the emotivists (Stevenson 1937; Ayer 1952) and expressivists (Blackburn 1998; Gibbard 1990; Silk 2015; Timmons 1999).

12 The non-contagion may be because our disgust level for incest and cannibalism is so high; but presumably so with homosexuality once upon a time.

13 Plakias's (2018, 5456) final reply to how disgust is inapt for homosexuality is that other emotions have also led to terrible actions and attitudes without disproving their general aptness. The other emotions she mentions are anger, guilt, pride, and moral conviction. I am not sure how this absolves, as opposed to exacerbates, the worry about relying on unwieldy emotions (of any sort) for moral assessment. Sometimes they are apt; sometimes they are not. The explanation for this difference cannot lie in the bare fact of the emotion itself.

14 In 2011, a single sperm donor fathered 150 children at the same sperm bank. These children will not know of their kin relation and may form socially approved sexual relations. Once the couples learn of their being half-siblings, we can imagine repugnance. Is our level of disgust less toward those who unknowingly engage in incest than toward childhood co-residents having sex?

CHAPTER FOUR

1 Moral luck literature accepts an unrefined account of luck focusing on whether an agent has control over her actions or not (Hartman 2019a, 3186; Statman 2019). For complaints, see Hales (2015); Latus (2003); Pritchard (2006).

2 Abigail may blame herself. We would be surprised if she did not (Wolf 2001, 10).

3 Williams claims that blame is due to the outcome (Williams 1981a, 23). His defence is that we regret our acts only when unsuccessful (29), but this does not show that an action is rationally justifiable only if successful; it shows only that we tend to regret actions that turn out badly.

4 Nagel's (1979) example has two WWII–era Germans, one of whom joins the army and is assigned to kill Jews in concentration camps. The other moves to Argentina with his family before inscription.

5 Hartman claims that circumstantial luck implies resultant luck by analogy (Hartman 2017, 106–7). Apart from Nyman's (2021) critique, I think he misses the point that people who focus only on resultant luck are not necessarily agreeing with circumstantial moral luck; only circumstantial luck. Cyr (2021) makes a similar slide from constitutional luck to constitutional moral luck without further ado.

6 For the claim that no one does, see Kneer and Machery (2019). It is also voiced by Bennett (1995, 59–60). Harm simply makes vivid how reckless the behaviour was.

7 Williams (1981a, 28) uses the fact of self-blame as justifying why we appropriately blame others – even when we know it is not their fault.

8 Enoch and Marmor (2007, 412) think the moral luck paradox dissolves once we distinguish blame from punishment ("blame-related reactions").

9 To say we would punish Bertha more than Abigail for deterrence, as Enoch and Marmor (2007, 413) suggest, would not explain why we also would not punish Abigail the same as Bertha. And punishment to appease the emotional wounds of outraged citizenry, as Riedener (2021, 709) and Strawson (2008, 23) suggest, sounds like an appeal to majority rule.

10 Social psychological studies show how situations affect behaviour. Milgram's (1963) study on obedience, for example, pairs well with Nagel's would-be Nazi living in Argentina (Nagel 1979, 26). Unless statistical propensity that people will *x* counts as knowledge that a particular person will *x*, such findings do not close the epistemic gap.

11 Jensen (1985) offers a similar distinction between overt blame and judgments of moral blameworthiness.

12 According to Latus (2019, 109), Nagel vacillates between asking whether luck can make a difference in a person's moral worth and asking whether luck can make a difference in what a person is morally responsible for. Moral luck skeptics can answer the first question negatively and the second positively.

13 For example, Duff (1986, 70); Fricker (2016); Scanlon (2008, 128); Macnamara (2015).

14 Hartman (2019b, 234) claims it is a mistake to infer equal blame from equal responsibility.

15 Williams (1981a, 23). We are often grateful "that morality does not always prevail" (37) nor is supreme (38).

16 See also Sand and Klenk (2021, 14) who recognize a limiting factor of blame is the cost to the blamer.

17 Following Hume, presumably, Riedener (2021, 698) offers this comparison. See also Sher (2006, 88).

18 Thinking of an objective morality in this way is a kind of fetishism, claims Riedener (2021, 706). By offering a subjective relative perspective on blame, Riedener thinks he provides a "somewhat reconciliatory" vindication of moral luck (694). I think it shows why moral luck is not a thing at all.

19 This condition is easier met for evolutionary contractarians as opposed to rational contractarians (Murray 2007).

CHAPTER FIVE

1 Sinnott-Armstrong (1988, 29) emphasizes the no-overriding principle. Not all agree, e.g., Mothersill (1996, 76).

2 See also Zimmerman (1996, 224–5).

3 Dahl (1996, 96) distinguishes deserved guilt from undeserved guilt and thinks this does not beg the question.

4 Ross (1930, 41) introduces priority rules within Kantianism to avoid this problem. For except-when clauses, see Donagan (1977, 154) and Hare (1981, 54).

5 Williams (1973, 180) dubbed it the *agglomeration principle*. Wright (1951, 3) calls it "conjunction," as does Copi (1954).

6 A worry specific to non-cognitivist theories concerns the application of logic to normative propositions that have no truth value. In reply, O(A)⊃~P(~A) is true, whether O(A) can be true or not.

7 McConnell 1978, 273. See also Brink 1994 and Smith 1986. Conee (1982, 88) shows us how from O(A) & ~O(A) we can derive O(~A) & ~P(~A), which claims you are obligated to do ~*A* when you are not permitted to do ~*A*. Still not a contradiction, but sufficient for showing the impossibility of moral dilemmas.

8 Another principle sometimes challenged is ought-implies-can (Sinnott-Armstrong 1988, 116; Zimmerman 1996, 99). If ought implies can, any act that you cannot do cannot be morally obligatory. If one of the obligations in a moral dilemma is impossible to fulfill (although we do not know which one), the ought-implies-can rule invalidates the unfulfilled duty. If ought need not imply can, an impossible duty would not be a problem for moral theory.

9 See also van Fraassen (1973); Goble (2000); Lemmon (1962, n2); Marcus (1980, 200).

10 Alternatively, we permit the rule of conjunction in non-dilemmas, but not in dilemmas (Beirlaen 2011; Horty 2003; Sinnott-Armstrong 1988, 134–5). This begs the question. We have moral dilemmas because the rule of conjunction does not apply. The rule of conjunction does not apply because we are faced with a moral dilemma.

11 I owe this example to Scott Woodcock.

12 I owe the napping example to Jan Narveson in lecture, memorable because Jan liked to nap in his office.

13 Feinberg (1978, 102) speaks of the difference between violation and infringement of rights, where infringements may not be morally wrong. A hiker breaks into a mountain cabin to survive a blizzard. In doing so, a rights infringement occurs, but not a rights violation. It would be a violation if, as one reviewer noted, the hiker burnt the Vermeer to stay warm. See also Thomson (1990, 122). When we call an infringement not morally wrong, I suggest, is when presumed consent may be reasonably imagined. But what if a sign is posted denying entry even in cases of surviving blizzards? Is entry now a violation or still just an infringement? Here we see that the presumed consent is mere shorthand for what rational, self-interested, amoral agents would agree to in an ex ante situation, not necessarily what actual agents would agree to in a particular case. See also Gauthier (1991, 25). Such agents would ask themselves, "Would it be in my overall interest to endorse a rule that forbids emergency entry to private property despite signs saying, Stay Out!?"

14 Technically, there needs to be a net benefit to the duty holder in accepting any positive in rem duty.

15 Thomson (1971) highlights how mandates against abortion fail each condition: (a) The cost to the one charged with the duty not to abort is exorbitant. (b) Only women can satisfy the duty.
16 A variant on the terrorist case discussed by Smart and Williams (1973, 98–9).
17 A real case, alas, in 2003, Germany.
18 Is active euthanasia a counter case? My promising my mother to get the doctors to kill her when the time comes is a positive in *personam* duty I have taken on. A conflict arises only if we think the doctors have a negative *in rem* duty against active euthanasia. Contractarians are not ones to think so.
19 Distinguishing psychological constraint from bad character may be difficult with positive *in rem* duties; less so with negative and in personam duties.
20 Rather than fixing the rules of a poorly constructed card game, she suggests stacking the deck before each round to prevent dilemmas.
21 See also Brink (1989).
22 Sinnott-Armstrong (1988, 192) opts for a moderate mind-independent realism.

CHAPTER SIX

An earlier version of this chapter appears in Murray (2017), wherein I claimed that blackmail was parametric (304). I was wrong about that. I have corrected the mistake in the present version, along with a few other revisions, updates, and replies to objections.

1 The puzzle about blackmail was raised by Campbell (1939), although many cite Williams (1954).
2 I call it "the puzzle." Berman (2011, 39) distinguishes the puzzle of moral blackmail from the puzzle of legal blackmail. To follow suit, I should say "the moral puzzle." Levy (2007, 1058) suggests the real puzzle about blackmail concerns "the contradiction between intuition and argument." A second puzzle about blackmail is introduced by DeLong (1993): why is it wrong for *A* to approach *B* asking for money for *A* to withhold sensitive information about *B* while it is fine for *B* to approach *A* offering money for *A* to withhold the same information?
3 See also Berman (2011, 38); Block (1999a, 3–4); Feinberg (1990, 238–40); Katz (1996, 133); Lindgren (1984, 716).
4 Both Berman (2011) and Shaw (2012) challenge this assumption. I take it up in section 2.5.3.

5 Some people view punishment as a case of two wrong acts. A harms B, so we harm A. If any intentional harm is wrong, then punishment is another wrong act. But this would not counter the claim that two wrong acts will never make a right act: only a case of two wrong acts making a wrong act. If we think punishment is a right act (suitably constrained), then we do not call the second act wrong, so, again, would not count as a case of two wrong acts making a right act. It would be simply a right act following a wrong act.

6 Feinberg (1990, 85–95) distinguishes between incriminating and embarrassing information and divides the latter category into four subsets: (i) falsehoods, (ii) legal but underhanded, (iii) non-saintly behaviour that would harm your reputation with "benighted" people, and (iv) pre-reform indiscretions. Posner 1993 distinguishes seven: (i) punished criminal acts, (ii) undetected criminal acts, (iii) wrongful, but not criminal acts, (iv) wrongful acts against the blackmailer (revenge), (v) disreputable, though non-criminal acts, (vi) embarrassing acts or conditions (e.g., bedwetting), and (vii) false accusations.

7 I omit some defences: for example, themes of dominance and subordination (DeLong 1993, 1691; Fletcher 1993, 1638), economic waste (Nozick 1974, 84–6), and a utilitarian argument that, while no harm ensues from blackmail, neither is there any benefit to society (Smilansky 1995).

8 I disagree. Sound arguments can be strengthened in aggregate form; a bunch of defeated arguments cannot.

9 Nozick (1969) defined coercion as the restriction of one's options, but it is not any restricted option that matters – only the option of remaining at the state of affairs one was in prior to the interaction.

10 For arguments along this line, see Katz (1996, 162–3); Levy (2007, 1076); Nozick (1974, 84–6).

11 Unlike blackmailers, businesses will not give their products/services for free, claims Altman (1993, 1640). Artists, prostitutes, farmers, overstocked prospectors in dead fads, however, often do so without rendering their activities immoral.

12 Another example: raising the price of EpiPens in bee country.

13 Levy (2007, 1082) claims that threats to reputation will likely cause greater fear and anxiety than threats against other supremely valued interests like life, liberty, and well-being.

14 Another comparison: plea bargaining. "You tell us x, and you get 5 years; otherwise 10 years."

15 We might go the reverse: when a law is generally disobeyed it may cease to become a law.

16 A danger when different groups have different concepts of morality, to be sure. A homophobic society might deem it morally required to shame homosexuals. A religious society might deem it appropriate to punish atheists.

17 Minimally, an epistemic uncertainty exists concerning our moral obligation to tell on adulterers (Gorr 1992, 55).

18 What if the blackmailer had not considered whether the threatened action is moral or not? Then the blackmailer is immoral for not giving due attention to moral deliberation concerning his proposed acts (Berman 2011, 70–1).

19 Many scholars highlight this feature: Coase (1988, 675); DeLong (1993, 1691); Fletcher (1993, 1626); Galoob (2016, 39); Murphy (1980, 166); Owens (1988, 507); Posner (1993, 1840); Shavell (1993, 1878).

20 Block (1999b, 26), however, notes that since courts can rule on matters concerning trade secrets, they could be set up to protect blackmailees' secrets. But a company going to court to protect trade secrets is not alarming; your spouse going to court to protect some undisclosed secret is.

21 This captures Epstein's (1983) worry about blackmail franchises. Paying off one blackmailing paparazzo will merely attract more blackmailing paparazzi. Blackmailers need to hold a monopoly on the information they are threatening to broadcast (Coase 1988, 675; Kipnis 1999, 21) – not that that would make it wrong (Owens 1988, 506). Greater competition would not make blackmail morally permissible, presumably.

22 A loss of $10,000 without divorce may be cheaper than a divorce, but see considerations (a) and (b).

23 Reasons (c) and (d) are inapplicable for blackmail scenarios that do not involve spouses.

24 Admittedly, the cost to the blackmailer to carry out the threat is minimal: an envelope and stamp, for example (Shavell 1993, 1189), or, for that matter, simply by gossiping (Lindgren 1993a, 1984).

25 Building one's reputation as a credible blackmailer has use only if blackmailers broadcast being blackmailers.

26 This may include responding to false accusations, like a scathing post about one's business, a post that would be taken down if money is paid.

27 They can lose if we add punishment costs. This is true of any game, however. That punishment affects outcomes shows only that punishment can deter, not that deterring someone is morally justified.

CHAPTER SEVEN

1 For a defence of evolutionary accounts, see Alexander (2023); Axelrod (1984); Binmore (1998); Danielson (1998); Joyce (2007); Kitcher (1993); Ruse and Wilson (1986); Skyrms (1996); Trivers (1971).
2 Other lost sailors include supererogation (chapter 1) and the inherent value of morality (chapter 9).
3 Among others, see D'Arms (2000); Darwall (2006); Kitcher (1999); Prinz (2009).

CHAPTER EIGHT

1 See Alexander (2007); Axelrod (1984); Binmore (1998); Danielson (1998); Joyce (2007); Kitcher (1993); Murray (2007); Skyrms (1996); Trivers (1971).
2 In competitive tournaments it is expected that everyone knows and follows the rules. But golf is more generally played by amateurs who compete only with themselves, or the course, not with other players.
3 Any moral theory proscribes positive and negative obligations. Anything not covered by the obligatory is by default morally permissible. That is, every action by humans will be under the auspices of a moral theory. For the supererogatory, see chapter 1.
4 Becker (1973, 369) argues that the difference between morality and etiquette does not concern the inescapability of the rules, but the scope of the rules. Moral considerations, he argues, are overriding considerations in ways that rules of etiquette or baseball are not. And "when we have 'considered everything' in so far as we feel bound to follow reason at all, we will feel bound unconditionally by the ought (the moral ought) we have reached."
5 One might, instead, defend a rule (or new rules, especially) by invoking the integrity, or spirit, of the game. This is the approach the USGA took to limiting the COR efficiency in drivers.
6 Foot (1972, 312) believes rules of etiquette are defeated by discovering their arbitrariness.
7 Golf may be an exception, given all the angry golfers.
8 This distinction belongs to Mackie (1977, 25–6), although directed to first- and second-order objectivity.

CHAPTER NINE

1 Irwin (1999) and Shields (2006) note that the Lydian shepherd's choosing instrumental self-gain over morality does not show that the Lydian shepherd does not deem morality to have intrinsic value. True enough, but Glaucon claims that the majority takes morality to be burdensome in itself and pursued for the sake of its consequences only (Plato, 358a). See also Paytas and Baima (2018).

2 Nor restricted to sociopaths (Verene 2010).

3 A rational, amoral, egoistic bargainer would rank from best to worst the following outcomes: 1. defect while other co-ops, 2. co-op while other co-ops, 3. defect while other defects, and 4. co-op while other defects. Since the third choice is the status quo, the state of affairs one was in prior to the interaction with the other, give this a 0. The one below it, being cheated upon, counts as −1. The level above 0 offers 1 utile. The first choice would, then, give 2 utiles.

4 Rather than RC, Gauthier (1986) speaks of a Constrained Maximizer (CM) to emphasize the revised notion of rationality. Perhaps he should say CR for Constrained Rationality. His CM (my RC) contrasts with what he calls a Straightforward Maximizer (SM), which I have represented as UD. SM and UD are not the same, since SMs may (however rarely) be in situations where they maximize utility by co-operating. SM represents for Gauthier the model of rationality he wishes to revise. Meanwhile, RC is but one type of reciprocal or conditional strategy. See also Axelrod (1984), Danielson (1992), Trivers (1971).

5 Another Nash Equilibrium is UD,UD, admittedly, assuming a shift from UD is co-operate, not reciprocally co-operate. The fact that RC,RC is a superior NE than UD,UD, however, gives us all that we need.

6 One may not wish to make this assumption. For example, is helping someone merely a contractual obligation? Is the wrongness of murder merely that murderers reneged on their word? Can we not do wrong even if everyone involved consented? The kernel of such worries is the ring of Gyges problem, so stay tuned.

7 Danielson (1992) calls this new disposition RC for reciprocal co-operation. One co-operates with another only so long as the other's co-operation is a reciprocation, not unconditional. What I call RC, Danielson calls CC for conditional co-operation.

8 An American comedian, b. 1939.

9 Natural realists vary on how they make their claims. See, for example, Bloomfield (2001); Boyd (1988); Casebeer (2005); McDowell (1980); Smith (1991); Sturgeon (1985).

10 Another option: non-natural (Moore 1903). I omit it primarily because I am unable to make sense of it, especially when all Moore's analogies to non-natural properties are natural properties, e.g., yellow. Another subset of the objective intrinsicality of morality is a logical view, captured by Kant. In the Kantian sense, we do not discover morality in the fabric of either the natural or spiritual world, but in the logical structure imposed on us by the world. Along with the non-natural, I ignore the logical and supernatural senses.

11 Of course, if Aristotle is right, maximizing self-interest (or self-love) is to be virtuous.

12 As Morris and Singpurwalla (2013) note, Kantianism suffers the same problem.

13 One may see this without accepting an evolutionary basis to morality. Taylor (2000, 93), for example, says, "What Plato never seems to have doubted is that there is such a thing as true justice, that it is something that is not a human fabrication."

14 Though it would not be "immoral" in such parlance. In contractarian language, morality is, and only can be, a subset of prudence (Gauthier 1986, 5). Contrast Copp (2007, 288), who believes that morality coinciding with self-interest is purely contingent.

15 Except in an analytic sense. If "morality" is the term to apply to rules like "Don't murder," then morality cannot be universally rational. If "morality" applies to reciprocal co-operation when reciprocal co-operation pays the reciprocal co-operator, then murder when "invisible" would not technically be "immoral," and so, in that sense, morality will always be universally rational, but few would care.

CHAPTER TEN

1 Another is the ring of Gyges. See chapter 9.

2 A conceptual difficulty: when rationality parts ways with morality, we can believe that either morality is not rational, or the claim to morality is misapplied. I side more with the latter.

3 Kavka (1983) dreamed up the toxin puzzle to disabuse people from thinking nuclear arms races are rational strategies. See also Kavka (1987).

4 "You are perfectly free to change your mind after receiving the money and not drink the toxin" (Kavka 1983, 34).

5 I ignore the model of morality that demands personal growth and well-being. Levy (2009, 273–4) considers and rejects the self-promise argument after (erroneously) crediting Gauthier as being committed to it (Levy 2009, nn29, 30). Another oddity: Levy treats Gauthier as committed to rule utilitarianism (277). True, Gauthier focuses on the rationality of dispositions rather than acts, but to pin utilitarianism to him is wildly amiss.

6 Apart from Kavka (1983), those who think you cannot rationally intend to drink the toxin in the toxin puzzle include Farrell (1989); Goetz (1988); Hieronymi (2006); Levy (2009); Mele (1992); Rudy-Hiller (2019).

7 Commitment to one's earlier intentions is needed in immoral action, too. When I go to rob a bank and wave my pistol about, I need to commit to shooting innocent people, even though the cost to me, if caught, is a longer prison term. Without that commitment, however, my threat may not be taken seriously, and my plans foiled.

8 Gauthier called the new strategy Constrained Maximization (CM).

9 It is also a useless cost to co-operate in a single interaction PD without worry about reputation or future interactions. While our normal PDs do not meet these criteria, the toxin puzzle certainly does. I shall return to this point in section 3.

10 "Reverting to UD" is not correct. The rational reverser is its own mixed strategy; call it "CD," a conditional defector, or "HF" for Hobbes's Foole.

11 In Harman's (1998) example, I do not form an intrinsic desire to drink toxin, I form an intrinsic desire to drink toxin to celebrate my success at winning a million dollars. That is how my wife treats champagne.

12 Epictetus would not bother interfering in *A's* abusing *B*, for example, since *B*'s pain is only what *B* decides is painful (v, xvi), and *A* obviously thought it right to abuse *B* (xlii), so who are we to interfere in what others take to be right?

13 Many have wondered whether the Ultimatum Game reflects real life. In what sense would our declining an unfair portion of a public resource make the resource just disappear into thin air? Consider the following scenario. Jones has a fishing pole, but a broken arm, and so cannot fish. Smith has no broken arm, but no fishing pole, and so cannot fish. The two come upon a stream filled with fish. Smith asks Jones to lend him the pole so Smith can catch some fish. Smith's reward to Jones? 10 per cent of the catch to Jones. If Jones declines, neither can get any fish.

14 Notice how this counteracts the concept of Pareto improvements. Paretianism would demand you accept an offer of zero for you and ten for the other, since no one is worse off and at least one person is better off. (If it were the offerer's pie to begin with, that would be a different matter.)

15 Reminiscent – albeit a different point – of Mele's (1992) compulsive toxin drinker. Whether one can intend to drink toxin when one knows one will be compelled to do so is the stumbling block for Mele. For example, compulsive hand washers do not really intend to wash their hands; they just find themselves doing so. But if one likes to drink toxin, one can easily intend to drink it.

16 For example, Bratman's (1998) future-regret avoidance model. One can regret drinking the toxin when the money is already in the bank, however. McClennen (1988) may convince us that if the intention is rationally derived, the resolution to execute the intention is rational as well, but that will never tell us whether the antecedent is affirmed.

17 Gauthier (1998, 22) noted and dismissed a closely aligned difference. In moral dealing, one's co-bargainer pays you based on your action, not your intention. In the toxin puzzle, the alien pays you for your intention, not your action. Gauthier did not think this difference troubling, since he argued that rational intentions lead RC agents to act on those intentions. Here, I emphasize that the reason for forming the intention needs to still apply at the time of execution for the benefit of compliance to take root. Otherwise, the sucker objection.

References

Alexander, Jason McKenzie. 2001. "Group Dynamics in the State of Nature." *Erkenntnis* 55 (2): 169–82.

Alexander, Jason McKenzie. 2007. *The Structural Evolution of Morality.* Cambridge: Cambridge University Press.

Alexander, Jason McKenzie. 2023. *Evolutionary Game Theory.* Cambridge University Press.

Alpers, Michael. 2007. "A History of Kuru." *Papa New Guinea Medical Journal* 50 (1–2): 10–19.

Altman, Scott. 1993. "A Patchwork Theory of Blackmail." *University of Pennsylvania Law Review* 141 (5): 1639–61.

Anscombe, Elizabeth. 1958. "Modern Moral Philosophy." *Philosophy* 33 (124): 1–19.

Anscombe, Elizabeth. 1961. "War and Murder." In *Nuclear Weapons: A Catholic Response*, edited by Walter Stein, 44–52. London: Sheed and Ward.

Aquinas, Thomas. 1945. *Summa Theologica.* In *Basic Writings of St. Thomas Aquinas*, edited by Anton Pegis. New York: Random House.

Archer, Alfred. 2015. "Are Acts of Supererogation Always Praiseworthy?" *Theoria* 82 (3): 238–55.

Aristotle. 1941. *Nicomachean Ethics.* In *The Basic Works of Aristotle*, edited by Richard McKeon, 935–1112. New York: Random House.

Aumann, Robert. 1981. "Correlated Equilibrium as an Expression of Bayesian Rationality." *Econometrica* 55 (1): 1–18.

Axelrod, Robert. 1984. *The Evolution of Cooperation.* New York: Basic Books.

Ayer, A.J. 1952. *Language, Truth, and Logic.* New York: Dover Publications.

Baggini, Julian. 2017. "Eating Humans." *The Times Literary Supplement.* https://www.the-tls.co.uk/articles/looking-for-the-causes-behind-our-taboo-against-cannibalism-essay-julian-baggini.

Baron, Marcia. 1987. "Kantian Ethics and Supererogation." *Journal of Philosophy* 84 (5): 237–62.
Barth, Frederik. 1975. *Ritual and Knowledge among the Baktaman of New Guinea.* Oslo: Universitetsforlaget.
Beals, Lawrence. 1952. "On Appearing Just and Being Unjust." *The Journal of Philosophy* 49 (19): 607–14.
Becker, Lawrence E. 1973. "The Finality of Moral Judgments: A Reply to Mrs. Foot." *The Philosophical Review* 82 (3): 364–70.
Beirlaen, Mathieu. 2011. "Ethical Consistency and the Logic of Ought." *Theoretical & Applied Ethics* 1 (3): 45–51.
Benn, Claire. 2014. "The Enemy of the Good: Supererogation and Requiring Perfection." *Utilitas* 30 (3): 333–54.
Benn, Claire. 2018. "Supererogation, Optimality, and Costs." *Philosophical Studies* 175 (1): 2399–417.
Bennett, Jonathan. 1995. *The Act Itself.* New York: Oxford University Press.
Berker, Selim. 2009. "The Normative Insignificance of Neuroscience." *Philosophy and Public Affairs* 37 (4): 293–329.
Berman, Mitchell. 1998. "The Evidentiary Theory of Blackmail: Taking Motives Seriously." *University of Chicago Law Review* 65 (3): 795–878.
Berman, Mitchell. 2011. "Blackmail." In *The Oxford Handbook of Criminal Law*, edited by J. Deigh and D. Dolinko, 37–106. New York: Oxford University Press.
Binmore, Ken. 1998. *Game Theory and Social Contract*, vol. 1: *Playing Fair.* Cambridge, MA: MIT Press.
Birkhead, T., K. Lee, and P. Young. 1988. "Sexual Cannibalism in the Praying Mantis Hierodula Membranacea." *Behaviour* 106 (1–2): 112–18.
Bittles, Alan. 2004. "Genetic Aspects of Inbreeding and Incest." In *Inbreeding, Incest, and the Incest Taboo: The State of Knowledge at the Turn of the Century*, edited by Arthur Wolf and W.H. Durham, 38–60. Stanford: Stanford University Press.
Blackburn, Simon. 1998. *Ruling Passions*. Oxford: Clarendon Press.
Block, Walter. 1997. "The Case for De-Criminalizing Blackmail: A Reply to Lindgren and Campbell." *Washington State University Law Review* 24 (2): 225–46.
Block, Walter. 1999a. "The Crime of Blackmail: A Libertarian Critique." *Criminal Justice Ethics* 18 (2): 3–10.
Block, Walter. 1999b. "Replies to Levin and Kipnis." *Criminal Justice Ethics* 18 (2): 23–8.

Bloomfield, Paul. 2001. *Moral Reality*. Oxford: Oxford University Press.

Bok, Sissela. 1982. *Secrets: On the Ethics of Concealment and Revelation.* New York: Pantheon.

Boorse, Christopher, and Roy Sorensen. 1988. "Ducking Harm." *The Journal of Philosophy* 85 (3): 115–34.

Borg, Jana Schaich, Debra Lieberman, and Kent Kiehl. 2008. "Infection, Incest, and Iniquity: Investigating the Neural Correlates of Disgust and Morality." *Journal of Cognitive Neuroscience* 20 (9): 1529–46.

Bostyn, Dries, S. Sevenhant, and A. Roets. 2018. "Of Mice, Men, and Trolleys: Hypothetical Judgment Versus Real-Life Behavior in Trolley-Style Moral Dilemmas." *Psychological Science* 29 (7): 1084–93.

Boyd, Richard. 1988. "How to Be a Moral Realist." In *Essays on Moral Realism*, edited by Geoffrey Sayre-McCord, 181–228. Ithaca: Cornell University Press.

Boyd, Richard, and Peter Richerson. 2002. "Norms and Bounded Rationality." In *Bounded Rationality: The Adaptive Toolbox*, edited by Gerd Gigerenzer and Reinhard Selten, 281–96. Cambridge, MA: MIT Press.

Bratman, Michael. 1998. "Toxin, Temptation, and Stability of Intention." In *Rational Commitment and Social Justice*, edited by Jules Coleman and Christopher Morris, 59–89. Cambridge: Cambridge University Press.

Brink, David. 1989. *Moral Realism and the Foundations of Ethics*. New York: Cambridge University Press.

Brink, David. 1994. "Moral Conflict and Its Structure." *The Philosophical Review* 103 (2): 215–47.

Burhenn, Herbert. 2004. "Understanding Aztec Cannibalism." *Archive for the Psychology of Religion* 26 (1): 1–14.

Burley, Mikel. 2016. "Eating Human Beings: Varieties of Cannibalism and the Heterogeneity of Human Life." *Philosophy* 91 (4): 483–501.

Butler, Joseph. [1726] 2017. *Fifteen Sermons Preached at the Rolls Chapel: And Other Writings on Ethics*, edited by David McNaughton. Oxford: Oxford University Press.

Campbell, A.H. 1939. "The Anomalies of Blackmail." *Law Quarterly Review* 55: 382–99.

Card, Claudia. 1996. *The Unnatural Lottery: Character and Moral Luck.* Philadelphia: Temple University Press.

Casebeer, William. 2005. *Natural Ethical Facts Evolution, Connectionism, and Moral Cognition.* Cambridge, MA: MIT Press.

Cecchetto, C., R. Rumiati, and V. Parma. 2017. "Relative Contribution of Odour Intensity and Valence to Moral Decisions." *Perception* 46 (3–4): 447–74.

Chapman, H.D., and A. Anderson. 2013. "Things Rank and Gross in Nature: A Review and Synthesis of Moral Disgust." *Psychological Bulletin* 139 (2): 300–27.

Chisholm, Roderick M. 1963. "Supererogation and Offence: A Conceptual Scheme for Ethics." *Ratio* 5 (1): 1–14.

Coase, Ronald. 1988. "Blackmail." *Virginia Law Review* 74 (4): 655–76.

Cofnas, Nathan. 2020. "Are Moral Norms Rooted in Instincts? The Sibling Incest Taboo as a Case Study." *Biology and Philosophy* 35 (5): doi 10.1007/s10539-020-09764-0.

Collinge, J., J. Whitfield, E. McKintosh, J. Beck, S. Mead, D. Thomas, M.P. Alpers. 2006. "Kuru in the 21st Century – an Acquired Human Prion Disease with Very Long Incubation Periods." *Lancet* 367 (9528): 2068–74.

Conee, Earl. 1982. "Against Moral Dilemmas." *The Philosophical Review* 41 (1): 87–97.

Conklin, Beth. 1995. "Thus Are Our Bodies, Thus Was Our Custom: Mortuary Cannibalism in an Amazonian Society." *American Ethnologist* 22 (1): 75–101.

Copi, Irving. 1954. *Symbolic Logic*. London: Macmillan.

Copp, David. 2007. "The Ring of Gyges: Overridingness and the Unity of Reason." In *Morality in a Natural World*, by David Copp, 284–308. Cambridge: Cambridge University Press.

Corey, J., S. Hayakawa, A. Foucart, M. Aparici, J. Botella, A. Costa, and B. Keysar. 2017. "Our Moral Choices Are Foreign to Us." *Journal of Experimental Psychology and Memory Cognition* 43 (7): 1109–28.

Costa, Michael. 1986. "The Trolley Problem Revisited." *The Southern Journal of Philosophy* 24 (4): 437–49.

Costa, Michael. 1987. "Another Trip on the Trolley." *The Southern Journal of Philosophy* 25 (4): 461–6.

Crisp, Roger. 2013. "Supererogation and Virtue." In *Oxford Studies of Normative Ethics*, vol. 3, edited by Mark Timmons, 13–34. Oxford: Oxford University Press.

Cyr, Taylor. 2021. "Inescapability of Moral Luck." *Thought: A Journal of Philosophy* 10 (4): 302–10.

Dahl, Norman. 1996. "Morality, Moral Dilemmas, and Moral Requirements." In *Moral Dilemmas and Moral Theory*, edited by H.E. Mason, 86–101. New York: Oxford University Press.

Daly, George, and Fred Giertz. 1978. "Externalities, Extortion, and Efficiency: Reply." *American Economic Review* 68 (4): 736–8.

Danielson, Peter. 1992. *Artificial Morality: Virtuous Robots for Virtual Games*. London: Routledge.

Danielson, Peter. 1998. "Evolutionary Models of Co-Operative Mechanisms: Artificial Morality and Genetic Programming." In *Modeling Rationality, Morality, and Evolution*, edited by Peter Danielson, 423–41. Oxford: Oxford University Press.

D'Arms, Justin. 2000. "When Evolutionary Game Theory Explains Morality, What Does It Explain?" *Journal of Consciousness Studies* 7 (1–2): 296–9.

D'Arms, Justin, and Daniel Jacobson. 2006. "Sensibility Theory and Projectivism." In *The Oxford Handbook of Ethical Theory*, edited by David Copp, 186–218. Oxford: Oxford University Press.

Darwall, Stephen. 2006. "Morality and Practical Reason: A Kantian Approach." In *The Oxford Handbook of Ethical Theory*, edited by David Copp, 282–320. Oxford: Oxford University Press.

Davis, Nancy. 1984. "The Doctrine of Double Effect: Problems of Interpretation." *Pacific Philosophical Quarterly* 65 (2): 107–23.

DeLong, Sidney. 1993. "Blackmailers, Bribe Takers, and the Second Paradox." *Pennsylvania Law Review* 141 (5): 1663–93.

Dennett, Daniel. 1984. "I Could Not Have Done Otherwise – So What?" *The Journal of Philosophy* 81 (10): 535–65.

Dentsoras, Dimitrios. 2023. "Supererogation in Christianity." In *Handbook of Supererogation*, edited by David Heyd, 293–314. Singapore: Springer.

Dole, Gertrude Evelyn. 1962. *Endocannibalism among the Amahuaca Indians*. New York: New York Academy of Sciences.

Donagan, Alan. 1977. *The Theory of Morality*. Chicago: University of Chicago Press.

Dorsey, Dale. 2012. "Weak Anti-Rationalism and the Demands of Morality." *Noûs* 46 (1): 1–23.

Dorsey, Dale. 2013. "The Supererogatory and How to Accommodate It." *Utilitas* 25 (3): 355–82.

Dreier, James. 2004. "Why Ethical Satisficing Makes Sense and Rational Satisficing Doesn't." In *Satisficing and Maximizing: Moral Theorists on Practical Reason*, edited by M. Byron, 131–54. Cambridge: Cambridge University Press.

Duff, Anthony. 1986. *Trials of Punishment*. Cambridge: Cambridge University Press.

Edmonds, David. 2014. *Would You Push the Fat Man?* Princeton: Princeton University Press.

Elger, M.A., and D.R. Nash. 1988. "Sexual Cannibalism in the Garden Spider Araneus Diadematus." *Animal Behaviour* 36 (5): 1511–17.

Enoch, David, and Andrei Marmor. 2007. "The Case against Moral Luck." *Law and Philosophy* 26 (4): 405–36.

Epictetus. 2004. *Enchiridion.* Translated by George Long. Mineola, NY: Dover Publications.

Epicurus. 1993. *Principal Doctrines.* In *The Essential Epicurus.* Translated by Eugene O'Connor. Buffalo: Prometheus Books.

Epstein, Richard. 1983. "Blackmail, Inc." *University of Chicago Law Review* 50 (Spring): 553–66.

Farrell, Dan. 1989. "Intention, Reason, and Action." *American Philosophical Quarterly* 26 (4): 283–95.

Feinberg, Joel. 1968. "Supererogation and Rules." *Ethics* 71 (4): 276–88.

Feinberg, Joel. 1978. "Voluntary Euthanasia and the Inalienable Right to Life." *Philosophy and Public Affairs* 7 (2): 93–123.

Feinberg, Joel. 1990. *Harmless Wrongdoing.* Oxford: Oxford University Press.

Firestone, Shulamith. 1970. *The Dialectic of Sex.* New York: William Morrow.

Fischer, John Martin. 1992. "Thoughts on the Trolley Problem." In *Ethics: Problems and Principles*, edited by John Martin Fischer and Mark Ravizza, 310–17. Fort Worth: Harcourt Brace Jovanovich College Publishers.

Fischer, Robert William. 2016. "Disgust as Heuristic." *Ethical Theory and Moral Practice* 19 (3): 679–93.

Fletcher, George. 1993. "Blackmail: The Paradigmatic Crime." *University of Pennsylvania Law Review* 141 (5): 1617–38.

Foot, Philippa. 1967. "The Problem of Abortion and the Doctrine of Double Effect." *Oxford Review* 5: 5–15.

Foot, Philippa. 1972. "Morality as a System of Hypothetical Imperatives." *Philosophical Review* 81 (3): 305–16.

Fraassen, Bas van. 1973. "Values and the Heart's Command." *Journal of Philosophy* 70 (1): 5–19.

Francis, K., C. Howard, I. Howard, M. Gummerum, G. Ganis, G. Anderson, and S. Terbeck. 2016. "Virtual Morality: Transitioning from Moral Judgment to Moral Action?" *Plos One* 11, no. 10. doi.org/10.1371/journal.pone.0164374.

Frankena, William. 1939. "The Naturalistic Fallacy." *Mind* 48 (192): 464–77.

Fricker, Miranda. 2016. "What Is the Point of Blame? A Paradigm-Based Explanation." *Noûs* 50 (1): 165–83.

Fritts, Megan, and Calum Miller. 2023. "Must We Be Perfect? A Case against Supererogation." *Inquiry* 66 (10): 1728–57.

Fritz, Kyle and Daniel Miller. 2018. "Hypocrisy and the Standing to Blame." *Pacific Philosophical Quarterly* 99 (1): 118–39.

Frowe, Helen. 2018. "Lesser-Evil Justifications for Harming: Why We're Required to Turn the Trolley." *The Philosophical Quarterly* 68 (272): 460–80.

Gallucci, F., and E. Ölafasson. 2007. "Cannibalistic Behaviour of Rock-Pool Copepods: An Experimental Approach for Space, Food, and Kinship." *Journal of Experimental Marine Biology and Ecology* 342 (2): 325–31.

Galoob, Steven. 2016. "Coercion, Fraud, and What Is Wrong with Blackmail." *Legal Theory* 22 (1): 22–58.

Gass, William. 1957. "The Case of the Obliging Stranger." *The Philosophical Review* 66 (2): 193–204.

Gauthier, David. 1982. "Three Against Justice: The Foole, the Sensible Knave, and the Lydian Shepherd." *Midwest Studies in Philosophy* 7 (1): 11–29.

Gauthier, David. 1986. *Morals by Agreement*. Oxford: Clarendon Press.

Gauthier, David. 1989. "Rethinking the Toxin Puzzle." In *Rational Commitment and Social Justice*, edited by Jules Coleman and Christopher Morris, 47–58. Cambridge: Cambridge University Press.

Gauthier, David. 1991. "Why Contractarianism?" In *Contractarianism and Rational Choice*, edited by Peter Vallentyne, 15–30. Cambridge: Cambridge University Press.

Gauthier, David. 1994. "Assure and Threaten." *Ethics* 104 (4): 690–721.

Geach, P.T. 1956. "Good and Evil." *Analysis* 17 (2): 33–42.

Gibbard, Alan. 1990. *Wise Choices, Apt Feelings: A Theory of Normative Judgment*. Cambridge, MA: Harvard University Press.

Goble, Lou. 2000. "Multiplex Semantics for Deontic Logic." *Nordic Journal of Philosophical Logic* 5 (2): 113–34.

Goetz, Stewart. 1988. "Reasons for Forming an Intention: A Reply to Mink." *Mind* 107 (425): 205–13.

Gorr, Michael. 1977. "Nozick's Argument against Blackmail." *The Personalist* 58 (2): 187–91.

Gorr, Michael. 1992. "Liberalism and the Paradox of Blackmail." *Philosophy and Public Affairs* 21 (1): 43–66.

Gould, Stephen Jay, and Elisabeth Vrba. 1982. "Exaptation – A Missing Term in the Science of Form." *Paleobiology* 8 (1): 4–15.

Graham, Peter. 2017. "Thomson's Trolley Problem." *Journal of Ethics and Social Philosophy* 12 (2): 168–90.

Greene, Joshua. 2014. "Beyond Point-and-Shoot Morality: Why Cognitive (Neuro)Science Matters for Ethics." *Ethics* 124 (4): 695–726.

Greene, Joshua, B. Sommerville, L. Nystrom, J.M. Darley, and J. Cohen. 2001. "An fMRI Investigation of Emotional Engagement in Moral Judgment." *Science* 293 (5537): 2105–8.

Greene, Joshua, D. Fiery, A. Cushman, L. Stewart, K. Lowenberg, L. Nystrom, and J. Cohen. 2009. "Pushing Moral Buttons: The Interaction between Personal Force and Intention in Moral Judgment." *Cognition* 111 (3): 364–71.

Greene, Joshua, L. Nystrom, A. Engell, J. Darley, and J. Cohen. 2004. "The Neural Bases of Cognitive Conflict and Control in Moral Judgment." *Neuron* 44 (2): 389–400.

Guevara, Daniel. 1999. "The Impossibility of Supererogation in Kant's Moral Theory." *Philosophy and Phenomenological Research* 59 (3): 593–624.

Haidt, Jonathan. 2001. "The Emotional Dog and Its Rational Tail: A Social Intuitionist Approach to Moral Judgment." *Psychological Review* 108 (4): 814–34.

Hale, Susan C. 1991. "Against Supererogation." *American Philosophical Quarterly* 28 (4): 273–85.

Hales, Steven. 2015. "A Problem for Moral Luck." *Philosophical Studies* 172 (9): 2385–403.

Halwani, Raja. 1988. "Virtue Ethics and Adultery." *Journal of Social Philosophy* 29 (3): 5–18.

Hanna, Robert. 1992. "Morality *De Re*: Reflections on the Trolley Problem." In *Ethics: Problems and Principles*, edited by John Martin Fischer and Mark Ravizza, 318–36. Fort Worth: Harcourt Brace Jovanovich College Publishers.

Hare, R.M. 1981. *Moral Thinking*. Oxford: Oxford University Press.

Harman, Gilbert. 1977. *The Nature of Morality*. New York: Oxford University Press.

Harman, Gilbert. 1998. "The Toxin Puzzle." In *Rational Commitment and Social Justice*, edited by Jules Coleman and Christopher Morris, 84–9. Cambridge: Cambridge University Press.

Harris, Marvin. 1977. *Cannibals and Kings*. New York: Random House.

Hart, H.L.A. 1968. "Intention and Punishment." In *Punishment and Responsibility: Essays in the Philosophy of Law*, by H.L.A. Hart, 113–35. Oxford: Oxford University Press.

Hartman, Robert. 2016. "Against Luck-Free Moral Responsibility." *Philosophical Studies* 173 (10): 2845–65.

Hartman, Robert. 2017. *In Defense of Moral Luck: Why Luck Often Affects Praiseworthiness and Blameworthiness*. New York: Routledge.

Hartman, Robert. 2019a. "Moral Luck and the Unfairness of Morality." *Philosophical Studies* 176 (12): 3179–97.

Hartman, Robert. 2019b. "Accepting Moral Luck." In *The Routledge Handbook of the Philosophy and Psychology of Luck*, edited by Ian Church and Robert Hartman, 227–38. New York: Routledge.

Heyd, David. 1980. "Beyond the Call of Duty in Kant's Ethics." *Kant-Studien* 71 (1–4): 308–24.

Heyd, David. 1982. *Supererogation: Its Status in Ethical Theory*. Cambridge: Cambridge University Press.

Heyd, David. 2015. "Can Virtue Ethics Account for Supererogation?" *Royal Institute of Philosophy Supplements* 77: 25–47. doi:10.1017/S1358246115000193.

Heyd, David. 2024. "Supererogation." In *The Stanford Encyclopedia of Philosophy*, edited by Edward N. Zalta and Uri Nodelman. https://plato.stanford.edu/archives/spr2024/ entries/supererogation.

Hick, John. 1966. *Evil and the God of Love*. London: Macmillan.

Hieronymi, Pamela. 2006. "Controlling Attitudes." *Pacific Philosophical Quarterly* 87 (1): 45–74.

Hill, Thomas. 1971. "Kant on the Imperfect Duty of Supererogation." *Kant-Studien* 62 (1–4): 55–76.

Hobbes, Thomas. [1651] 1988. *The Leviathan*. Buffalo: Prometheus Books.

Holbo, John. 2002. "Moral Dilemmas and the Logic of Obligation." *American Philosophical Quarterly* 39 (3): 259–74.

hooks, bell. 1989. *Talking Back: Thinking Feminist, Thinking Black*. Boston: South End Press.

Horty, John. 2003. "Reasoning with Moral Conflicts." *Noûs* 37 (4): 557–605.

Huemer, Michael. 2005. *Ethical Intuitionism*. New York: Palgrave Macmillan.

Hume, David. [1739] 1978. *A Treatise of Human Nature*, edited by L.A. Selby-Bigge and P.H. Nidditch. Oxford: Oxford University Press.

Hume, David. [1751] 1989. *Enquiries Concerning the Principles of Morals*, edited by L.A. Selby-Bigge and P.H. Nidditch. Oxford: Clarendon Press.

Hursthouse, Rosalind. 2006. "Are Virtues the Proper Starting Point for Morality?" In *Contemporary Debates in Moral Theory*, edited by J. Dreier, 331–44. Abingdon: Routledge.

Igneski, Violetta. 2008. "Defending Limits on the Sacrifices We Ought to Make for Others." *Utilitas* 20 (4): 424–46.

Irvine, William. 1989. "Cannibalism, Vegetarianism, and Narcissism." *Between the Species: A Journal of Ethics* 5 (1): 11–17.

Irwin, T.H. 1999. "Republic 2: Questions about Justice." In *Plato 2: Ethics, Politics, Religion and the Soul*, edited by Gail Fine, 164–85. Oxford: Oxford University Press.

Jacobson, Daniel. 2013. "Moral Dumbfounding and Moral Stupefaction." In *Oxford Studies in Normative Ethics*, vol. 2, edited by Mark Timmons, 289–316. Oxford: Oxford University Press.

Jacquette, Dale. 2001. "Aristotle on the Value of Friendship as a Motivation for Morality." *Value Inquiry* 35 (3): 371–89.

Jensen, Henning. 1985. "Morality and Luck." *Philosophy* 59 (229): 323–30.

Joyce, Richard. 2001. *The Myth of Morality*. Cambridge: Cambridge University Press.

Joyce, Richard. 2007. *The Evolution of Morality*. Cambridge, MA: MIT Press.

Kagan, Shelly. 1988. "The Additive Fallacy." *Ethics* 91 (1): 5–31.

Kahan, D. 1999. "The Progressive Appropriation of Disgust." In *The Passions of the Law*, edited by S. Bandes, 63–79. New York: New York University Press.

Kamm, Francis. 2007. *Intricate Ethics*. Oxford: Oxford University Press.

Kant, Immanuel. [1785] 1981. *Grounding for the Metaphysics of Morals*. Translated by J.W. Ellington. Indianapolis: Hackett.

Kant, Immanuel. [1797a] 1996. *The Metaphysics of Morals*. Translated by Mary Gregor. Cambridge: Cambridge University Press.

Kant, Immanuel. [1797b] 2012. "On a Supposed Right to Lie from Philanthropy." In *Immanuel Kant: Practical Philosophy*, translated by Mary Gregor, 605–16. New York: Cambridge University Press.

Kass, Leon. 1994. *The Hungry Soul: Eating and the Perfecting of Our Nature*. Chicago: University of Chicago Press.

Kass, Leon. 1997. "The Wisdom of Repugnance." *The New Republic* 216 (22): 17–26.

Katz, Leo. 1996. *Ill-Gotten Gains: Evasion, Blackmail, Fraud, and Kindred Puzzles of the Law*. Chicago: University of Chicago Press.

Kavka, Gregory. 1979. "The Numbers Should Count." *Philosophical*

Studies 36 (3): 285–94.

Kavka, Gregory. 1983. "The Toxin Puzzle." *Analysis* 43 (1): 33–6.

Kavka, Gregory. 1984. "A Reconciliation Project." In *Morality, Reason, and Truth*, edited by David Copp and David Zimmerman, 297–319. Lanham, MD: Rowman and Allenheld.

Kavka, Gregory. 1987. *Moral Paradoxes of Nuclear Deterrence.* Cambridge: Cambridge University Press.

Kawall, Jason. 2009. "Virtue Theory; Ideal Observers, and the Supererogatory." *Philosophical Studies* 146 (2): 179–96.

Kekes, John. 1992. "Disgust and Moral Taboos." *Philosophy* 67 (262): 431–46.

Kelly, Daniel. 2011. *Yuck: The Nature and Moral Significance of Disgust.* Cambridge, MA: MIT Press.

Kipnis, Kenneth. 1999. "Blackmail as a Career Choice: A Liberal Assessment." *Criminal Justice Ethics* 18 (2): 19–22.

Kitcher, Philip. 1993. "The Evolution of Human Altruism." *The Journal of Philosophy* 90 (10): 497–516.

Kitcher, Philip. 1999. "Games Social Animals Play: Commentary on Brian Skyrms' *Evolution of the Social Contract.*" *Philosophy and Phenomenological Research* 59 (1): 221–8.

Kneer, Markus, and Edouard Machery. 2019. "No Luck for Moral Luck." *Cognition* 182: 331–48. doi: 10.1016/j.cognition.2018.09.003.

Kraus, Jody. 1993. *The Limits of Contractarianism.* Cambridge: Cambridge University Press.

Kujundzic, Neb. 2013. "Thought Experiments, Puzzles, and Paradoxes." *Philosophy Study* 3 (8): 750–7.

Kumar, Victor, and Richmond Campbell. 2012. "On the Normative Significance of Experimental Psychology." *Philosophical Psychology* 25 (3): 311–20.

Latus, Andrew. 2000. "Moral and Epistemic Luck." *Journal of Philosophical Research* 25: 149–72. 10.5840/jpr_2000_21.

Latus, Andrew. 2003. "Constitutive Moral Luck." *Metaphilosophy* 34 (4): 460–74.

Latus, Andrew. 2019. "Thomas Nagel and Bernard Williams on Moral Luck." In *The Routledge Handbook of the Philosophy and Psychology of Luck*, edited by Ian Church and Robert Hartman, 105–12. New York: Routledge.

Lemmon, E.J. 1962. "Moral Dilemmas." *Philosophical Review* 71 (2): 139–58.

Levy, Ken. 2007. "The Solution to the *Real* Blackmail Paradox: The Common Link between Blackmail and Other Criminal Threats." *Connecticut Law Review* 39: 1051–96.

Levy, Ken. 2009. "On the Rationalist Solution to Gregory Kavka's Toxin Puzzle." *Pacific Philosophical Quarterly* 90: 267–89.

Liao, M., A. Wiegmann, J. Alexander, and G. Vong. 2011. "Putting the Trolley in Order: Experimental Philosophy and the Loop Case." *Philosophical Psychology* 25 (5): 661–71.

Lieberman, D., and T. Lobel. 2012. "Kinship on the Kibbutz: Coresidence Duration Predicts Altruism, Personal Sexual Aversions, and Moral Attitudes among Communally Reared Peers." *Evolution of Human Behavior* 33 (1): 26–36.

Lindenbaum, S. 1979. *Kuru Sorcery: Disease and Dangers in the New Guinean Highlands*. Mountain View, CA: Mayfield Publishing.

Lindgren, James. 1984. "Unraveling the Paradox of Blackmail." *Columbia Law Review* 84 (3): 670–717.

Lindgren, James. 1989. "Blackmail: On Waste, Morals, and Ronald Coase." UCLA *Law Review* 36 (3): 597–608.

Lindgren, James. 1993a. "Blackmail: An Afterword." *University of Pennsylvania Law Review* 141 (5): 1975–89.

Lindgren, James. 1993b. "The Theory, History, and Practice of the Bribery-Extortion Distinction." *University of Pennsylvania Law Review* 141 (5): 1695–740.

Lorenz, Konrad. 1988. *Here Am I – Where Are You? The Behavior of the Greylag Goose*. New York: Harcourt Brace.

Lu, Matthew. 2013. "Explaining the Wrongness of Cannibalism." *American Catholic Philosophical Quarterly* 87 (3): 433–58.

MacIntosh, Duncan. 1992. "Preference-Revision and the Paradoxes of Instrumental Rationality." *Canadian Journal of Philosophy* 22 (4): 503–29.

MacIntosh, Duncan. 2013. "Assuring, Threatening, a Fully Maximizing Theory of Practical Rationality, and the Practical Duties of Agents." *Ethics* 123 (4): 625–56.

Mack, Erik. 1982. "In Defence of Blackmail." *Philosophical Studies* 41 (2): 273–84.

Mackie, J.L. 1977. *Ethics: Inventing Right and Wrong*. Harmondsworth: Penguin.

Macnamara, Coleen. 2015. "Reactive Attitudes as Communicative Entities." *Philosophy and Phenomenological Research* 90 (3): 546–69.

Marcus, Ruth Barcan. 1980. "Moral Dilemmas and Consistency." *The Journal of Philosophy* 77 (3): 121–36.
May, J. 2014. "Does Disgust Influence Moral Judgment?" *Australasian Journal of Philosophy* 92 (1): 125–41.
McClennen, Edward. 1988. "Constrained Maximization and Resolute Choice." *Social Philosophy and Policy* 5 (2): 95–118.
McConnell, Terence. 1978. "Moral Dilemmas and Consistency in Ethics." *The Canadian Journal of Philosophy* 8 (2): 269–87.
McConnell, Terence. 1980. "Utilitarianism and Supererogatory Acts." *Ratio* 22 (1): 36–8.
McConnell, Terence. 1981. "Moral Blackmail." *Ethics* 91 (4): 544–67.
McConnell, Terence. 1996. "Moral Residue and Dilemmas." In *Moral Dilemmas and Moral Theory*, edited by H.E. Mason, 36–47. New York: Oxford University Press.
McDowell, John. 1980. "Values and Secondary Qualities." In *Morality and Objectivity*, edited by Ted Honderich, 110–29. London: Routledge and Kegan Paul.
McDowell, John. 1998. *Mind, Value, and Reality*. Cambridge, MA: Harvard University Press.
McIntyre, Alison. 2001. "Doing Away with Double Effect." *Ethics* 111 (2): 219–55.
McKenna, Michael. 2012. *Conversation and Responsibility*. Oxford: Oxford University Press.
Mele, Alfred. 1992. "Intentions, Reasons, and Beliefs: Morals of the Toxin Puzzle." *Philosophical Studies* 68 (2): 171–94.
Milburn, Josh. 2016. "Chewing Over In Vitro Meat: Animal Ethics, Cannibalism and Social Progress." *Res Publica* 22 (3): 249–65.
Milgram, Stanley. 1963. "Behavioral Study of Obedience." *The Journal of Abnormal and Social Psychology* 67 (4): 371–8.
Mill, J.S. [1863] 1987. *Utilitarianism*. Buffalo: Prometheus Books.
Moore, G.E. [1903] 1986. *Principia Ethica*. Cambridge: Cambridge University Press.
Morris, Christopher, and Rachel Singpurwalla. 2013. "Ring of Gyges." In *The International Encyclopedia of Ethics*, edited by Hugh LaFollette, 4641–6. Oxford: Blackwell.
Mothersill, Mary. 1996. "The Moral Dilemmas Debate." In *Moral Dilemmas and Moral Theory*, edited by H.E. Mason, 65–85. New York: Oxford University Press.
Murphy, Jeffrie. 1980. "Blackmail: A Preliminary Inquiry." *Monist* 63 (2): 156–71.

Murray, Malcolm. 2007. *The Moral Wager: Evolution and Contract.* Dordrecht: Springer.

Murray, Malcolm. 2008. "Rational Choice and Evolutionary Fit." In *Moral Psychology Today: Essays on Values, Rational Choice, and the Will*, edited by David Chan, 225–38. Dordrecht: Springer.

Murray, Malcolm. 2017. *Morals and Consent: Contractarian Solutions to Ethical Woes.* Montreal: McGill-Queen's University Press.

Nagel, Thomas. 1979. "Moral Luck." In *Mortal Questions*, by Thomas Nagel, 24–38. Cambridge: Cambridge University Press.

Nagel, Thomas. 1986. "Ethics." In *The View from Nowhere*, by Thomas Nagel, 164–88. Oxford: Oxford University Press.

Narveson, Jan. 1988. *The Libertarian Idea.* Philadelphia: Temple University Press.

Nash, John. 1950. "Equilibrium Points in *n*-Person Games." *Proceedings of the National Academy of Sciences* 36 (1): 48–9.

Norcross, Alastair. 1995. "Should Utilitarianism Accommodate Moral Dilemmas?" *Philosophical Studies* 79 (1): 59–83.

Nozick, Robert. 1969. "Coercion." In *Philosophy, Science, and Method: Essays in Honor of Ernest Nagel*, edited by Sidney Morgenbesser, Patrick Suppes, and Morton White, 440–72. New York: St Martin's Press.

Nozick, Robert. 1974. *Anarchy State, and Utopia.* New York: Basic Books.

Nussbaum, Martha. 2004. *Hiding from Humanity: Disgust, Shame, and the Law.* Princeton: Princeton University Press.

Nyman, Anna. 2022. "The Parallelism Argument and the Problem of Moral Luck." *Philosophical Studies* 179 (3): 955–71.

Otsuka, Michael. 2009. "Moral Luck: Optional, Not Brute." *Philosophical Perspectives* 23 (1): 373–88.

Owens, David. 1988. "Should Blackmail Be Banned?" *Philosophy* 63 (246): 501–14.

Parfit, Derek. 1978. "Innumerate Ethics." *Philosophy and Public Affairs* 7 (4): 285–301.

Parfit, Derek. 1986. *Reasons and Persons.* Oxford: Oxford University Press.

Paytas, Tyler, and Nicholas Baima. 2018. "Intrinsic Valuing and the Limits of Justice: Why the Ring of Gyges Matters." *Phronesis* 64 (1): 1–9.

Perkins, Rollin, and Ronald Boyce. 1982. *Criminal Law and Procedure: Cases and Material.* Mineola, NY: Foundation Press.

Pinheiro Walla, Alice. 2015. "Kant's Moral Theory and Demandingness." *Ethical Theory and Moral Practice* 18 (4): 731–43.

Plakias, Alexandra. 2018. "The Response Model of Moral Disgust." *Synthese* 195 (12): 5453–72.

Plato. 1945. *The Republic*. Translated by F.M. Cornford. New York: Oxford University Press.

Posner, Richard. 1993. "Blackmail, Privacy and Freedom of Contract." *University of Pennsylvania Law Review* 141 (5): 1817–47.

Poundstone, William. 1990. *Labyrinths of Reason*. New York: Anchor Books.

Prinz, Jesse. 2009. *The Emotional Construction of Morals*. New York: Oxford University Press.

Pritchard, Duncan. 2006. "Moral and Epistemic Luck." *Metaphilosophy* 37 (1): 1–25.

Pritchard, H.A. 1912. "Does Moral Philosophy Rest on a Mistake?" *Mind* 21 (81): 21–37.

Pummer, Theron. 2016. "Whether and Where to Give." *Philosophy and Public Affairs* 44 (1): 77–95.

Quine, Willard Van Orman. 1976. *The Ways of Paradox and Other Essays*. Cambridge, MA: Harvard University Press.

Quinn, Warren. 1989. "Actions, Intentions, and Consequences: The Doctrine of Double Effect." *Philosophy and Public Affairs* 18 (4): 334–51.

Rachels, James. 1975. "Active and Passive Euthanasia." *The New England Journal of Medicine* 29 (2): 78–80.

Rault, Jonathan, Eric Benoît, and Jean-Luc Gouzé. 2013. "Stabilizing Effect of Cannibalism in a Two Stages Population Model." *Acta Biotheoretica* 61 (1): 119–39.

Rawls, John. 1971. *A Theory of Justice*. Cambridge, MA: Harvard University Press.

Raz, Joseph. 1998. *The Morality of Freedom*. Oxford: Oxford University Press.

Reiter, P. 1999. "From Shakespeare to Defoe: Malaria in England in the Little Ice Age." *Emerging Infectious Diseases* 6 (1): 1–11.

Rescher, Nicholas. 1993. "Moral Luck." In *Moral Luck*, edited by Daniel Statman, 141–66. Albany: State University of New York Press.

Richards, David A.J. 1971. *A Theory of Reasons for Action*. Oxford: Clarendon Press.

Richards, Norvin. 1993. "Luck and Desert." In *Moral Luck*, edited by Daniel Statman, 167–80. Albany: State University of New York Press.

Riedener, Stefan. 2021. "Don't Make a Fetish of Faults: A Vindication of Moral Luck." *Philosophical Studies* 178 (3): 693–711.

Rini, Regina. 2013. "Making Psychology Normatively Significant." *The Journal of Ethics* 17 (3): 257–74.

Ross, W.D. 1930. *The Right and the Good.* Oxford: Oxford University Press.

Royzman, Edward, Kwanwoo Kim, and Robert Leeman. 2015. "The Curious Tale of Julie and Mark: Unraveling the Moral Dumbfounding Effect." *Judgment and Decision Making* 10 (4): 296–313.

Rozin, P., J. Haidt, and C.R. McCauley. 2008. "Disgust." In *Handbook of Emotions*, 3rd ed., edited by M. Lewis, J.M. Haviland-Jones, and L.F. Barrett, 757–76. New York: Guilford Press.

Rozin, P., L. Lowery, S. Imada, and J. Haidt. 1999. "The CAD Triad Hypothesis: A Mapping between Three Moral Emotions (Contempt, Anger, Disgust) and Three Moral Codes (Community, Autonomy, Divinity)." *Journal of Personality and Social Psychology* 76 (4): 574–86.

Rozin, P., L. Millman, and C. Nemeroff. 1986. "The Laws of Sympathetic Magic in Disgust and Other Domains." *Journal of Personality and Social Psychology* 50 (4): 703–12.

Rudy-Hiller, Fernando. 2019. "So Why Can't You Intend to Drink the Toxin?" *Philosophical Explorations* 22 (3): 294–311.

Ruse, Michael, and E.O. Wilson. 1986. "Moral Philosophy as Applied Science." *Philosophy* 61 (236): 173–92.

Russell, Daniel. 2008. "That 'Ought' Does Not Imply 'Right': Why It Matters for Virtue Ethics." *Southern Journal of Philosophy* 46 (2): 299–315.

Russell, Pascale Sophie, and Roger Giner-Sorolla. 2013. "Bodily Moral Disgust: What It Is, How It Is Different from Anger, and Why It Is an Unreasoned Emotion." *Psychological Bulletin* 139 (2): 328–51.

Sainsbury, Mark. 1996. *Paradoxes.* Cambridge: Cambridge University Press.

Sand, Martin, and Michael Klenk. 2021. "Moral Luck and Unfair Blame." *The Journal of Value Inquiry* 57 (4): 701–17.

Sartre, Jean-Paul. [1946] 2007. *Existentialism Is a Humanism.* New Haven: Yale University Press.

Sayre-McCord, Geoffrey. 1992. "Normative Explanations." *Philosophical Perspectives* 6: 55–71.

Scanlon, Thomas. 2008. *Moral Dimensions: Permissibility, Meaning, Blame.* Cambridge, MA: Harvard University Press.

Schinkle, Anders. 2009. "The Problem of Moral Luck: An Argument Against Its Epistemic Reduction." *Ethical Theory and Moral Practice* 12 (3): 267–77.

Schnall, Simone, Jonathan Haidt, Gerald Clore, and Alexander Jordan. 2008. "Disgust as Embodied Moral Judgment." *Personality and Social Psychology Bulletin* 34 (8): 1096–109.

Schutt, Bill. 2017. *Cannibalism: A Perfectly Natural History*. Chapel Hill: Algonquin Books.

Searle, John. 1964. "How to Derive an 'Ought' from an 'Is.'" *Philosophical Review* 73 (1): 43–58.

Seidel, Angelika, and Jesse Prinz. 2013. "Sound Morality: Irritating and Icky Noises Amplify Judgments in Divergent Moral Domains." *Cognition* 127 (1): 1–5.

Shand, John. 2010. "Abhorrence and Justification." *Ethical Perspectives: Journal of European Ethics Network* 17 (4): 515–28.

Shavell, Steven. 1993. "An Economic Analysis of Threats and Their Illegality: Blackmail, Extortion, and Robbery." *University of Pennsylvania Law Review* 141 (5): 1877–903.

Shaw, James. 2012. "The Morality of Blackmail." *Philosophy and Public Affairs* 40 (3): 165–96.

Sher, George. 2006. *In Praise of Blame*. Oxford: Oxford University Press.

Shields, Christopher. 2006. "Plato's Challenge: The Case against Justice in *Republic* II." In *Blackwell Guide to Plato's Republic*, edited by Gerasimos Santas, 63–83. Oxford: Blackwell.

Silk, Alex. 2015. "How to Be an Ethical Expressivist." *Philosophy and Phenomenological Research* 91 (1): 195–222.

Singer, Peter. 1972. "Famine, Affluence, and Morality." *Philosophy & Public Affairs* 1 (3): 229–43.

Singer, Peter. 2016. *Ethics in the Real World: 82 Brief Essays on Things That Matter*. Princeton: Princeton University Press.

Sinnott-Armstrong, Walter. 1988. *Moral Dilemmas*. Oxford: Blackwell.

Skyrms, Brian. 1996. *The Evolution of the Social Contract*. Cambridge: Cambridge University Press.

Skyrms, Brian. 2004. *The Stag Hunt and the Evolution of Social Structure*. Cambridge: Cambridge University Press.

Slote, Michael. 1989. *Beyond Optimizing*. Cambridge, MA: Harvard University Press.

Smart, J.J.C., and Bernard Williams. 1973. *Utilitarianism: For and Against*. Cambridge: Cambridge University Press.

Smilansky, Saul. 1995. "May We Stop Worrying about Blackmail?" *Analysis* 55 (2): 116–20.

Smilansky, Saul. 2007. *Ten Moral Paradoxes*. Oxford: Blackwell.

Smith, Holly. 1986. "Moral Realism, Moral Conflict, and Compound Acts." *The Journal of Philosophy* 83 (6): 341–5.

Smith, Michael. 1991. "Realism." In *Companion to Ethics*, edited by Peter Singer, 399–410. Oxford: Blackwell.

Smith, Michael. 1994. *The Moral Problem*. Oxford: Blackwell.

Sorensen, Roy. 2003. *A Brief History of the Paradox*. Oxford: Oxford University Press.

Stangl, Rebecca. 2016. "Neo-Aristotelian Supererogation." *Ethics* 126 (2): 339–65.

Statman, Daniel. 2019. "The Definition of 'Luck' and the Problem of Moral Luck." In *The Routledge Handbook of the Philosophy and Psychology of Luck*, edited by Ian Church and Robert Hartman, 195–205. New York: Routledge.

Stevenson, Charles. 1937. "The Emotive Meaning of Ethical Terms." *Mind* 46 (181): 14–31.

Strawson, P.F. 2008. "Freedom and Resentment." In *Freedom and Resentment and Other Essays*, by P.F. Strawson, 1–28. New York: Routledge.

Sturgeon, Nicholas. 1985. "Moral Explanations." In *Morality, Reason and Truth*, edited by David Copp and David Zimmerman, 49–78. Totowa, NJ: Rowman and Allenheld.

Styron, William. 1980. *Sophie's Choice*. New York: Bantam Books.

Suter, Renata, and G. Hertwig. 2011. "Time and Moral Judgment." *Cognition* 119 (3): 454–8.

Swanton, Christine. 2004. "Satisficing and Perfectionism in Virtue Ethics." In *Satisficing and Maximization*, edited by M. Byron, 176–89. New York: Cambridge University Press.

Swift, Jonathan. [1729] 2008. "A Modest Proposal for Preventing the Children of Poor People from being a Burthen to Their Parents or Country, and for making them Beneficial to the Publick." Project Gutenberg. https://www.gutenberg.org/files/1080/1080-h/1080-h.htm.

Swinburne, Richard. 1996. *Is There a God?* Oxford: Oxford University Press.

Taurek, John. 1977. "Should the Numbers Count?" *Philosophy and Public Affairs* 6 (4): 293–316.

Taylor, Richard. 2000. *Good and Evil*. New York: Prometheus.

Thomson, Judith Jarvis. 1971. "A Defense of Abortion." *Philosophy and Public Affairs* 1 (1): 47–66.

Thomson, Judith Jarvis. 1973. "Rights and Deaths." *Philosophy and Public Affairs* 2 (2): 146–59.

Thomson, Judith Jarvis. 1976. "Killing, Letting Die, and the Trolley Problem." *The Monist* 59 (2): 204–17.

Thomson, Judith Jarvis. 1985. "The Trolley Problem." *The Yale Law Journal* 94 (6): 1395–415.

Thomson, Judith Jarvis. 1990. *The Realm of Rights*. Cambridge, MA: Harvard University Press.

Thomson, Judith Jarvis. 2008. "Turning the Trolley." *Philosophy & Public Affairs* 36 (4): 359–74.

Thomson, Judith Jarvis. 2015. "Kamm on the Trolley Problem." In *The Trolley Problem Mysteries* by Francis Kamm, 113–33. Oxford: Oxford University Press.

Timmerman, Jens. 2005. "Good but Not Required? – Assessing the Demands of Kantian Ethics." *Journal of Moral Philosophy* 2 (1): 9–27.

Timmons, Mark. 1999. *Morality without Foundations: A Defence of Ethical Contextualism*. Oxford: Oxford University Press.

Tooley, Michael. 1980. "An Irrelevant Consideration: Killing versus Letting Die." In *Killing and Letting Die*, edited by Bonnie Steinbock, 56–62. Englewood Cliffs: Prentice-Hall.

Tralau, Johan. 2013. "Incest and Liberal Neutrality." *The Journal of Political Philosophy* 21 (1): 87–105.

Trivers, Robert. 1971. "The Evolution of Reciprocal Altruism." *Quarterly Review of Biology* 46 (1): 35–57.

Tybur, J.M., D. Liebermann, R. Kurzban, and P. DeScioli. 2013. "Disgust: Evolved Function and Structure." *Psychological Review* 120 (1): 65–84.

Ullmann-Margalit, Edna. 2011. "Considerateness." *Iyyun* 60 (July): 205–44.

Urmson, J.O. 1958. "Saints and Heroes." In *Essays in Moral Philosophy*, edited by A.I. Melden, 198–216. Seattle: University of Washington Press.

Valdesolo, P., and D. DeSteno. 2006. "Manipulations of Emotional Context Shape Moral Judgment." *Psychological Science* 17 (6): 476–7.

Vallentyne, Peter. 1989. "Two Types of Moral Dilemmas." *Erkenntnis* 30 (3): 301–18.

van Ackeren, Marcel, and Martin Sticker. 2015. "Kant and the Problem of Demandingness." *Ethical Theory and Moral Practice* 18 (1): 75–89.

van Zyl, Liezl. 2011. "Right Action and the Non-Virtuous Agent." *Journal of Applied Philosophy* 28 (1): 80–92.

Varden, Helga. 2010. "Kant and Lying to the Murderer at the Door … One More Time: Kant's Legal Philosophy and Lies to Murderers and Nazis." *The Journal of Social Philosophy* 41 (4): 403–21.

Velleman, David. 2012. "Against the Right to Die." In *Questions of Life and Death: Readings in Practical Ethics*, edited by Christopher Morris, 337–45. New York: Oxford University Press.

Verene, Donald Phillip. 2010. "The Sociopath and the Ring of Gyges: A Problem in Rhetorical and Moral Philosophy." *Philosophy & Rhetoric* 43 (3): 201–21.

Viminitz, Paul. 2005. "A Defence of Terrorism." *Journal of Philosophical Research* 30 (Supplement): 397–408.

Vytal, K., and S. Hamann. 2010. "Neuroimaging Support for Discrete Neural Correlates of Basic Emotions: A Voxel-Based Meta-Analysis." *Journal of Cognitive Neuroscience* 22 (12): 2864–85.

Watson, Gary. 2004. "Responsibility and the Limits of Evil: Variations on a Strawsonian Theme." In *Agency and Answerability* by Gary Watson, 219–59. Oxford: Clarendon Press.

Wertheimer, Alan. 1987. *Coercion*. Princeton: Princeton University Press.

Westermarck, Edward. 1891. *The History of Human Marriage*. London: Macmillan.

Wiggins, David. 1980. "What Would Be a Substantial Theory of Truth?" In *Philosophical Subjects: Essays Presented to P.F. Strawson*, edited by Zak van Straaten, 189–221. Oxford: Oxford University Press.

Wiggins, David. 1987. *Needs, Values, Truth*. Oxford: Blackwell.

Williams, Bernard. 1973a. "Consistency and Realism." In *Problems of the Self*, by Bernard Williams, 187–206. London: Cambridge University Press.

Williams, Bernard. 1973b. "Ethical Consistency." In *Problems of the Self*, by Bernard Williams, 166–86. London: Cambridge University Press.

Williams, Bernard. 1981a. "Moral Luck." In *Moral Luck*, by Bernard Williams, 20–39. New York: Cambridge University Press.

Williams, Bernard. 1981b. "Utilitarianism and Moral Self-Indulgence." In *Moral Luck*, by Bernard Williams, 40–53. New York: Cambridge University Press.

Williams, Glanville. 1954. "Blackmail." *Criminal Law Review* 79: 162–72.

Wisniewski, Jeremy. 2004. "A Defence of Cannibalism." *Public Affairs Quarterly* 18 (3): 265–72.

Wisniewski, Jeremy. 2007. "Murder, Cannibalism and Indirect Suicide: A Philosophical Study of a Recent Case." *Philosophy in the Contemporary World* 14 (1): 11–21.

Wisniewski, Jeremy. 2014. "Cannibalism." In *Encyclopedia of Food and Agricultural Ethics*, edited by D. Kaplan, 355–61. doi: 10,1007/978-94-007-6167-4_28-8.

Wolf, Arthur. 2004. "Explaining the Westermarck Effect: Or What Did Natural Selection Select For?" In *Inbreeding, Incest, and the Incest Taboo: The State of Knowledge at the Turn of the Century*, edited by Arthur Wolf and W.H. Durham, 76–92. Stanford: Stanford University Press.

Wolf, Susan. 1982. "Moral Saints." *The Journal of Philosophy* 79 (8): 419–39.

Wolf, Susan. 2001. "The Moral of Moral Luck." *Philosophic Exchange* 31 (1): 5–19.

Woodcock, Scott. 2017. "When Will a Consequentialist Push You in Front of a Trolley?" *Australasian Journal of Philosophy* 95 (2): 299–316.

Wright, G.H. von. 1951. "Deontic Logic." *Mind* 60 (237): 1–15.

Zimmerman, Michael. 1996. *The Concept of Moral Obligation.* Cambridge: Cambridge University Press.

Zimmerman, Michael. 2002. "Taking Luck Seriously." *Journal of Philosophy* 99 (11): 553–76.

Zwart, Hub. 2014. "The Donor as an 'Object *a*': A Lacanian Perspective on Organ Donation and Transplantation Medicine." 17 (4): 559–71.

Index